The Party's Over

The Party's Over

How the Extreme Right Hijacked the GOP
and I Became a Democrat

Charlie Crist

and Ellis Henican

DUTTON
— est. 1852 —

DUTTON
—• est. 1852 •—

Published by the Penguin Group
Penguin Group (USA) LLC
375 Hudson Street
New York, New York 10014

USA | Canada | UK | Ireland | Australia | New Zealand | India | South Africa | China
penguin.com
A Penguin Random House Company

LIBRARY OF CONGRESS CATALOGING-IN-PUBLICATION DATA
has been applied for.

ISBN 978-0-525-95441-5

Printed in the United States of America
10 9 8 7 6 5 4 3 2 1

To my dear mother and father, Charlie and Nancy, the people who taught me what is truly important in life—for that I will be forever grateful.

To my three sisters, Margaret, Elizabeth, and Catherine, whom I love with all my heart, for helping me understand how precious women are.

Finally, to my beautiful wife, Carole, the love and light of my life, who knows me better than anyone and completed me as a man.

The Party's Over

Introduction

"Thank you!" I called out to the massive crowd in front of me. "What an incredible night! Optimism is in the air."

I was deep inside enemy territory. That's what my old friends were telling me. It was Thursday, September 6, 2012, a couple of minutes after 8:30 P.M., and I had never stood before a throng so huge: more than twenty thousand men and women, a loud and raucous mix of anticipation and fun, in the TV glare of the Time Warner Cable Arena in Charlotte, North Carolina—every age, race, region, and hat style you could imagine. Most of them were jammed onto tiny folding chairs. Others were crowding the narrow aisles. As I peered over the top of an oversize, wooden podium, I could see hundreds—was it thousands?—of white-on-blue Obama-Biden posters and many, many pole signs. "MINNESOTA." "TENNESSEE." I found "FLORIDA" off to my right. Halfway back in my home-state delegation, one poster said "I-4 Obama," a little play on the highway that connects Tampa and Daytona Beach, always a crucial swing-vote corridor. But as I moved through my opening pleasantries, I have to say, the applause sounded a little tepid to me.

I got the distinct feeling that the audience was holding back. It was as if all these people were taking a careful measure of me, trying to decide whether I'd fully earned the right to be here.

Were they happy to see me? Were they asking themselves, "Who the hell is this guy? Who invited him?" I hadn't seen any polling data or focus group reports. But I'd been around this business long enough to know: People with résumés like mine weren't supposed to speak at Democratic National Conventions. This wasn't the way that game was played.

I'd been the low-tax, pro-life, pro-gun Republican governor of Florida. As a young state senator, I'd been such an anti-crime crusader, people called me "Chain Gang Charlie"—and I considered it a compliment. Heck, I'd named my boat *Freedom*. Was that Republican—or what? I'd risen through the ranks from education commissioner to attorney general to governor, always running with an "R" next to my name. In the 2008 presidential campaign, I'd worked diligently for John McCain, even making his short list for vice president. At various points along the way, I had referred to myself as a "Ronald Reagan Republican."

And here I was with a prime-time, Thursday-night speaking role at the 2012 Democratic National Convention, preparing to sing the praises of Barack *Hussein* Obama. That's how many of my old party mates liked referring to him, as if he weren't just a president from a different party but a highly suspect, otherworldly creature and probably a Muslim too.

No, this wasn't politics as usual.

I was addressing this Democratic crowd the same night the president was. My slot was after Caroline Kennedy and just before John Kerry and Joe Biden. The big addresses from Michelle and Barack Obama were coming right after that. You'd have to look long and hard in the annals of American politics to find a fish more out of water than I was that night.

I'd even joked with my wife, Carole, when I first got the call from Jim Messina, who was managing the president's reelection campaign: "Didn't anyone do a background check?"

I wasn't even invited when Republican delegates gathered August 27 to 30 for their national convention in Tampa, just a short drive from my rented condo in St. Petersburg. Why would I be? I wasn't one of theirs anymore. They were brimming with Tea Party fervor and anti-Obama zeal. I'm pretty sure they wouldn't have enjoyed what I had to say.

"What an honor to be here with you to stand with President Barack Obama," I told the Democratic crowd.

A small fan was whirring at my feet. I always like a fan at the podium when I give a big speech. You have no idea how hot those TV lights can be. But I could still feel tiny beads of sweat forming on my forehead. I don't usually get nervous giving speeches. My heart was pumping now.

Before I got to the business at hand, I wanted to address the elephant in the room. Never before, I thought, had that old expression been quite so apt.

"Half a century ago," I began, "Ronald Reagan, the man whose optimism inspired me to enter politics, famously said that he didn't leave the Democratic Party, but the party left him. Well, listen, I can relate. I didn't leave the Republican Party. It left me."

It had been a while, I was sure, since Ronald Reagan was quoted so approvingly at a Democratic convention. "Then again," I added, "my friend Jeb Bush recently noted Reagan himself would have been too moderate, too reasonable for today's GOP."

People clapped at that. Right there, I could feel it. I had the attention and the support of the room. We might have come from different places. But I could tell—and they could tell—we were talking the same language and talking the same way. It had taken me a while to get here, but I felt thoroughly at home.

I had already changed my registration from Republican to Independent. By the time the year was over, I would officially be a Democrat. But despite those changing labels, I felt the same way I always had. I had the same basic values. I'd never been an ideologue. It was just that, in an ugly bow to extremism, the party I'd grown up in had abandoned people like me. And the place I was heading, I was happy to see, wasn't run by enforcers with mandatory checklists.

Standing at the podium in Charlotte, I wanted to share with the Democratic delegates some of the causes I cared most about. Not the divisive, hot-button issues so many Republican politicians seemed suddenly obsessed with—birth control, abortion, gays, and guns. Not the nasty caricatures that fueled so much of talk radio and cable TV news. Just as I always had, I wanted to talk about issues that touch all people's lives, whatever their party might be.

So I did.

"We must create good middle-class jobs so we can have an economy built to last," I said. "We must rebuild our roads and bridges and improve our public schools. And particularly important to me and my state is the challenge of saving Medicare and Social Security so we can keep our promise to seniors."

These shouldn't be divisive issues at all.

"As a former lifelong Republican," I said, "it pains me to tell you that today's Republicans—and their standard-bearers, Mitt Romney and Paul Ryan—just aren't up to the task. They're beholden to my-way-or-the-highway bullies, indebted to billionaires who bankroll ads and are allergic to the very idea of compromise. Ronald

Reagan would not have stood for that. Barack Obama does not stand for that. You and I won't stand for that."

I was laying everything right out there. It sure felt great. I had to mention the hug.

"One of the president's first trips in office brought him to Fort Myers, Florida, where I was proud to embrace him and his plan to keep our teachers, police, and firefighters on the job," I said. "Well, that hug caused me more grief from my party than you can ever imagine."

Embracing Barack Obama had made me an instant pariah in the eyes of some Republicans. Yet the president and I, coming from different places, had been on similar journeys all along.

"I'll be honest with you," I told the Democratic delegates. "I don't agree with President Obama about everything. But I've gotten to know him, I've worked with him, and the choice is crystal clear. When he took office, the economic crisis had already put the state of Florida on the edge of disaster. The foreclosure crisis was consuming homeowners, the tourists we depend on couldn't afford to visit, and our vital construction industry had come to a standstill. President Obama saw what I saw: a catastrophe in the making. And he took action."

Then I delivered the formal endorsement I had come to Charlotte to make.

"When I look at President Obama," I said, "I see a leader with a cool head, a caring heart, and an open mind, a president who has demonstrated through his demeanor and through his deeds that he is uniquely qualified to heal our divisions, rebuild our nation, and lead us to a brighter future together.

"That's the leader Florida needs. That's the leader America needs. And that's the reason I'm here tonight, not as a Republican, not as a

Democrat, but as an optimistic American who understands that we must come together behind the one man who can lead the way forward in these challenging times: my president, our president, Barack Obama!"

And the people went wild.

It felt so liberating, saying those words to that crowd on that night and being received the way that I was.

There was one last line in my written text I had planned to end my speech on. It was a funny line, I thought, a little self-deprecating and 100 percent accurate. But the reaction to what I'd said was just so warm and so genuine—and so earsplittingly loud—those final fourteen words felt almost gratuitous. The point had been made and received. I had done as well as I could.

"If you see the president before I do," I was going to say, "give him a hug for Charlie!"

But I didn't use the line. I didn't think I needed to. Whatever hug the president needed had already been delivered by me and by this grateful Democratic crowd.

I waved. I said, "God bless you, God bless America, and thank you so much." Then I left the stage.

What a ride these last few years have been!

I have gone from lifelong Republican to the Nowheresville of being an Independent to finally becoming a Democrat. Some of my friends tell me I've always been a Democrat—it just took me fifty-six years to figure that out. I wish someone had mentioned something sooner. Everything was rolling smoothly along. I loved being governor of Florida, helping people, high in the polls, showing the warring parties of Tallahassee how they could actually get along. Then,

I had this notion about bringing our bipartisan Florida values to Washington. It was just about then that a band of crazy extremists hijacked the party I'd grown up in. Pedal to the metal, they drove it off an ideological cliff. I got banged up riding with these unsavory characters. But thankfully, I leapt to safety just in time. Now I'm happier than I've ever been and feeling thoroughly at home.

Along the way, I got to see American politics as few others have seen it—up close and personal at the very highest levels and from both sides of the aisle. I've been appalled at the cynicism I have seen as my former party slipped into the clutches of the Tea Party haters and extremists of various sorts. I have felt sympathy and then sadness as people I'd been close to decided they had to accommodate these rising demands. But I have been truly inspired by the goodness in the hearts of the vast majority of people. I have learned some unexpected lessons along the way—about where we are headed as a nation and the great possibilities that are ahead for us.

That night in Charlotte—*me! addressing a Democratic convention!*—was one amazing stop on this unexpected journey. But it didn't start in Charlotte, and it certainly didn't end there. And as I look to the future, here's the part I'm most excited about: I'm convinced this journey of mine has truly only begun.

Chapter 1

I never became a Republican. I was born that way.

My father is a lifelong Republican. His father voted Republican until the day he died at ninety-six. The members of my mother's family were Republicans too. Most of the people I knew growing up in St. Petersburg, Florida, were Republicans. Even though Florida was a heavily Democratic state at the time, the west coast was a relative bastion of Republicanism, mostly because so many people had moved down from the Republican Midwest. Political parties are like religions that way. They choose us even more than we choose them. Very few people actually conduct a comparative study before they declare "I'm a Republican" or "I'm a Democrat," any more than they interview clergymen or weigh doctrines before deciding to be a Baptist, a Hindu, or a Jew. My three sisters and I were Republicans for the same reason we were Methodists. Those before us had been, and we just were.

That said, I felt perfectly comfortable with the party I found myself in. The basic beliefs of the Republicans, as I understood them when I was growing up and becoming curious about the world, sounded pretty sensible to me. Don't waste the people's money. Maintain a strong national defense. Respect the views of others. Keep government on a fairly short leash. Who's not for that?

I've always believed that it matters where a person comes from. We are all, in part, products of our upbringings and environments. That's why I still like to ask people when I first meet them, "Where ya from?" I am hugely grateful to come from the family, the city, and the state that I do. The original family name was Christodoulos. They came from Cyprus, a small island nation in the eastern Mediterranean just south of Turkey and five hundred miles south of mainland Greece. Cyprus is divided between Greeks and Turks, who get along about as well as Washington Republicans and Democrats. My father's father, Adam Christodoulos, traveled to America in 1912 at the age of fourteen for the same reasons immigrants have always come: for freedom and opportunity and the chance to build a better life. Family photos show a tall, lean boy with thick black hair. Everyone said he had a cheery, upbeat demeanor. I've always thought I inherited that. His older brother was the one who was supposed to make the trip. But on the dock in Cyprus, the assertive young Adam said, "Let me go instead"—and his more reserved older brother quickly agreed. Adam didn't have the proper papers. Some people today might call him an illegal immigrant. He was certainly too young to be making the journey to America alone. When the boat finally reached Ellis Island, he was allowed onshore only after a helpful gentleman said, "Come here, son"—and whisked him through immigration. But soon enough, the kind man disappeared into the swirling crowd of the reception center's giant auditorium, leaving young Adam to fend for himself. He was sitting on a bench, trying to figure out what to do next, when another man walked over and said to him in Greek: "You need a job?"

"I felt like the sun came out when I heard those words," Pappap told me years later. We always called him Pappap.

The Greek-speaking man owned a shoe-shine parlor in a gritty railroad-and-steel-mill city called Altoona, Pennsylvania. As a boy, my grandfather spoke little English. He had a third-grade education. He earned five dollars a month shining shoes.

It's a great immigrant story, the kind of story modern America is built on. When World War I broke out, the immigrant shoe-shine boy from Altoona joined the US Army and fought in Belgium. Earning an honorable discharge, he was eligible to become a citizen of the United States—not so different from today's immigrant "Dreamers" nearly a hundred years later.

He saved his money and married a local girl named Mary Khoury, whose people were of Lebanese descent. They started their own family, raising seven children in all. My grandfather eventually opened a café, a bar, and a hat-cleaning shop and bought some real estate. He was proud to be an American and especially proud of his right to vote.

Most new immigrants—then as now—joined the Democratic Party. In industrial cities like Altoona, ward bosses and precinct captains helped to steer them in. But my grandfather considered himself a businessman. "If you're a businessman," he would often tell people, "you're a Republican."

My father, Charles Joseph Christodoulos, was born in 1932, Pappap and Grandma's sixth child. People had big families back then. Like the children of many immigrants, my father wasn't too interested in the ways of the old country. He never learned to speak more than a few words of Greek. He was still in high school when he and his older brother, my uncle Harry, went down to the courthouse in Altoona and shortened their last names to Crist.

"No one can spell it, and no one can pronounce it," he said to Pappap.

My grandfather didn't mind. "We're Americans now," he said.

One day my dad asked his father to attend a parent-teacher conference at school. Pappap said he'd rather not. "My accent's too heavy," he told his son. "I might embarrass you. Your mother should go instead." Pappap hated any sign that he might not be fully American. With his own lack of schooling, he believed deeply in education. He wanted all his children to learn the value of working hard and to get as much education as they possibly could.

My father had after-school jobs in his father's little businesses. One day, my dad sliced off part of his right index finger, trying to fix a fan in Pappap's appliance-repair shop. Dad thought the fan was broken. It was not. He attended Pennsylvania State University, where he joined a fraternity and majored in science, in that order. His grades weren't stellar, but he did okay, and he had a large circle of friends. On campus, he met a blue-eyed, brown-haired young woman from a well-off Scots-Irish family. Her name was Nancy Virginia Lee.

He was outgoing and gregarious. She was quiet and more reserved. They fell hopelessly in love. He was twenty-one and she was nineteen in February of 1954 when they drove to Virginia and got married. Her parents did not approve. They didn't want their daughter settling for "that Greek boy." The newlyweds rented an apartment near the campus in State College and got busy starting a family of their own. My older sister, Margaret, arrived later that year as my father was thinking about applying to medical school.

The Americanized son of immigrants kept being reminded how Greek he was. One of the schools he applied to was Jefferson Medical College in downtown Philadelphia. He went for an interview, and the admissions officer spoke frankly to him.

"Your grades are good enough," he said. "You did well on the admissions exam. But we already have our quota of southern Europeans. We won't be able to offer you a place."

It wasn't anything like the prejudice African Americans and others have experienced in our society. But it was real. And it made my father push himself harder. He went back to Penn State, began working on a master's degree in biochemistry, and tried again, applying to another round of medical schools. But he was starting to doubt he would ever get in. Late one night, as he loved to tell the story, he was working at the lab on an experiment that involved the digestive system of a cow. He was having trouble proving his thesis. He hadn't heard from the medical schools. His pregnant wife was home with their baby daughter. As far as he was concerned, things weren't going too well.

On his two-mile walk back home, he said a quiet prayer.

"God, please help me."

He woke up the next morning. His experiment had been proved valid. He received a letter in that day's mail saying he'd been accepted to Emory University's highly regarded School of Medicine in Atlanta. And a couple of days later, July 24, 1956, I showed up. I was born at Altoona Hospital. My parents named me Charles Joseph Crist Jr., for my dad. When I was six weeks old, my father, mother, older sister, and I piled into my mom's parents' car—we didn't have our own yet. Her parents and the four of us and all our suitcases made the long drive south to Decatur, Georgia. My mom says I fussed the whole way. Only after we got settled into a small apartment near the med school did Dad go and buy a family car, a maroon-and-cream-colored Packard.

My father loved medical school, especially when he got a chance to interact with real patients. While many of his classmates were drawn to narrow specialties, he liked treating the whole person the way that family doctors do. On his occasional free afternoons, he'd play with me and Margaret in the backyard or go fishing with his medical school friends. Halfway through med school, the family grew to five when my younger sister Elizabeth was born.

After my dad graduated from Emory in 1960, he had to choose where to do a one-year internship. My mother's family had been spending winters in St. Petersburg since the 19-teens. Why not do the year there? He knew he'd be working horrible hours at the hospital. But in St. Pete at least Mom could get some babysitting help from her family. We arrived in June of 1960, a month before my fourth birthday, part of a giant postwar influx to the booming Sunshine State. We moved into a rental house for a year while Dad built us a new home in the rising Pinellas Point subdivision at the southern tip of St. Petersburg. The area was growing rapidly. Everyone in Florida seemed to be moving, buying, and trading up back then.

My dad felt immediately at home in Florida, and so did the rest of us. The winters were perfect—especially compared to central Pennsylvania's. The breezes off the Gulf of Mexico and Tampa Bay made the summers much more bearable than Georgia's. There was water everywhere, and everyone—rich people, poor people, kids, and adults—seemed to have a boat. The fishing opportunities—kingfish, mackerel, grouper—were spectacular. For at least part of the year, my mother had relatives around. "We're never going back to all that snow," my father said, and no one argued with him. That was the day, I think, we really became Floridians.

After his internship, my dad took a medical position at Mound Park Hospital, what is now called Bayfront Medical Center. It's the oldest hospital in Pinellas County and its only trauma center. He began seeing patients as a general-practice family doctor—just like that levelheaded Marcus Welby on TV—providing hands-on care to young families and settled retirees. He was hugely dedicated to his patients, and they loved him back. I'll bet he's treated at least half of St. Pete by now. He always saw both white patients and black patients, which wasn't too common in those days. What I remember is that he was constantly in motion, phoning in prescriptions, fielding emergencies, running back to the hospital, even making house calls.

Our new one-story house on Colony Drive South was right on Tampa Bay. We had a deck out back and thick Bermuda grass. I could easily walk the one mile to Bay Vista Elementary School. My mom stayed home with the children. There was nothing she wouldn't do for us. It was eggs sunny-side up for breakfast and frequent little tips on how to behave. She and Dad were both big believers in doing things correctly.

"Sit up straight at the table," Mom would say.

"Keep your left hand in your lap."

"The little boat goes out to sea," reminding us to move our soup spoons forward, not back.

Dad insisted on "yes, sir," "yes, ma'am," and firm, look-'em-in-the-eye handshakes.

We always had lively conversations at the family dinner table. Even when my sisters and I were little, Dad would go around the table and ask:

"What did you do today?"

"Have you started your homework yet?"

"How did your team do in the game?"

"Did you hear what the president said?"

We were expected to have answers and to deliver them—early

training, I've always thought, for a lifetime of speeches and interviews.

I was seven years old when President John F. Kennedy was assassinated in 1963. At such a young age, I didn't fully understand what that meant. But the teachers at school all seemed worried, and some of them cried. I knew what getting shot was. I'd seen that happen in cowboy movies and on TV. I knew that President Kennedy was the youngest president ever, and he had a very pretty wife. I knew their daughter, Caroline, who had her own pony, was a grade younger than I was. I knew she had a little brother who liked to climb on things and under them. His name was John. I saw him on television, saluting at the funeral. I knew it was all very sad. Given the family I grew up in, we talked a lot at dinner about what happened in Dallas and what it all meant.

But mostly, the life we had together was just about idyllic. My dad loved his work. My mom loved being a mom. My sister Cathy, the youngest, arrived in 1964. My three sisters and I had every advantage we could possibly ask for, and that included the biggest one: We always knew we were loved.

Leave It to Beaver had nothing on the Crists of St. Pete. We were so darn wholesome, a friend of mine once joked: "Compared to you guys, Wally and the Beav are almost criminals."

As the only son, I developed a special bond with my father. He would take me everywhere—to the hospital, on Saturday-morning errands, even sometimes on house calls. In 1966, when I was almost ten, my dad decided to run for the Pinellas County School Board— as a Republican, of course.

I guess you'd call my dad fiscally conservative and socially moderate. He liked low taxes. He wanted local businesses to thrive. He was naturally suspicious of President Lyndon Johnson's Great Society and other big-government solutions from Washington. But he was troubled by the racial segregation that lingered in Florida and elsewhere. He very much believed in equal opportunity and social programs that worked.

My dad had never shown the slightest interest in running for office. But as a family physician, he'd gotten involved with a new federal program called Head Start. He loved the idea of Head Start, preparing children for school long before the first day of kindergarten. He'd clearly taken his father's education advice. But he didn't like the way the local Head Start office was being operated. He knew the school board was supposed to have oversight. So he decided to run.

Apparently, it never occurred to him that he might also have to campaign.

He didn't give any speeches. He didn't buy any ads. And he hadn't raised any money. I don't think he felt too comfortable asking people for their votes. Finally, a man at the county Republican office suggested maybe he should attend some local political events. "You're going to have trouble getting elected," the man said, "if you don't do something."

Dad decided to print up a stack of palm cards with his picture on one side and his educational credentials on the other. One Saturday afternoon he heard about a Republican Party fish fry at Lake Maggiore.

"Feel like coming along?" he asked me.

"Sure," I said.

"All right," he said. "Come on. We'll go see what's going on over there."

After we got to the fish fry, Dad sat down at one of the big round tables and began talking to some of the adults. He handed me a little stack of his cards.

"Go hand these out," he told me.

"Okay," I said.

I walked from table to table along the side of the lake, talking with the people as I went, handing each one of them one of my father's cards.

"I hope you'll vote for my dad," I said. "He's running for the school board."

I don't remember my father going around to any of the tables, but he might have. What I do remember was how much fun I had. Talking with the people. Asking for their votes. Working the fish fry like a seasoned, pint-size political pro.

Everyone was nice to me. They listened to what I said. And I thought it was kind of neat that my dad was running for office as the Republican candidate for the Pinellas County School Board. I definitely hoped he would win.

When it was time to go, my father told me how impressed he was. He said he'd noticed how comfortable I seemed. "You did more campaigning than I did," he said.

Something must have clicked. He won fairly easily and added "school board member" to all the other things going on in his life.

In those years, race was never far off the public-education agenda. For the schools in Pinellas County, integration was still a work in progress. Some of the schools were integrated. Some were not. We escaped a lot of the rancor of other cities. But busing became an issue. And my dad felt like it was his responsibility to set what examples he could.

Gibbs High School, which at the time had only black students, needed a team doctor for the football team.

"We can't find anyone," the principal said at the school board meeting one day.

My father volunteered to do it. "But there's one condition," he said. "Only if my son Charlie can be on the sidelines with me."

He never told me why he did that. But I think he realized we lived a fairly comfortable lifestyle. He wanted to make sure I began to get a broader view of life. Those were the kinds of people who raised me—open, generous, always leading by example. And I was gradually figuring out who I was.

I spent hours on Tampa Bay, looking at sea life, taking my sisters for rides in the family boat, a seventeen-foot Glasspar with a 75-horsepower Johnson outboard. It wasn't anything fancy, but to me, that was like having my own car on water. My friends could come along. I could go and see nature whenever I felt like it.

I was a friendly, energetic kid who was always taking on some fresh project or getting involved in something new at school. I was the boy who organized the class recycling program and raised the money by holding a school dance. I had a knack for bringing people together. I discovered that early. It gave me a special place in the crowd, and it brought real pleasure to me. While I was still in seventh grade, Dad began building a new two-story house on Snell Isle, a small peninsula in Tampa Bay. The street was called Brightwaters Circle. The house had white columns out front, a pool and a patio and a dock in the back. I moved from Bay Point to Riviera Junior High in time for eighth grade. I was the new kid, which is always awkward. I didn't know anyone in the new school. But late in the year, with Dad's encouragement, I decided to run for student council president, hoping at least I'd meet some new friends.

I sealed the race on Speech Day. The whole student body was in the gym, which doubled as the school auditorium, to hear from the candidates.

"Stand up," I told everyone as I began my remarks.

The students glanced at one another, not quite sure what to do. But they were used to being bossed around by teachers and coaches. Everybody stood.

What if they hadn't? That was a little risky.

"Now please sit down," I said. And everyone did.

I let them all settle down and then I said: "Look how much power I have over you, and I haven't even won yet."

"Power" isn't a word I used often, then or now. And the gesture was totally pointless. It didn't achieve a thing.

Except for this: The students thought it was hilarious. And of the six hundred who voted, I believe I got about five hundred votes.

I don't think my opponent knew quite what hit him.

Up through junior high, the schools my sisters and I attended were all white. But St. Petersburg High School drew from across the city and was racially integrated. I wouldn't say we had a lot of racial tension when I got to St. Pete High in 1971. But there was some. I noticed little clumps of students—blacks with blacks, whites with whites—sitting at separate tables in the school cafeteria. One time, the crowd had to be cleared from the gym before a basketball game, as rumors of a big fight were flying around, but I don't believe anything actually materialized. Compared to some places I'd read about, in the Deep South especially, St. Petersburg in the early 1970s was an island of relative tranquility. I know I never had any personal problem attending an integrated school, and I think football was one of the reasons why. Without a doubt, the best interactions I had were on the field. Our team—*go, Green Devils!*—was totally integrated. Coach Forrest Page didn't care what race you were. If you could run, block, tackle, throw, catch, or kick a football, he would find a place for you on the team. He wanted to win games.

Don Collins, Mark McGarry, Jerry Lewis, and the others—we were a high-spirited and highly loyal group of guys, brothers on and off the field. Football teaches important lessons for life. I could see that even then. Everyone had much to contribute, and we all had to work together for a common cause. We'd only win if we pulled together.

I loved playing football, especially as I developed my skills as a quarterback. The coach had the vision and the overall game plan. But the quarterback got to call the plays, throw the football, and create the whole tempo of the offense. It was the quarterback who got to lead on the field. I liked that. And, no, being quarterback didn't hurt my dating opportunities.

I wasn't big—six foot one, 180 pounds. But I had a strong arm and was a good, accurate passer. Junior year, I was actually getting recruited to play at colleges like Rice University and the University of Virginia. Then, one day at Stewart Field in a game against our rivals from Northeast High, I dropped back to pass. Northeast had a linebacker named Gilbert Mavro. I'd gone to junior high with Gil. He came roaring up the middle at me, slamming my left knee with his shoulder. My knee bent off to the side at a highly unnatural angle. I went down instantly, a fiery pain shooting through my leg. The doctors said I'd torn my medial meniscus. All I knew was that it felt like someone had jammed a rusty fish-scaling knife deep into cartilage and wiggled it around in there. Over Christmas break, I had an operation at St. Anthony's Hospital in St. Petersburg, praying I'd be able to play my senior year. The doctor called the surgery a success. But my recovery was painful and slow. I was still in a full-leg cast at the junior prom. My father called Lenox Hill Hospital in New York to find out about the special knee brace that Joe Namath had worn. Broadway Joe had the most famous messed-up knees in football. But just like Namath, I never got all my speed and agility back.

This was extremely frustrating to me. For a moment, I was pretty sure my whole life was over. Long-term perspective is not something most teenagers excel at. I certainly didn't. I'd dreamed of playing big-time college football—*somewhere*. That disappointment, I believe, is a big part of the reason I turned my attention to that other extracurricular where I thought I could be a leader.

Politics.

My father's service on the school board and our lively dinner-table talk must have stuck in my head somehow. I'd always kept up with the news and always admired great leaders. Watergate was the big news story when I was in high school. What President Richard Nixon and those around him did, I thought, was terrible. It was cheating. It was wrong. And it was unnecessary. Even without the dirty tricks, he probably would have beaten George McGovern in a landslide.

At the end of junior year, I ran for senior class president. My opponent was a young lady named Sarah Snyder, who was very smart and nice. We had a short campaign, nothing like the endless marathons I'd go through later. We made our speeches, but there weren't too many issues that I recall. Who's more popular—that's usually the issue in high school campaigns. When the votes came in, Sarah and I were in a dead-even tie. The principal, Ron Hallam, floated the idea of us being co-presidents. But we decided to have a runoff instead, and I squeaked in.

I really enjoyed helping my fellow students. But even with the responsibilities of senior class president—even with the blown-out knee—I still wasn't entirely done with football. No more recruiters had me on their call sheets. I knew I'd never get to play at a football powerhouse like University of Florida or Florida State. But thankfully, I still had some other options. I was happy to be accepted at Wake Forest University in Winston-Salem, North Carolina. The Wake Forest football team plays in Division I of the Atlantic Coast Conference. It's the smallest Division I school in the country. I didn't have a football scholarship. I wasn't guaranteed anything. I just walked onto the practice field my freshman year and asked for a shot.

I didn't make the big team. But I played junior varsity and ran the scout team for the varsity. Like a surrogate preparing a politician for an upcoming debate, we scrimmaged as the opposing team. No great accomplishments. But this was college football, and I was thrilled just being there.

Academically, Wake Forest was a tough school. When I saw my grades, I consoled myself recalling that my father hadn't done so well in college either, and he'd made something of himself. And I made some really good friends, especially on the football team. But I missed my family. I missed the Florida sunshine. And I discovered something I hadn't paid adequate attention to before. North of Atlanta, the weather is cold and gray in the winter. I didn't like that at all. After my second season of Wake Forest football, I transferred back home to Florida State University in Tallahassee.

I knew the Seminole football program was far out of my league. The legendary coach Bobby Bowden arrived the same week I did. The 'Noles were a Division I powerhouse. With my taped-up left knee and my JV experience, I was Division Forget-About-It. I joined a fraternity, Pi Kappa Alpha, and found my way back into student politics. What can I say? It's who I am. I was elected to the Student

Senate from the College of Education. Small-world alert: Steve Geller, who would become Senate Democratic leader when I was governor, was the one who recruited me to run.

When the student body president was impeached for some alleged impropriety, the vice president moved up to president and I was chosen by my fellow senators for the VP job. I vowed to pull my grades up so I might have a prayer at law school.

As a large public university, Florida State drew a wide diversity of students—rural, urban, people from different family backgrounds and different parts of the state. There were moderates, liberals, and conservatives on campus. This was Florida State—not Berkeley. Politically, I'd say I was somewhere in the middle of the pack.

The fall of my junior year, President Gerald Ford, who'd taken over after President Nixon was forced to resign, faced a challenge from Jimmy Carter, the Democratic governor of Georgia. This was the first year I was old enough to vote for president. I liked President Ford. I believed he was doing his best to heal the country after Watergate. Carter campaigned as an outsider with a fresh approach.

College students aren't always the most organized people, and Election Day somehow crept up on me. At noon on November 2, I was in the living room of the fraternity house, pacing back and forth and feeling frustrated with myself for being there.

"I can't believe I didn't vote absentee," I told my friend Tom Dzien.

"Me neither," said Tom, who, like me, came from St. Petersburg.

Tom and I jumped into my red Mustang. We took the old way home, Apalachee Parkway east to US 19, south to SR 589 south, almost exactly 250 miles. We walked into the polling place, St. Raphael Catholic Church on Snell Isle Boulevard, just south of the Shore Acres Bridge. This was thrilling, our first time voting in a presidential race. I turned the lever on the voting machine for President Ford and his running mate, Senator Bob Dole, two moderate Republicans. Tom told me he did the same. Then we got back into the Mustang and headed straight to Tallahassee.

It was very late when we finally got back to campus. That was a lot of driving for one day. But it was worth it. It made me think about Pappap and all he'd struggled for. Voting felt mighty good to me.

I was disappointed when my guy lost. But Jimmy Carter seemed like a decent, hardworking man to me. I figured President Carter would do his best for the country. And I was proud that, the first chance I got, I'd been a full participant in an inspiring system of self-government. I had helped elect the leader of the free world, the president of the United States.

Win or lose, I still feel that way every time I vote.

Florida State was a great place to go to college. I made wonderful friends. I really did develop some confidence there. Senior year, I started dating a beautiful, blond-haired girl named Amanda Morrow, who came from Palm Beach County. She was active in student government and a member of Tri Delta, one of the top sororities on campus. She ran for student body vice president with my friend Cory Ciklin. I felt lucky to have Mandy as my girlfriend. She was smart, cute, and fun.

But just after we all returned to school from Christmas break, the whole Tallahassee campus was badly shaken by an absolutely harrowing event. Around 2:45 A.M. on January 15, an unknown man walked into the Chi Omega sorority house and savagely beat four young women. He then broke into a basement apartment eight blocks away and attacked another Florida State student.

It took three weeks for the assailant to be caught. He was a former law student from Washington State named Ted Bundy, on a cross-country, multiyear murder spree. Before he was finally put to death in 1989, he confessed to thirty murders in seven states between 1974 and 1978. The true total could be much higher. The attacks left me with an intense empathy for crime victims that has followed me through my life. It also cemented my interest in attending law school.

But first I had to get in.

I earned good grades at Florida State, but my average was dragged down a bit by my three semesters at Wake Forest. My LSAT scores were okay, but not great.

The first few schools I applied to didn't make me wait long for an answer. "No thanks," they said right away.

My dad knew a lawyer in St. Pete named Joe Fleece whose son had applied to a law school in Birmingham, Alabama, called Cumberland, which was part of Samford University. The word was that Cumberland wasn't so hard to get into, at least back then. I submitted my application, and my dad followed up with a call to Dean Don Corley.

"My son's applied to these other schools," he said, "and he hasn't gotten in. But he was vice president of the student body at Florida State. He played football at Wake Forest. Charlie will make you proud. Just give him a chance."

Cumberland's one-man admission committee gave me a chance. To this day, when people ask me why I attended Cumberland School of Law at Samford University in Birmingham, Alabama, I have a four-word answer:

"Because they took me."

Once you've been attorney general, you can joke about that. I would end up being the fifth Florida governor to attend law school at Cumberland. I believe that's even more than the University of Florida has.

Being accepted to law school was a life-changing moment for me. It was my version, two generations later, of how my grandfather must have felt when he was offered a job by that man on Ellis Island. I too felt like the sun had come out. *Yes,* I thought, *I can see my future now. I'm going to law school. I'm going to be a lawyer. I am going to make it in life.*

Was I getting ahead of myself?

My first year at Cumberland was a nightmare. Before classes started, I read a book called *One L* by Scott Turow. I should never have read that book. It was about the first year of law school. That book scared the crap out of me. When I first arrived on campus in August of 1978, I met a guy in the class ahead of me who was out on a porch having a beer. Dorian Damoorgian was his name.

"I'm worried about school," I told him.

"Hey, man," he said, shooting me a big grin. "I'm from Florida too. If you just read the cases, you'll be fine. If I can make it, anybody can."

When I became governor, I ended up appointing Dorian to an appellate judgeship. He hid a super-sharp mind behind that laid-back attitude.

Law was a whole new language for me. I read with a dictionary open on my desk. Torts, contracts, real property, constitutional law—and your whole grade hanging on a single exam at the end of the term. I was pretty sure I was going to flunk out.

I came home at Christmas after my final exams and told my father, "I've washed out."

"Maybe so," he said calmly. "But let's go on a little duck hunting trip, and you can tell me about it." My dad had a friend named Eric Whitted, who was an assistant county school superintendent with a hunting lodge in Chassahowitzka on the Nature Coast. That's about seventy-five miles north of St. Petersburg.

On the drive up, my dad started asking me:

"Tell me about your contracts exam. What was it like? What were the questions? How did you answer?"

I told him as well as I could recall.

"What about real property?" he asked. I explained that too.

Finally, he said: "You know this stuff. You're not gonna flunk out. You've got a lot of knowledge in your head. I think you're going to be okay."

And I was. I didn't make Law Review. I wasn't at the top of my class. But when the grades came out, I did all right. And Dad felt vindicated, I think. I know the dean breathed a sigh of relief.

"What's coming next might not always be easy," my father told me. "But I'm pretty sure you're going to find your way."

Chapter 2

I appreciated my father's stirring confidence. But this whole grown-up thing, I kept discovering, was a little tougher than it looked.

I really liked Mandy Morrow. One Sunday afternoon during my first year at Cumberland Law, she was visiting me in Birmingham. We were sitting on the couch in my apartment. I hated that she had to head back to Tallahassee.

"Let's get married," I said.

"Really?" she asked.

"Yeah," I said. "Why not?"

"Okay," she said.

Mandy called that night and asked, "Are you sure about what you said this afternoon? We're kind of young." We were both twenty-one.

"Yeah," I told her. "It's exactly what I want to do."

We had a big wedding that summer in Delray Beach, where her family lived. During the ceremony, we were sitting in front of the minister when a candle shattered its glass holder at the end of one of the pews. *That's a weird omen,* I thought.

My family liked Mandy, and I believed her family liked me. We went to the Bahamas for our honeymoon. She moved to Birmingham, got a job as an urban planner, and we started arguing about silly stuff. Who was cleaning the apartment. Which brand of toothpaste to use. Stupid, trivial things. I hated to argue. I still do.

One night, I was talking on the phone with my father. "You doing okay?" he asked me.

"Yeah, I'm doing fine," I said.

"Why don't you call me tomorrow when I'm at the office."

"What's going on?" he asked me the next morning. "Is something wrong? Your voice didn't sound right."

"My marriage is not going well," I told him. "We're arguing all the time. I don't think I'm ready for this."

"What do you want to do?" he asked me.

"I don't know," I said.

"What about getting out?"

Nobody in my family had ever been divorced before, not that I'd ever heard about. I didn't even like saying the word. But when my dad said "What about getting out," it was like a light went on. I told Mandy: "You're a great person, but I just can't do this anymore. It's not good for either of us."

We cared for each other. She was a lovely person. She still is. It just didn't work out for us. The first person I told outside my family was Mike Hamby, one of my closest law school friends. Mike's parents were divorced.

"You're both great people," he said. "People are going to ask you what happened. When they do, just say, 'It didn't work out.'"

I do think the experience made me think long and hard before marrying again, and it made me a believer in living together before marriage.

I am grateful for what I learned at Cumberland, especially how to focus on complex issues and see the core principles buried in there. Law school is a perfect training ground for that. I ended up connecting with a lot of people from Florida, and I got my first up-close look at Bill Clinton.

He was our Law Day speaker in 1979, a young, first-term Democratic governor from Arkansas who hardly anyone had heard of before. But the speech he gave that day—and especially the way he connected with the students one-on-one—inspired everyone at Cumberland, Democrats and Republicans. And I remember saying to one of my friends: "That guy could be president one day." And I wasn't the only one who thought that.

By the grace of God and with a lot of grinding work, I graduated from Cumberland in 1981. But I flunked the Florida bar exam. After an internship in the state attorney's office in St. Petersburg and a brief stint in the graduate tax program at Emory University School of Law—what was I thinking? I hated math!—I got a job as general counsel at the National Association of Professional Baseball Leagues. That's the commissioner's office for minor league baseball.

The association's president, John Johnson, was a veteran of the New York Yankees organization and a wonderful man. I'm convinced the only reason he hired me was because the office manager, Barbara Douglas, had been a neighbor of ours. She must have told Mr. Johnson: "He's a good kid. He comes from a nice family." They started me at $19,000 a year.

I couldn't believe my good fortune. The job mixed law and sports, two things I loved. I reviewed contracts and protected trademarks. I settled territorial disputes among the different minor leagues, whose owners sometimes had conflicting needs and easily bruised feelings. That was ideal training for politics. I went to the baseball winter meetings in Honolulu and to the player drafts in New York. I got to work under baseball commissioners Bowie Kuhn and Peter Ueberroth.

And then I flunked the bar exam a second time.

I was devastated. I was sure I'd be fired from my baseball-lawyer job. I wondered, *Am I ever going to get my license? Is my law career over before it even begins?* I went into Mr. Johnson's office to face my future.

"I've got some bad news," I said. "I didn't pass the bar again. I'm not sure what to do or what your thoughts are."

"Don't worry about it," he told me. "Stay on. You'll do administrative stuff. Take the exam again. How many times can you take it?"

"I don't think there's a limit," I said. "As many as you want."

"Just study harder, and take it again."

Talk about a lifeboat! Mr. Johnson gave me a shot and another chance. Years later, when my Republican friends were in an uproar over my efforts to restore the rights of Florida felons, I would remember that. Everyone deserves a second chance—or, in my case, a third chance.

I passed the next time. I'd like to think I was beating a path for John Kennedy Jr., who needed three tries too. I was on my way.

I was gaining confidence. I was meeting people. I was growing up. I was making my way into the world of politics. I joined the local Rotary Club. I liked their slogan, "Service Above Self." I also became active with the St. Petersburg Area Chamber of Commerce. And I joined the Pinellas County Young Republicans. I thought that these groups might be a base for something. I didn't know what. I stayed with minor league baseball for five years, until I left to practice law with my sister Margaret's husband, J. Emory Wood.

This was the early and middle 1980s, a time of large leaders and a changing world. Ronald Reagan was president. The Berlin Wall hadn't fallen yet, but Communism was definitely on the run. And the threats we faced in the world—Grenada! Nicaragua!—sound pretty puny now. Reagan wasn't universally beloved. The Iran-contra scandal was brewing. But he found a way to work with Tip O'Neill, the Democratic Speaker of the House of Representatives. The Republican president's sunny personality and human touch created a whole new political category, Reagan Democrats.

Florida's Democratic governor, Bob Graham, also had a broad appeal, even though Florida, like the rest of the South, was becoming more Republican. He had captured public attention by working eight-hour shifts as a teacher, a busboy, a police officer, a railroad engineer—jobs of regular Floridians. Once in office, he focused on improving education and diversifying Florida's economy beyond tourism and agriculture. He had a real commitment to Florida's natural environment, creating our Save the Everglades program. Even many Republicans loved Bob Graham.

And things kept puttering along in Pinellas County. The county was still more Republican than many parts of Florida. Our local congressman, Bill Cramer, was a Republican. He was followed by Bill Young, another Republican. Bob Dole came to Guy Lombardo's Port O' Call Resort in Tierra Verde for the party's Lincoln Day Dinner one year. I was impressed with how down-to-earth Senator Dole was for a Washington political powerhouse. I didn't realize at the time that the days of his kind of Republican were as numbered as they were.

In 1986 I made my first run for office. I was twenty-nine years old. Some friends in the Republican Party reached out to me and suggested I might try for a state senate seat in St. Petersburg. They knew I was active in the community groups and I'd grown up in St. Pete. That's a very typical path into politics.

I campaigned door-to-door. I had a slogan—"Crist: A Name You Can Trust"—which I printed on yard signs and leaflets. It wasn't exactly the snappiest slogan. But I thought it might remind some folks of my dad, the trusted family doctor, and our family more generally. My big issue was education. I said we had to improve the public schools. I didn't raise much money. But I did well enough in my interview with the editorial board at the *St. Petersburg Times* that I got the paper's endorsement in the Republican primary.

In a tight four-candidate field, I made it to the Republican primary runoff, then lost by about two hundred votes. The Republican candidate who beat me, a local optometrist named Bob Melby, was then defeated by the Democratic incumbent, Jeanne Malchon, who went off to Tallahassee for another four years. Incumbents still have a real advantage in a race like that.

It would have been wonderful to win. But I never really expected to. I just considered the race a valuable first experience.

Around that time, Connie Mack was just establishing himself on the statewide political scene. Connie was my idea of a Republican politician—tall, lean, graying hair, warm, gracious, able to talk with anyone, clear on his principles of low taxes and an open business climate. By the time I got to know him in 1988, he was a three-term congressman from Cape Coral near Fort Myers with his eye on Lawton Chiles's Senate seat. To me, he already looked like a senator from central casting and always carried himself that way.

His real name was Cornelius Alexander McGillicuddy III, but everyone called him Connie Mack, the same name people used for his grandfather. The original Connie Mack was first-string baseball royalty. Born in 1862, he joined the Washington Nationals in 1886 for a ten-year playing career in the National League. He was a pretty good catcher—not a powerful hitter—who was nonetheless credited early in his career with several lasting innovations to the game. Baseball historians say he was the first catcher to position himself immediately behind home plate and the first to begin needling batters to distract them. But it was as a manager and co-owner of the Philadelphia Athletics that Cornelius Alexander McGillicuddy Sr. earned his place in the Baseball Hall of Fame. He managed the team for half a century, from 1901 to 1950. He always wore a coat and tie to the ballpark, and there are a bushel full of managerial records still listed in his name: most wins (3,731, nearly a thousand more than anyone else), most losses (3,948), and most games managed (7,755).

The baseball great wasn't the only achiever in Connie III's lineage. His maternal grandfather, Morris Sheppard, was a congressman and US senator from Texas. When Senator Sheppard died, his widow quickly married a second US senator from Texas, Tom Connally.

"I think my grandmother must have liked being married to a senator," Connie often joked.

We don't pick our leaders by heredity in America. We got rid of that when we booted the British out. But over the centuries—think Adams, Roosevelt, Kennedy, Bush—some families have certainly provided more than their share. Years later, Connie Mack IV would serve in the Florida House of Representatives, win his father's old seat in Congress, and marry a congresswoman, Mary Bono Mack of California, who was herself the widow of a congressman, the late entertainer Sonny Bono.

Connie III had been a Democrat as a young man, just like his Philadelphia family members were. He told me it was Ronald Reagan's cheerfulness and clarity that inspired him to get involved in politics and run for Congress as a Republican in 1982. Midway through his third term, he declared that he would give up his seat in Congress to run against the powerful Senator Chiles. That seemed like political suicide.

But when the popular Democrat finally did decide to retire from the Senate, all of a sudden a bunch of other, better-known Republicans were ready to jump into the primary race. They included Congressman Bill McCollum of Orlando. I sent a letter to the editor of the *St. Petersburg Times*, saying Republicans ought to support Connie in the primary. I stressed that he was the only one who'd had the guts to take on the giant Chiles.

No one asked me to do that. It was just how I felt. Connie got the Republican nomination and the chance to face Democratic congressman Buddy MacKay in November. Connie's campaign manager, Mitch Bainwol, took me to lunch at Bennigan's on 4th Street North in St. Pete and asked me who might be a good choice to direct the ground game in Pinellas County.

I suggested a couple of prominent local Republicans.

"What about you?" Mitch asked.

"I'm thirty-one years old," I reminded him. "I lost my election for the state senate."

"You'll be fine," he said.

The Mack-MacKay race was described at the time as a real Irish slugfest. The incredibly close results might have been the original precursor to Bush versus Gore.

"I'm mainstream conservative, and he's a liberal Democrat," Connie asserted during the only televised debate.

"I'd use labels too," Buddy shot back, "if I had a record like

Mr. Mack." Buddy liked to call himself a conservative Southern Democrat.

That's what passed for mudslinging in the Florida Senate race of 1988. It was clearly a gentler era. Both of these candidates were at heart truly decent men.

On Election Night, each of them was within a whisker of 50 percent. It was the closest US Senate race in Florida history. We didn't know the winner for days, which has become much more of a pattern in recent years. But Connie pulled it out in the end.

Buddy would go on to serve as lieutenant governor when his best friend, Lawton Chiles, was elected governor. Almost eight years later, in a bittersweet twist, Buddy himself served briefly as governor—for twenty-four days—when Lawton died before Jeb Bush was sworn in. And before Connie took office at the start of 1989, Mitch Bainwol asked me join the new senator's staff as state director. I set up and ran six Senate offices across Florida and went to Washington occasionally.

I can't imagine a better way to learn public service from the ground up.

People called and walked into those Senate offices all day long, looking for help with an extraordinary variety of issues. Veterans benefits. Late Social Security checks. A problem with the IRS. A child with a dream of attending one of the military academies. If it had anything at all to do with the federal government—and, often, even if it didn't—we'd try to help.

This was frontline constituent service, the basic human link between an elected officeholder and his boss, the people, the ones who elected him. It was my job—and the job of Senator Mack's other aides—to help those people any way we could. A phone call to some obscure federal agency. An application for an SBA loan. It could be almost anything. A big part of the job was just lending a sympathetic ear.

It was truly an honor to do that. It was thoroughly gratifying how much you could genuinely help people if you took the time to try. And people were immensely appreciative.

I look at that period as the start of my real career and my real education in politics. I became totally convinced that serving the public was how I wanted to spend my life. I didn't care so much about making money. It wasn't the fame or the power that drove me. This might sound corny—I don't know—but the joy of helping people was almost indescribable. I felt like I had found my purpose in life. I knew I had to learn the ropes. I was lucky to be working for a real professional. I imagined that, at some point, I might want to run for office again, though I had no idea when or for what. But in signing on full-time with Connie Mack and being his link with the people who sent him to Washington, public service went from an interest and a passion for me to something more than that—a full-time career and commitment that would follow me for the rest of my life.

I traveled with the senator when he was home. I got to know tons of people all across Florida. I learned how to deal competently—and compassionately—with the myriad of concerns that constituents bring to their elected officials.

Back then and still today, I always had my boss's words in my head: "Listen to the people. Try to help them. Constantly remind them that we work for them."

As I spent time around Florida's new senator, I kept remembering a story my mother used to tell about me when I was a boy. Some adult would ask her what I wanted to do when I grew up.

"I think he wants to go into politics," my mother would answer proudly.

"He's too nice to be a politician" was the inevitable reply.

Connie proved that theory wrong. He helped me see that a nice human being really could succeed in politics.

Given Connie's family history, it was no surprise that he would find a way to help Florida get its own major league baseball team. Lots of teams came south for spring training. Plenty of minor league teams played in Florida. But baseball commissioner Fay Vincent wasn't convinced that a major league franchise could succeed in the state.

Connie disagreed. He highlighted the close ties between baseball and Florida. He reminded baseball officials how many fans lived in Florida. He might have even mentioned baseball's antitrust exemption, a law that let the teams coordinate in ways that normal businesses could not. Baseball was the only major sport that had that exemption. A quiet campaign like that, coming from a senator named Connie Mack—well, before you knew it, plans were moving forward for what we now know as the Miami Marlins and Tampa Bay Rays.

Was that liberal? Was that conservative? Was it Democratic or Republican? Connie didn't care. His only question was: Is it good for Florida?

He and I went to a spring training game together at Al Lang Stadium in St. Petersburg. I had been coordinating with local business groups while Connie was pushing the levers of real power in Washington. He walked into that game like a conquering hero. Everyone knew Connie Mack. He was fighting for them.

Over the years, I would get to know and work with quite a few

Republican officeholders who had that special knack for thinking creatively and working across any aisle. John McCain was a master at that, using his gruff, tell-it-like-he-sees-it demeanor to beat his own independent paths. Bob Dole was a natural too. There was no Democrat in Washington he couldn't find something in common with, no matter where on the political spectrum that person stood. Jack Kemp, Mel Martinez—there were many others: loyal, dedicated, effective Republicans who didn't think it was a crime to be open and nice.

Both parties used to be teeming with leaders like those. Connie Mack was that kind of leader. If I ever got elected to anything, I told myself, that's the kind of leader I wanted to be.

But for now, I was learning my way around politics. I was loving the work I was doing for Connie and the people of Florida. I was totally happy where I was. I was beginning to think I might run again for something someday, though I wasn't immediately sure what.

Chapter 3

I
t didn't take long.

    On November 3, 1992, the same day Bill Clinton won the White House from George H. W. Bush, I was elected to the Florida Senate. I was thirty-six years old, almost exactly ten years younger than the new president was. I defeated a longtime Democratic senator named Helen Gordon Davis, though that didn't exactly make me a giant killer. The district lines had been redrawn after the 1990 census, and Helen's strength was Tampa. The new district included more of Republican-leaning St. Petersburg. My three-pronged message—pro-education, pro-environment, anti-crime—seemed to connect with the voters. And spending time on Connie Mack's staff had given me the valuable opportunity to interact with thousands of civic leaders, business people, and regular folks—not just around St. Petersburg but across the state.

    Election Night, my mom, my dad, all three of my sisters, a bunch of my old friends, and a couple of media people gathered at the Firehouse, a bar and restaurant in downtown St. Pete. It took a while for the final results to trickle in. Finally, Steve Nichols, a reporter with Tampa Bay's WTVT/Channel 13, got a tip from his news desk.

"You're down by twenty percent," he said.

Really? I plopped into a chair like the wind was kicked out of me. *Not again*, I thought.

But a minute later, Steve was back.

"I'm really sorry," he said. "We got that wrong. You're *up* by twenty. It's confirmed now."

Yes, every vote really does count, a crucial lesson in Florida politics.

Winning a real election was everything I imagined it would be. I felt instantly exhilarated. The months of door-to-door campaigning, the many friends who helped, waking up early on Election Day to wave campaign signs outside the Tyrone Square Mall—all of it seemed totally worth it now. We had won. I'll tell you how excited I was. I danced that night in the Firehouse to the Sister Sledge song "We Are Family."

We are family.
Get up ev'rybody and sing.

And I really don't like dancing at all.

It just so happened that my election ended the Democrats' 128-year control of the Florida Senate. With me there, the legislature's upper chamber was evenly split, twenty Republicans and twenty Democrats. Now, every single vote counted, every single day. So when I arrived in Tallahassee, my new Republican colleagues were very happy to see me.

I focused immediately on the issue of crime and criminals. No one had to tell me how rattling violent crime could be—and not just because of my criminal law courses at Cumberland. I remembered Ted Bundy from Florida State. Growing up, I'd known several other crime victims. My heart really went out to these people and their families. Carjackings, home-invasion robberies, drive-by shootings along with horrible rapes and murders and assaults: In the early 1990s, Florida was the number-one state in America for violent crime. And the serious felonies seemed to be spreading into middle-class neighborhoods. An elderly deaf couple were savagely beaten in St. Petersburg, leaving the man in critical condition and the woman dead. A fired insurance claims adjuster shot his former supervisors, killing three and wounding two. The frustrated police erected most-wanted billboards along state highways. Tourism was even starting to suffer. People on South Beach were wearing T-shirts reading "Sunshine, Sand, Murder." Our governor, Lawton Chiles, made a trip to Miami after a German visitor was killed near the airport. Before the governor got out of the SUV, he took off his jacket and put on a bulletproof vest. That made headlines around the world.

One thing I noticed was that many people who went to prison in Florida didn't seem to stay very long. It wasn't unusual for prisoners—even murderers—to pack their stuff and go home after 20 or 25 percent of their terms. The criminal justice system had plenty of justice for the criminals and almost none for the victims of their crimes. So I sponsored legislation requiring inmates to serve at least 85 percent of their sentences. STOP, it was called, for Stop Turning Out Prisoners. It flew through the legislature. Governor Chiles allowed the change to become law without his signature, going along with it while hinting he wasn't exactly thrilled.

But it was the chain gangs that really got me noticed in Tallahassee. In 1995, Alabama had revived the practice of shackling prisoners together and sending them out to work with armed guards, often collecting litter along the highways. The practice had been abandoned in most places in the 1940s. Still, I thought reinstituting appropriate punishment was an important concept, and I decided on a dramatic way of making the point. So one day in the Senate chamber, I hoisted a set of chains above my head—and, boy, were they heavier than I thought! With Robert Wexler, a very liberal Democrat from South Florida, I co-sponsored a chain gang amendment. "It's as popular in my district as it is in yours," Robert told me.

It was Martin Dyckman, an editorial writer at the *St. Petersburg Times*, who first coined the nickname "Chain Gang Charlie." I can assure you it was not meant as a term of endearment. But soon enough, people across the state were calling me "Chain Gang," and I didn't mind it one bit. My Republican friends certainly didn't mind. They appeared proud of me. "Your political career is set, son," said Malcolm Beard, a very fatherly senator from the Tampa area, shaking my hand energetically. Before serving in Tallahassee, he'd been the Hillsborough County sheriff. Being tough on criminals was fine with Republicans. So was the law I co-sponsored creating charter schools. So was the time I grilled Governor Chiles in the Ethics and Elections Committee on Election Eve scare calls to seniors. The calls made wildly exaggerated claims about Jeb Bush, the governor's Republican challenger, threatening Social Security—political dynamite in a state like Florida. Grilling Democratic governors is guaranteed to delight Republicans, even if the governor is personally exonerated, as Lawton Chiles was.

These were heady times to be a Republican—in Florida and across America. As Republicans in Tallahassee discovered what it meant to be a majority party—you actually got to have your way!—our colleagues in Washington were making similar inroads. Newt Gingrich was orchestrating a Republican takeover in Congress and pushing his Contract with America, as the Republican disdain for Bill Clinton began flying into overdrive and ultimately to impeachment.

I didn't really get the anti-Clinton outrage. To me, he seemed like a fairly levelheaded leader who was pushing the Democratic Party more toward the middle, something Republicans should be pleased about. When the Monica Lewinsky scandal blew up, I felt sad for everyone involved, the families especially.

The truth is, all of that felt like a million miles away from the Florida capital. I was having a fine time in Tallahassee. I got along well with the other senators, including the Democrats. I loved being able to find an issue people cared about—and really seize on it. I did that on education funding. And protecting the environment. But it wasn't all handshakes and back pats in the Florida capital. I learned that lesson when I strayed from the party line on abortion. Now *that* was playing with fire. Republicans in the Senate didn't like their members, especially new members, crossing party lines on such a hot-button issue.

A bill came before the legislature in the spring of 1995, seeking to impose a mandatory, twenty-four-hour waiting period before a woman could have an abortion. There was no medical justification for this, no practical reason at all—other than the desire of some abortion opponents to throw up every imaginable roadblock. When the proposal came before the Health Care Committee, I voted with the Democrats, creating a 3–3 tie and killing the legislation for that session. Abortion opponents were outraged. Some had appeared before the committee with gruesome abortion photos. Senator Robert Harden, a Republican from Fort Walton Beach who'd sponsored the bill, vowed to find another way to get it approved.

Looking back, that vote took some nerve for a first-term Republican, but it didn't feel huge to me at the time. While I didn't like abortion personally, I was equally opposed to government inserting itself into such a personal medical decision. I thought this should be a woman's decision—period—with whatever input she sought from her doctor, her partner, or her clergy. I was only voting my judgment and my conscience. Isn't that what legislators were supposed to do? I knew I couldn't be the only Republican who believed that.

Some of the Senate's Republican staffers had watched the committee meeting on closed-circuit TV. When I got back to the office, several of them quietly congratulated me. "Great vote, boss," said my administrative assistant, Ronda Federspiel. I'd call Ronda a moderate Republican.

Lucy Morgan called from the *St. Petersburg Times*. She asked me why I'd voted that way.

"I generally don't like the government telling people what to do," I said.

Who does, really?

"I believe in individual rights and freedom," I told Lucy, "That's why I'm a Republican."

Not too many Republican officeholders would give an answer like that today, not unless they wanted to attract angry opposition in their next primary run. But the answer seemed natural enough back then. True, the party was pro-life, and I didn't personally like abortion. But I was raised with three sisters and no brothers. I didn't like telling women what to do with their bodies. It just seemed to me that people should make their own decisions on an issue as personal as that.

Lucy quoted me in her piece. But no one yelled at me. No one tried to throw me out of the Republican caucus. Party discipline wasn't so strict back then. In the clubby culture of the Florida Legislature, the legislators were permitted certain individual quirks. The people had elected us, after all. All of our districts were different. Some people might be upset or not like a vote or even feel abandoned. But there were limits to how confrontational the personal exchanges got.

Mostly, disapproval was expressed with what I came to think of as "the look."

After the abortion vote, I got the look from Senator John Grant of Tampa, staring disapprovingly at me over his reading glasses. I just smiled back.

I got the look any time I did something in Tallahassee that wasn't from the usual Republican playbook. When I supported teacher salary increases. When I raised funds for conservation in the Everglades by suggesting a charge for new vanity license plates. It was never overtly hostile. It was more of a raised eyebrow and a shaking head: "Really? Do you have to?" But it was when I championed lower electric rates that some of my Republican colleagues got really steamed. Florida Power had raised its rates abruptly. People were livid when they opened their bills. We had a hearing in the Senate on the rate hike. But I felt like I should do something more personal and direct.

I sued Florida Power, though not as a state senator. I filed as myself, a consumer. I didn't have the state pay the legal bills. I paid for the suit myself. Some of my fellow Republicans were definitely shaking their heads at that. In a few special cases—this was one of them—the look was put into words.

"What are you doing?" Senator Grant wanted to know. "These are our friends. These are the guys who support us and help get us elected and raise money for us. You'll regret this. They're too powerful to mess around with."

"I respect how you feel," I told him. "But it's not how I feel. They're being unfair to the people who elected me, and I can't let that stand. What they're doing is wrong."

Back then, I could get away with that and not be treated like a Republican pariah. The people had sent me to Tallahassee. I was getting lots of publicity. No one in the close-knit Republican caucus really wanted to take me on, so we stayed friendly.

With all the attention I'd been getting since "Chain Gang Charlie," people started asking me about running for something larger than a state senate seat. Al Austin, a politically astute real estate developer who had contributed to my campaigns, took me to lunch one day in Tampa. "If this keeps up," he said, "you should probably be thinking about running statewide."

I figured, why start small? Bob Graham's Democratic Senate seat was up in 1998. Graham was a beloved figure in Florida politics, even more than I knew. But as Al told me: "The Republicans will need to run someone against him." I decided to give up my seat in the Florida Senate and make the big leap to Washington.

Let's just call the idea highly premature.

The campaign was beyond tough. I had trouble raising money. No one really thought I could win. Everybody I met seemed devoted to Senator Graham. Later, I found out why. He was always kind to everyone, including an absurdly long-shot challenger like me. Mitch Bainwol, who'd moved from Connie Mack's staff to run the Recording Industry Association of America, called with a heads-up late on Election Day.

"You know," he said, "sometimes in these elections, the media will declare a winner, like, one minute after the polls close. I just want you to be ready for that."

That's exactly what happened. I believe the race was called at 7:01. Just as Mitch predicted, the words were right there on the screen. "SEN. GRAHAM WINS." He clobbered me by twenty-six points. But it wasn't a total loss, I told myself. I got some statewide name recognition, and I got credibility and credit in the Florida Republican Party for taking on such a towering Democrat.

Jeb Bush had a better night than I did.

As I was being creamed by Bob Graham, the second son of George and Barbara Bush was elected the forty-third governor of Florida.

Jeb grew up in Houston, attended the University of Texas at Austin, and moved to Florida after his father was elected vice president in 1980. He quickly began building a political career. In 1986, he was named Florida's secretary of commerce, a position he kept for two years until he left to help his father campaign for president. After losing the governor's race to Democrat Lawton Chiles in 1994 by less than two percentage points, he ran again four years later, portraying himself as a consensus-building pragmatist. He made a real effort to court the state's moderate Hispanic voters. This time, he sailed past Democrat Buddy MacKay with 55 percent of the vote. On the same day, Jeb's older brother, George W. Bush, won a second term as the governor of Texas.

Jeb had real leadership qualities. I could see that from the day he showed up in Florida. He connected well with people. He was super-smart. He had unparalleled Republican connections. He was highly ambitious. And for the next eight years, he was the central figure in Florida politics.

Jeb and I had a friendly relationship. He saw me as an up-and-comer, I believe. I was certainly no threat to him. After my sacrificial-lamb role against Bob Graham, Jeb appointed me to a nice—if slightly obscure—position as deputy secretary of business and professional regulation, overseeing Florida's cosmetologists, veterinarians, real estate agents, pari-mutuel wagering clerks, and others who needed licenses to operate. It was fun meeting all those people in all those different occupations and trying to solve problems in their fields. The $90,000 annual salary seemed like a princely sum to me. It was far more money than I had ever earned before.

But I missed serving the public in elected office. I liked being out there, dealing with a wide range of issues, helping folks with whatever their problems were. I was grateful to Jeb for the appointment. It was an important job. But being a deputy secretary inside a sprawling government agency wasn't exactly how I wanted to spend the rest of my life. It was inevitable I would run for office again.

The 2000 election hit Florida like a Category 5 hurricane—and talk about a personal brush with history: I was on that infamous ballot too, right there with George W. Bush, Al Gore, and something called a hanging chad. Thankfully, Crist versus Sheldon, the 2000 race for state commissioner of education, wasn't quite the nail-biter that Bush versus Gore turned out to be. With my good friend David Rancourt running my campaign, I outpolled former Democrat state representative George Sheldon of Tampa by a comfortable seven percentage points. So I went to bed November 7, 2000, with a smile on my face, still not knowing who the next president would be but pleased with how my race came out.

I woke up the next morning with a terrible pain in my gut. No one had won. No one had conceded. But I figured we'd know soon enough who won Florida and the White House—Bush or Gore— probably sometime that afternoon.

Not quite.

The whole thing was a total fiasco, from beginning to end.

Lines had stretched for hours. Older voters had been thoroughly confused. The results were painfully close. The voting system was a total mess. Oh, and the Florida governor's big brother was one of the candidates.

There was that.

As the whole world quickly discovered, Florida was utterly unable to handle a close election. The wide variety of ballot types, the lack of reliable paper trails, the angry mobs outside the election counting rooms, the lawyers rushing into state and federal court, county election officials who looked like they might be castoffs from an especially low-rated reality TV show. The hours turned into days, which turned into weeks. No one knew how ridiculously long this state of confusion might continue.

"STATE OF CONFUSION": That would have made a perfect headline—and maybe a new slogan for Florida's license plates.

To this day, I don't think anyone really knows which candidate got more votes for president in Florida that year. The only honest answer is "It depends." It depends on how the votes were counted, who counted them, when they were counted, what exactly counted as a vote, and how much influence over the process Secretary of State Katherine Harris really had.

It was bad.

For thirty-five excruciating days and nights, Florida squirmed and stumbled under a twenty-four-hour media spotlight. For anyone who cared about the state, this was truly painful to watch. And the final result was a direct affront on the sacred concept of democracy. Not that George W. Bush ended up on top. Someone had to. The problem was how: a 5-to-4 vote by the United States Supreme Court, following a predictable conservative-liberal split, installing a new president in a process that alienated millions and millions of patriotic Americans who believed the people were supposed to make that choice.

Electing a president is the single greatest obligation the voters have in a representative democracy. This was certainly no way to do that.

The echoes of the 2000 election would bounce around Florida for many years to come. What happened that fall affected me in countless ways, as it affected many others in Florida. I had nothing to do with running that election. As the newly elected education commissioner, I certainly didn't have any power to change the way that elections were held. But as all this exploded around me, I developed a whole new appreciation for the importance of fair and competent elections. And I vowed, if I ever got the chance, I would do whatever I could to help Florida achieve a system we could all be proud of.

In the meantime, as the incoming education commissioner, I had a serious job to do: improving the quality of Florida teaching and lifting the standards of our schools. This was not something that could possibly be placed on long-term hold.

Our state needed an educated population so people could find jobs, solve problems, and live better lives. Yet Florida had a history of shoddy, underfunded public education, and the state had clearly suffered as a result. That had to change, I thought. I worked with local school districts, with education experts, and with parent and teacher groups. To his credit, Jeb Bush had made education reform a top priority of his administration. So I got some solid support in the governor's office. We both wanted results. Jeb was pushing charter schools and standardized testing, concepts I generally supported. I was working on making teachers more accountable and getting the good ones paid well. Working together, we made some genuine progress. Reading scores improved. Parents got more choices about the schools their children attended. The legislature got a little less stingy about paying the bills.

But I did get the look again from some of my fellow Republicans, who thought I pushed the cause of public education too hard. "Some teachers in our school systems should earn a hundred thousand dollars a year," I said one day, unapologetically.

"The teachers' unions aren't exactly friends of ours," I was reminded more than once. "Republicans are more interested in private and religious schools."

None of this seemed complicated to me. If we wanted good teachers, we should pay them decently. When it came to public education, I had the benefit of personal experience. My three sisters and I all went to public schools. Two of my sisters became educators. My mom and dad both went to Penn State. I'd finished college at Florida State. I always have—and always will—fight for public education.

And you know who else seemed to agree? Our Republican president, George W. Bush. His No Child Left Behind program was downright progressive compared to the stuff being advanced by some public school haters. He traveled to public schools across the country to promote the plan. And when the terror attacks occurred on September 11, 2001, where was the president? He wasn't ripping public education. He was reading to school children at the Emma E. Booker Elementary School in Sarasota. Oddly, on September 7, the day Bush's visit was announced, 9/11 hijackers Mohamed Atta and Marwan al-Shehhi traveled to Sarasota and enjoyed drinks and dinner at a Holiday Inn two miles down the beach from where the president was scheduled to stay.

In 2003, the job of state education commissioner was turning into an appointed position. Jeb and I were working well together. I had no reason to think he wouldn't have appointed me. But I had already decided to run for attorney general, a job with far broader responsibilities and a much higher profile. This wouldn't be an easy race. I had to get past two Republican primary opponents and Democrat Buddy Dyer, a state senator from Orlando who was a famously tough campaigner.

I campaigned hard. I promised to be a pro-consumer attorney general. I said I'd continue my efforts on education reform. I vowed to make an impact on Florida civil rights. During a campaign, I spoke to a forum at the Florida NAACP—the only candidate, Republican or Democrat, to do that.

Buddy threw some punches on the general election campaign trail. One of his ads carried a tagline that said: "Charlie Crist: unqualified, unethical, incompetent. Are these really the qualities we want in our next attorney general?" Buddy never quite spelled out what was so awful about me. So I never really had to defend myself.

I didn't take any of it personally. I had better statewide name recognition than Buddy did, and I raised more money. And the popular Jeb Bush was at the top of the Republican ticket, also championing education reform. As the Republican candidate for attorney general, I would have had a tough time losing that year.

I defeated Buddy with 53 percent of the vote. The next year, Buddy was easily elected mayor of Orlando, a job he still holds today, developing into one of the finest big-city mayors in recent Florida history. I became Florida's first Republican attorney general and joined the state's first all-Republican cabinet along with Chief Financial Officer Tom Gallagher and Agriculture Commissioner Charles Bronson. With both houses of the legislature also solidly in Republican hands, Florida government was now truly in the grip of Republicans.

That placed certain expectations on me. A big team had been assembled here, and I was supposed to be on it. As I was about to start my term, several Republican advisers told me: "You gotta fire everybody in that office. They're all Democrats. We won. We get the fruits of our victory. Go hire a bunch of Republicans. That's how politics works."

That didn't sound like good advice to me.

I'll be new, I thought to myself. *Everyone else in the office will be new. No one will know how the office is run.* My view was that most of the people in the office were just hardworking professionals who were doing their jobs. Until I saw otherwise, I didn't think mass firings were the way to begin my term.

I just went to work.

We did all the stuff an attorney general usually does, representing the state in lawsuits, giving state agencies legal advice. But we also got the legislature to change the law in Florida to allow the attorney general to bring civil rights cases without going through the US Justice Department first.

"We've got this new law," I said. "Let's go use it."

What could be more important to our democracy than basic civil rights? The right to vote. The right to equal protection under the law. The right to fair treatment in employment, housing, and public accommodation. If these rights aren't in place, we don't have a democracy. That's not a liberal or conservative opinion. It's not Republican or Democratic. It's an American value that everyone should embrace.

The first civil rights case I brought was against a hotel in Perry, Florida, outside Tallahassee. It was called the Southern Inn. An African American family was having a reunion at the hotel. The owner went out to the pool and began to yell at the children: "No coloreds in the pool." This was the summer of 2003.

We sued the hotel. I'm not sure if all my fellow Republicans thought that was such a great use of our office resources. But at the conclusion of the case, the hotel owner could never again do business in Florida.

Later, we reopened an ancient civil rights case that had never been solved. On Christmas night in 1951, a bomb went off beneath the home of Harry and Harriette Moore, local educators and top leaders in the Florida NAACP. It was their twenty-fifth wedding anniversary. They'd been working hard making sure local African Americans weren't denied their right to vote. Both of them were killed. Some historians call the Moores America's first civil rights martyrs. No one was ever charged in their deaths. We disproved old rumors that linked Sheriff Willis McCall to the crime. But we determined the murders had been the work of violent members of a Central Florida klavern of the Ku Klux Klan, one of eleven bombings against black people in the state that year. We identified four men as directly involved, including Earl J. Brooklyn, who had floor plans to the Moores' house and had recruited the others. All four had already died.

Being Florida attorney general is a wonderful job. Far more than most government positions, it is defined by the individual who holds it. It seemed to me the people had elected me, and I should fight for them. Consumers. Rate payers. Policyholders. Credit card customers. Mortgagees. Far too often, they were being treated unfairly by large corporations and utilities. Shouldn't the people have a lawyer too? I'd tested that proposition when I was in the state senate. Now I had the platform to do much more.

I spoke with my chief of staff, George LeMieux.

"These phone bills are getting outrageous," I said. "All the add-ons that no one really reads or notices—that's not fair to people. They're slipping stuff by and taking advantage. That's just wrong."

George told me the same thing John Grant had when I was in the Senate. "These are our friends, you know?" he said. "You want to go after them?"

And I answered similarly: "Absolutely. Republicans pay those bills too."

George nodded. But I knew what he thought.

I hired Jack Shreve, who had been Florida's public counsel, the state's official consumer watchdog. The day I hired Jack, we had a small press conference.

"Did you ask him what party he is in?" Lucy Morgan asked.

"No," I answered. Then, turning to Jack: "What party are you in?"

"I'm a Democrat," he said. "Is that a problem?"

"No," I said. "I don't care."

I didn't think I had to. Jack was an excellent hire, whatever party he was in.

He was hugely knowledgeable—and hugely effective—at keeping regulatory heat on. Inside the attorney general's office, Jack had actual influence with the rate-setting Public Service Commission. He saved Florida consumers hundreds of millions of dollars over the years.

Again, no one called up and said, "You stupid ass. You can't do this." But the skeptical looks were coming more frequently, and increasingly, the skepticism was being expressed out loud.

"Really? You want to do that? Are you sure?"

I was sure.

The truth is I was never that much of a partisan. How could any thinking person be? I believed in the power of political parties. I liked having allies. People have to come together somehow to get things done. But give up my own priorities and judgment? Let others do my thinking for me? Be such a loyal team player that I forget who I am? No thank you to any of that.

As I began to build my political career, you wouldn't call me a rebel. I wasn't picking constant fights. I always preferred bringing people together instead of squabbling with them. I was a Republican. No one missed that. I checked all the boxes Republicans do: low taxes, tough on crime, support for a strong national defense—not that I had too much need for that last one as I climbed the ladder of Florida state politics. But in all the jobs I've had—and I've had a few—I tried to remain true to the things I cared about and always tried to be my own man. That could point me conservative. It could point me liberal. I wasn't big on labels. If I stuck with causes I believed in, I told myself, the politics would take care of themselves. And I could admire leadership talent wherever it turned up.

Even at a Democratic Party convention.

I got a blast of that on Tuesday, July 27, 2004, watching the keynote address at the Democratic National Convention on TV. This was the year the Democrats nominated John Kerry and John Edwards for president and vice president. As the Republican attorney general of Florida, I certainly wasn't showing up at the FleetCenter in Boston in person. The big opening speech was delivered by an Illinois state senator whose name I had never heard before that week: Barack Obama. He had just achieved an unexpected victory in the Democratic primary for a US Senate seat. He was clearly a rising star in his party.

It was a moving speech from beginning to end, delivered with passion and precision and natural drama. But the part that struck me most was when this young state senator said:

"There is not a liberal America and a conservative America— there is the United States of America. There is not a black America and a white America and Latino America and Asian America— there's the United States of America. The pundits like to slice and dice our country into Red States and Blue States; Red States for Republicans, Blue States for Democrats. But I've got news for them too: We worship an awesome God in the Blue States, and we don't like federal agents poking around in our libraries in the Red States. We coach Little League in the Blue States, and, yes, we've got some gay friends in the Red States. There are patriots who opposed the war in Iraq, and there are patriots who supported the war in Iraq."

In seventeen minutes, he was interrupted thirty-three times by applause. I'm not sure if he could hear me clapping or not.

For many Republican politicians, it was easy to sign on with the extremists in the Terri Schiavo case. It was impossible for me.

Terri was a young woman who had lived with her husband, Michael, in an apartment a few blocks from my place in St. Petersburg. I had never met either of them. But early in the morning of February 25, 1990, at the age of twenty-six, Terri had collapsed in a hallway. Her husband called 9-1-1. The paramedics found her unconscious and facedown. She wasn't breathing and had no pulse at all. Failing to revive her, the paramedics rushed her to Humana Northside Hospital. As well as doctors could figure, an extreme weight-loss diet had kicked off a condition known as hypokalemia, whose symptoms can include "sudden arrhythmia death syndrome." Whatever the cause, her heart gave out and Terri fell into what doctors called a "persistent vegetative state." She lay in bed day and night, year after year after year, connected to machines, taking drips of nourishment through a feeding tube, never regaining full consciousness again.

It's hard to imagine a situation any more tragic. Or any more painful for the family involved. Or any less appropriate for politicians to barge in on.

Michael and the doctors tried everything. Experimental treatments. Cross-country trips to specialists. Endless bedside hours with never a glimmer of hope.

In 1998, Michael Schiavo petitioned the Sixth Circuit Court of Florida in Pinellas County to remove Terri's feeding tube. She would never want to live this way, he told the judge. On October 15, 2003, with the court's approval, Terri's feeding tube was finally removed.

That's when things really blew up. I didn't see the full scope of it at first. I didn't realize how fundamental a change was on the way. But this was the first time that a growing intolerance and extremism inside the Republican Party got played out on such a large and prominent stage. It was something scary to behold!

It wasn't just Terri's parents. Within a week, they were joined by a well-organized band of anti-abortion activists who knew how to raise money, get media attention, mobilize clergy, and lobby Republican politicians. They had three things political people are always scared of—passion, adamancy, and organizational skill brought in by anti-abortion activists. With media-savvy organizer Randall Terry at the front of the pack, they rushed to the Florida Legislature. As protesters marched in Tallahassee and talk radio hosts conjured up comparisons to Nazi death camps, Republican State Representative Frank Attkisson and his colleagues passed "Terri's Law," giving Jeb Bush authority to intervene in the case.

The legislature? The governor? Overruling the husband, the doctors, and the courts? I'd never seen blind zeal like this. Or was it blind politics?

Jeb immediately ordered the feeding tube reinserted. He then sent the Florida Department of Law Enforcement to remove Terri from her hospice bed, against her husband's wishes, sending her to the Morton Plant Rehabilitation Hospital in Clearwater.

It was one of the cruelest things I have ever witnessed in my life. And the case spun even further out of control.

When the Florida Supreme Court found "Terri's Law" unconstitutional, Jeb turned to his brother, President George W. Bush, who got a nice twofer out of the deal: He could be helpful to his brother and cement his own ties with social conservatives. Congressional Republicans jumped in with both feet. Bill Frist, the Senate

Republican leader, who was also a physician, even began diagnosing Terri's condition from Washington—without ever examining her. Republicans in the Congress subpoenaed both Terri's parents and Michael—at one point even calling Terri!—demanding that the family members come to Washington and testify. A sad family tragedy was truly spinning into Looney Land and being milked for political gain.

The Washington Republicans and their staunch allies would stop at nothing. They came up with another plan. With the authority of Congress, they would sidestep the Florida judges who'd been ruling against them—and hand the whole case to the federal courts.

The Senate agreed to this on March 20, 2005. The House gave its approval March 21 at 12:41 A.M. President Bush flew back to the White House from his vacation in Texas, signing the bill into law at 1:11 A.M.

As all this craziness unfolded in Florida and Washington, it seemed there was only one Republican officeholder in either place who wasn't bellowing loudly about Terri Schiavo and what she and her husband should want.

The Republican attorney general of Florida.

The chief law-enforcement officer of the state where the life-or-death drama was unfolding, whose own party was riding the case like a holy crusade.

Me.

I thought the whole thing was an abominable circus and a cruel embarrassment. The best evidence we had said Terri would never wish to live like this. I certainly understood it. Neither would I.

The attorney general of Florida, unlike the attorney general of the United States, is an independently elected official. In this job, we work for the voters. We don't serve at the governor's pleasure or whim.

I think Jeb expected me to leap into the fracas on his side, doing everything I legally could to frustrate the wishes of Michael Schiavo and the courts. I was, after all, Florida's first Republican attorney general.

I did no such thing.

I wouldn't agree.

I understood the passions and the politics, but I didn't think the people of Florida had elected me to second-guess a suffering family at a time like that.

I didn't publically attack the governor. I didn't call press conferences and denounce him. I didn't see the point of open warfare between Jeb and me over an issue he felt so strongly about and would never be swayed on.

I just didn't participate. I made no statements. I filed no suits. I didn't go along. And my point was clearly made. Jeb's staff and my staff communicated regularly. His preferences were clear. But he never asked me directly. So there was never a personal confrontation. I just pointedly declined to jump on the government-knows-best train. And I think history shows I was right.

Most of the people in the attorney general's office were supportive of my refusal to carry Jeb's water on this one. There were the usual looks and rumblings from my old Republican friends. George LeMieux urged me to think twice before saying no to the Bush brothers. But I detected something else this time: the approval of Democrats and independents.

Those who thought I'd been respectful.

Those who appreciated my refusal to jump in.

Those who thought the case was already too much of a mob scene.

A state appellate judge even pulled me aside in a restaurant one night. "Excellent how you handled the Schiavo thing," a state judge told me. "Don't let 'em suck you in."

One evening in early 2005, I walked over to the Governor's Mansion for a visit with Jeb. Yes, Jeb and I had experienced some tension over Terri Schiavo. But he was the sitting governor of Florida. He was one of the leaders of the Republican Party. He was an undeniably smart guy.

The Governor's Mansion is an elegant two-story home on North Adams Street in Tallahassee with large white columns and a sweeping gallery across the front. The house was designed in 1956 by Palm Beach architect Marion Sims Wyeth to resemble Andrew Jackson's Hermitage in Tennessee, although the completed home had fewer rooms than originally planned due to a shortfall in the state budget. But after Bob and Adele Graham installed the Florida Room in the early 1980s—Jeb and Columba Bush's library was just being planned—no one could call the fifteen-thousand-square-foot mansion remotely cramped.

There's a room on the first floor of the mansion with couches, a large coffee table, pecky cyprus paneling, high ceilings, a flat-screen TV—a real man cave. It's a perfect place to sit and talk.

"What would you like to drink?" Jeb asked as soon as I walked in.

"Whatever you're having," I said.

Jeb liked Scotch. I don't ordinarily drink Scotch. For me, it's usually a dirty vodka martini or a glass of red wine. But he poured us each a Glenlivet single-malt, an old one—I don't know my Scotches.

I just remember it was smooth and sweet and far less mediciney than the Scotch I'd sipped before.

We talked about elections and getting support and raising money and all the energy it takes to campaign in a state like Florida.

At one point Jeb glanced up at the TV. One of the cable news channels was on. "That guy thinks he's so damned smart," Jeb said about one of the commentators. I wondered who he was talking about, but I couldn't see. That was about our only interruption.

We talked about how large and diverse Florida was becoming. "Running statewide's quite a challenge," I said. By that point, I'd done it three times already—in 1998 for US Senator against Bob Graham, in 2000 for education commissioner, and in 2002 for attorney general—twice successfully. I didn't have Jeb's experience. But I felt like I had learned a few things.

"The two guys in this room know how hard it is, maybe better than anybody," he said. "Not many have walked in our shoes."

We just reflected together on where each of us was, one who'd been the governor for seven years already, one who'd been attorney general for three.

I wasn't really asking for anything, not yet at least. There'd be plenty of time for politics. This was more of a personal moment and a social call.

It was quiet in there, just Jeb and me, very different people sharing something just the same. As I left the mansion that night, I did think to myself: *I could definitely see living here.*

Chapter 4

T he People's Governor"—that's what I was going to be. The corporations had their attorneys. The special interests had their lobbyists. The rich and famous had their twenty-four-hour flacks. Shouldn't the people have someone who was looking out for them?

That was the campaign I wanted to run for governor of Florida in 2006—as a Republican. And I didn't see one thing strange about a Republican approaching the office that way. Why should Democrats be the only ones championing the people?

That's the kind of attorney general I'd been. Now I wanted to take my consumer and civil rights approach into the big job.

The idea of running for governor had bubbled up gradually. As attorney general, I had a solid statewide base of support. I discussed the idea with my mom and dad and my sisters. I spoke to some of my smartest and best-connected friends. By late 2005, the political pros in Tallahassee were telling me they thought I had a good shot. I knew it wouldn't be easy. I knew I'd have to raise a lot of money and would need a lot of help. But the pieces were coming together, and I was as ready as I would ever be.

Nationally, the Republican brand was getting hammered. George W. Bush's popularity, sky-high after the terror attacks of 2001, had taken a real beating from the long war in Iraq. Young people, women, blacks, gays, Asians, Latinos—quite a few groups were feeling alienated from the Republican Party. And the incompetent way the administration handled Hurricane Katrina in August of 2005 hadn't helped at all.

But that was Washington. I was in Florida. I didn't consider myself bound by what was happening up there. We were our own kind of Republican in Florida, I figured—at least I knew that I was.

As a state senator, education commissioner, and attorney general, I had built a record as a solid fiscal conservative with an independent heart. I knew the independent part wouldn't please some of the party stalwarts. But at this point, Republican candidates were still allowed to exhibit moderation and independence. John McCain, Chuck Hagel, Richard Lugar, Lindsey Graham—these were broadly respected voices among Republicans. The party hadn't screeched off the right cliff yet. There were still some well-grounded Republican strategists who understood: It was better to win elections with popular, moderate candidates than to lose with inflexible ideologues.

Term limits meant that Jeb Bush couldn't run for reelection again. Before I announced anything, I had lunch with him at a little restaurant near the Capitol. I didn't expect him to endorse me in the Republican primary. He was still hoping his lieutenant governor, Toni Jennings, would run and become the first female governor of Florida. As I read the politics, the best I could hope for was that Jeb would stay neutral in the primary. I was a little nervous before our lunch. There were still some raw feelings from Terri Schiavo, his voting-reform reversals, and a couple of other disagreements. But Jeb was perfectly gracious, and we spoke openly.

"I'm pretty sure I'm going to run," I told him. "If you can, I'd love you to endorse me."

Hey, why not ask?

"But if you can't," I added, "at least think about staying neutral. I would really appreciate that. Just be Switzerland."

Jeb was already there. "That's what I'm thinking of doing," he said. He didn't like picking sides in a Republican primary. That was certain to alienate some of his supporters. And on balance, he and I had gotten along pretty well.

Instead of the lieutenant governor, my opponent in the Republican primary was Tom Gallagher, Florida's chief financial officer. Tom was a confident and self-assured man. He always had a big smile, whatever job he was in. He'd been the Florida House minority whip, education commissioner, treasurer, insurance commissioner, and fire marshal. You couldn't say Tom wasn't durable. He had run for governor twice, in 1986 and 1994, and as the 2006 campaign moved forward, he just exuded victory. He was known for promoting a ten-year tax freeze and was a staunch social conservative. He had the structure of the Florida Republican Party behind him. And he was expected to outraise me. But that only encouraged me to reach out to a younger generation of active Republicans. Like me, they tended to be a little more socially moderate.

I spoke in favor of embryonic stem cell research, disagreeing with President Bush's decision to veto a stem cell bill. I came out for gay civil unions. I understood that the word "marriage" was still awfully rattling to many people, Republicans and Democrats. I can see now

I was heading in that direction. Like a lot of politicians, I just wasn't there yet. But it seemed clear to me even then that gay men and women deserved their legal rights. For a Republican primary candidate, I sounded awfully moderate on most issues. Speaking up for civil rights enforcement. Promising to support high-quality public education. I vowed to restore the threatened Everglades, a broadly popular idea. I even got an endorsement from Arizona Senator John McCain, who just about defined "moderate Republican" in Washington.

As the primary campaign heated up, people started throwing all kinds of stuff at me. They floated rumors I was gay. I denied those outright, telling interviewer Jim DeFede on WINZ radio: "The point is, I'm not. There's the answer. How do you like it? Not that there's anything wrong with that, as they say on *Seinfeld*. But I just happen not to be."

At around the same time, anonymous faxes began appearing at a Florida newspaper saying that, eighteen years earlier, I had fathered a child with a woman from St. Petersburg.

Apparently my anonymous critics couldn't decide: Was I gay? Or was I a womanizing deadbeat dad?

I knew the woman. But I wasn't the father of the infant daughter she had put up for adoption nearly two decades before. I'd even signed a legal document when she had raised that possibility at the time, saying fatherhood was "not possible" in this case "as I never consummated the act necessary for parenthood."

"It's just absolutely false," I said when reporters outside First Baptist Church in Jacksonville asked about the anonymous faxes they'd been receiving.

The Gallagher campaign insisted they weren't behind either story, and I had no solid proof that they were.

When abortion came up—on the Republican campaign trail, it almost always does—I didn't poll-test or focus-group my position. I didn't clear it with anyone from the Religious Right. I didn't do any of that. I just said what I'd always said: "I'm pro-life."

And when the reporters probed a little deeper, I explained what I meant by that.

"If you're pro-life," they asked, "would you outlaw abortion?"

"No," I answered.

"How's that pro-life?"

"I'm personally pro-life," I said. "But I'd rather change hearts than change laws. I'm a live-and-let-live kind of guy. That's how I am."

That was not the usual Republican answer, even in 2006. It conflicted with the party's national platform, which called for a constitutional amendment banning abortion. Several Republican consultants had warned: "You're playing with fire on this one." But here's the surprising thing I discovered. There was still a big Republican audience for tolerance and common sense. People's hearts are rarely as rigid as written platforms are. I saw it in Florida. I assumed it was true across the country. My answer didn't hurt me, even in a competitive Republican primary. Most of the voters, I think, actually agreed with me—or at least didn't disagree too strongly or had other things they cared more about.

That, I thought, was the best way of looking at a hugely divisive issue that could actually bring people together. Believe what you want to, and give others the same courtesy. I couldn't imagine anyone living through the Terri Schiavo case and not seeing the perils of government reaching into places it had no business being.

In the end, none of these hot-button issues or personal hits seemed to do me much harm. In the September 5 Republican primary, I rolled past Tom with 64 percent of the vote. I even won some positive notice from Florida Democrats.

I faced Jim Davis in the general election. Jim was a real gentleman, a Democratic congressman who represented Tampa and some of its suburbs. Like me, he was pretty much a centrist. In Washington, he even co-chaired the New Democrat Coalition, a group of House members trying to steer the Democratic Party in a moderate direction. The main issue in the race—if there was one—was which one of us would do a better job rolling back property taxes and homeowner-insurance rates.

Jim had an armload of Democratic endorsements—former president Bill Clinton, Florida Senator Bill Nelson, even Illinois Senator Barack Obama. But his primary campaign against State Senator Rod Smith had left hard feelings. The barbs they were trading had turned quite personal. Some of Rod's supporters even came over to me. Also, Jim was trying to juggle his duties in Washington with the demands of a competitive governor's race, and he wasn't very successful. At one point, we discovered Jim had the worst attendance record of all 535 members of Congress.

Stuart Stevens and Russ Schriefer, my campaign strategists, made a biting TV commercial featuring an empty chair where Jim should have been. A lot of people noticed that.

As my running mate, I chose a moderate Republican legislator from Cape Coral, Jeff Kottkamp. I'd known Jeff since my 1998 Senate run. When I was attorney general, he'd sponsored the bill that gave me the power to prosecute civil rights without having to go through the Justice Department. He was also a personal-injury attorney with Morgan & Morgan, a top personal-injury law firm that would play a big role in my own life a few years later.

Republicans don't usually turn to plaintiffs' lawyers like Jeff. But even business lobbyists in Tallahassee didn't seem rattled by the pick or my campaign. "Charlie is the kind of guy who has trial lawyer support, business support; it's just the kind of guy he is," said Jon Shebel, who for years led the Associated Industries of Florida, one of the most powerful Tallahassee business lobbies. "He's the man of everybody."

Nationally, 2006 was a Democratic year. Animosity over the war in Iraq and the unpopularity of George W. Bush were hurting Republicans everywhere. The media called the race harsh and vitriolic. But the campaign was also expensive—the most expensive governor's race in Florida history. I outraised and outspent Jim three-to-one. By the time the race was over, I would have raised and spent $60 million.

In the final couple of weeks, I was fairly confident with where we were. The polls were looking solid. Our ads were everywhere. But anything is possible in the final days of a close Florida contest, and Jim was running hard right up to the end. George LeMieux, my former chief of staff in the attorney general's office, who was managing my campaign for governor, kept telling me: "We'll just keep pushing 'til Election Day."

Our final schedule was all mapped out well in advance: St. Petersburg, Tampa, Orlando, Delray Beach, Fort Lauderdale, Miami, Cape Coral, and Jacksonville. We had a great wrap-up planned. John McCain had already agreed to campaign with me on Election Eve in Jacksonville. John was such an independent guy, he could attract Republicans and Democrats. Jacksonville has a big military presence, and as a war hero, John could certainly connect with those folks. He was the perfect closer for me. The Panhandle and most of North Florida looked fairly solid. But the I-4 corridor and the northeast coast, Jacksonville especially, could still go either way.

This wasn't exactly the moment I expected to walk into a national Republican buzz saw.

Ten days before the election, I got a call from someone letting me know that President Bush was planning to come to Pensacola for a rally the day before the vote. Would I be able to be with him?

I would have been happy to. I certainly didn't want to ignore the president. He'd been pretty good to me. His brother was our governor. And I knew the president had been taking a lot of heat in Washington over his handling of Hurricane Katrina and the war in Iraq. A little Florida sunshine might be good for him. But I explained to the aide on the phone that Senator McCain was already coming to campaign with me in Jacksonville, and I'd agreed to be with him.

I took it upon myself to call Jeb.

"You know, Governor," I said, "I've been notified that the president, your brother, is planning to come to Pensacola on Monday before Election Day. I've got a conflict. I'm already doing something with John McCain over in Jacksonville."

Jeb sounded like this was the first he was hearing of any conflict. "Do you know if the Pensacola tickets have been printed yet?" he asked me.

"No, I don't," I said.

"Well," Jeb said, "let's see what's going on with that. Let me call Karl. I'll see what I can do." Karl Rove, of course, was chief political adviser and strategist to George W. Bush. The two of them went all the way back to the president's first run for governor of Texas. Karl had gotten his old friend elected president—twice. There'd been a whole book about Karl called *Bush's Brain*.

"Great," I told Jeb. "I just wanted to give you a heads-up. I don't want anyone to be embarrassed because I'm not gonna be there."

Jeb thanked me, and we hung up.

I had a sense this could be trouble. But as the day got closer, I didn't hear from anyone connected to the president. I did hear through my campaign staff that he was coming anyway. Jeb could certainly greet him, I figured. Maybe some of the other Republican candidates could be there.

I didn't call Jeb again. I knew if he was going and I wasn't, we wouldn't have a very pleasant talk. I was busy campaigning. That was one conversation I didn't need to have.

So the president came to Pensacola. From what I heard, he had a very nice rally there. His wife, Laura, was with him. So was Jeb. So was the local Republican congressman, Jeff Miller, and former secretary of state Katherine Harris, who was running for the US Senate against Democrat Bill Nelson. Now a congresswoman from Sarasota, the controversial Harris had made a national name for herself in the 2000 presidential election, becoming a pariah to Democrats and maybe some Republicans. Though she came to the rally, she still wasn't invited to appear on the stage with the president.

He did say some kind words to the crowd about me, even though I was 350 miles away in Jacksonville.

"Tomorrow, you get to vote for a new governor, and I strongly suggest you vote for Charlie Crist," the president said before flying off in Air Force One for preelection rallies in Arkansas and Texas. "He's experienced. He's compassionate. He'll work hard on behalf of the citizens of this state."

I appreciated that.

When the reporters asked me later if I was avoiding the president because of his low approval ratings or the rising unpopularity of the war in Iraq, I said, not at all. "I'm glad he's come to our state," I said, "but I've got to get around Florida."

The reporters had noticed that my name was on the invitation as the person who'd be introducing the president. I saw in the media and heard secondhand that Karl Rove had been complaining all day about my absence.

When the traveling reporters asked where I was, he didn't bother explaining. He just grumbled: "Ask George LeMieux."

"Rather than being with the governor and the president and 10,000 people in Pensacola, they made a last-minute decision to go to Palm Beach," one piece quoted him as saying. "Let's see how many people show up in Palm Beach on 24 hours' notice versus 8,000 or 9,000 people in Pensacola."

Actually, I wasn't going to Palm Beach—but whatever.

My day had been terrific. McCain was at his absolute best. Funny, warm, enthusiastic, connecting with everyone. If I got elected governor, he said at one point, "it puts him on the national stage, particularly in the ranks of Republican leaders."

Thank you, John.

The next morning, Election Day, I was back at home in St. Petersburg, where I was planning to vote and watch the returns come in. I was outside my condo building in the little breezeway where we pull our cars in. My cell phone rang. It was Karl Rove.

You've never been yelled at until you've been yelled at by Karl Rove. "You chickenshit!" he bellowed, almost cutting off my hello. "I can't believe you didn't show up last night to be with the president! What a chickenshit thing to do. You were going to get elected anyway."

I barely knew Karl Rove. Maybe we'd met once or twice. He certainly wasn't someone I had a relationship with. And now he was screaming at me on my cell phone over a scheduling conflict?

"I can't believe you did that," he yelled. "Who do you think you are?"

He sounded so agitated, he was yelling so loud, I had to pull the phone back from my ear. I knew he was under pressure. I really thought he might have a heart attack or he might explode. I had never heard a political professional lose it like that. He was scolding me like I was ten years old and he was my unreasonably angry father.

I didn't know what to say to the guy. I tried to calm him down.

"I'm sorry you're disappointed," I said. "I certainly didn't mean to cause you guys a problem. I thought I should be with Senator McCain as planned."

Nothing I said seemed to make headway. I was trying to be conciliatory. Rove just kept on fuming at me. I'm not sure if the president cared or even noticed that I had other campaign obligations on Election Eve.

But clearly, at the highest levels of the Republican Party, the mood was turning darker. Some people in power were starting to feel beleaguered. The easy popularity of earlier years was getting tougher to achieve. Instead of reaching out and becoming more open to a variety of approaches and points of view, some people were turning harsher, nastier, and less tolerant. A with-us-or-against-us mind-set was definitely creeping in.

But to me that day, Karl Rove just seemed like a jerk.

Jim Davis won the South Florida counties by large margins, as Democrats normally do. But he couldn't overcome our strength around the rest of the state. Jim, who was at the Grand Hyatt Tampa Bay, called me in my room at the Vinoy Renaissance hotel in St. Petersburg. He graciously conceded. I was elected the forty-fourth governor of Florida by a comfortable margin of 52 to 45 percent.

My mom and dad were there for the grand ballroom victory celebration. So were all three of my sisters. I had school friends and political colleagues and people I'd known for years. The media expected me to win. So there was quite an armada of reporters and TV-satellite trucks.

In my speech, I thanked God, my parents, and Jim Davis for running a "spirited and honorable" campaign.

"Tonight, we all come together as one," I said, sticking closely to my all-in-this-together theme. "Not as Republicans, Democrats, or Independents but as one, as Floridians. Each Floridian will have a voice in all we do, and I will serve every Floridian with all my heart."

And here's the thing that I think surprised a lot of people. I really meant what I said.

Chapter 5

For almost as long as Florida has been electing governors, those governors have been celebrating their glorious victories with lavish inaugural balls. Jeb Bush had two major blowouts, one for each time he was elected—just like most of his predecessors did—with dinner, dancing, and free-flowing champagne.

But as Inauguration Day grew closer, I grew more and more uncomfortable with the whole idea. For one thing, our plans were even more extravagant and more expensive than what Jeb and the earlier governors had done—to the tune of $2 million. For another, this was the worst possible time to be dressing up in tuxedos and evening gowns for a self-congratulatory romp.

As 2006 was coming to a close, Florida's economy, just like the nation's, was sinking deeper into recession. Foreclosures were soaring. Home prices were tumbling hard. Jobs were getting more and more difficult to find. Insurance and property taxes were starting to feel like shakedowns. And here we were putting on this party that was somewhere between a formal state dinner and a Kardashian wedding night.

I did something I don't think anyone really expected, something I instinctively knew was right. On Saturday, December 9, three weeks before Inauguration Day, I canceled the Governor's Inaugural Ball. It wouldn't be right, I said, to put on this high-priced party, paid for by a bunch of trade associations and lobbyists, while so many Floridians were suffering as badly as they were.

And let's be honest: Those fancy dinner-dances are almost always a tedious bore. I'm uncomfortable dancing. I do it only when I have absolutely no other choice. Personally, I'd be just as happy if I were never forced to attend anyone's ball again.

My decision wasn't too popular inside the campaign office or around Tallahassee. I started getting blowback from some of my biggest donors.

"You're kidding, right?" one of them asked, his eyes almost bulging out of his head. "My wife already bought her gown."

Yes, people take these things very seriously in Tallahassee.

They were proud of our victory, several of my supporters said, as proud as I was. They'd written checks, they reminded me, and they'd all worked hard. "The governor's ball is a long Florida tradition," they emphasized. "This is our night to celebrate."

"I'm sorry," I said. "But I'm going with my heart on this one. I'm just not comfortable having some lavish party when Floridians are struggling so hard."

I was a Republican, yes. But that didn't mean I had to lose touch with all the regular people on my first day in office. Canceling the governor's ball sent an early signal that this was not going to be your typical Republican administration, not the kind people had come to expect over the years. Things would be different now—in the governor's office, at least.

As I walked onto the east steps of the Old Capitol on January 2 to take my oath of office as the forty-fourth governor of Florida, the band was playing Aaron Copland's *Fanfare for the Common Man*, a song I chose. That seemed a whole lot better to me than Stephen Foster's "Old Folks at Home (Swanee River)," which is Florida's official state song. I'm not kidding. It really is. Frankly, I didn't want to be inaugurated to a minstrel song whose original lyrics included "darkeys" and "still longing for de old plantation"—even if the words were altered to "brothers" and "still longing for my old connection" after complaints got raised in past years. That wasn't exactly the inclusive message I had in mind.

Jeb was on my right as I sat on the dais. My mom was on my left. My dad was next to her. Three other previous Florida governors were up there too—Claude Kirk, Reubin Askew, and Bob Martinez. So were US Senator Mel Martinez and ex-senator Connie Mack, two legendary Florida Republicans I had really come to admire. Also on the dais were four prominent Democrats, US Senator Bill Nelson, Congressman Robert Wexler, Florida House Minority Leader Dan Gelber, and Alex Sink. Alex was our new chief financial officer and the wife of Bill McBride, who'd been the Democratic candidate for governor in 2002. You couldn't get a broader mix of Florida politicos, and these people all meant something to me.

Tampa's poet laureate, James E. Tokley Sr., read "A Meeting of the People," a poem he wrote for the occasion. It said in part:

Not Republican, nor Democrat, but we meet as one, somehow
And our minds are independent, based upon a greater sight.

For a poet, he's not a bad prognosticator.

The program was running a little ahead of schedule, which seldom happens in politics, and the new governor is supposed to take office right at noon. So we had a few minutes to kill. I climbed off the dais with Jeff Kottkamp, my lieutenant governor, and we made our way into the crowd, thanking people and posing for pictures.

"Congratulations, Governor," one man said, reaching out his hand.

"Just Charlie," I answered, exchanging a warm, two-handed grip.

"Charlie," he said, smiling.

The oath was going to be delivered by Florida Supreme Court Chief Justice Fred Lewis, a towering jurist and genteel man who'd been appointed to the court by Governor Lawton Chiles. As I walked toward Justice Lewis, the crowd began to chant:

"Charlie . . . Charlie . . . Charlie."

I raised my right hand. I placed my left one on a family Bible. I pledged to uphold the constitutions of Florida and the United States—"so help me God."

Just then, a couple of historic cannons sounded on Apalachee Parkway, down the hill from the Capitol. They fired off a nineteen-gun salute. Twenty-one is reserved for presidents. Governors get nineteen. And as the boom of the cannons began to fade, two F-15 fighter jets from the 125th Fighter Wing of the Florida Air National Guard came zooming in overhead. They were fast and loud and very low.

As the jets flew over the Capitol, they tipped their wings to the right. Jeb tapped me on the shoulder and asked: "You know what that was? They are saluting . . . you. As the new governor."

It was totally over the top. It was also amazingly cool. That, for me, was when the idea really sank in: *I'm the governor*, I thought to myself. *All I have to do now is go and run the state.*

In my speech, I thanked my parents. I saluted Jeb as the outgoing governor and President Gerald Ford, who had died the previous week. And I tried to strike an optimistic tone. "The sun shines upon our faces," I said. That was a little strange since the sky was gray and overcast with temperatures in the fifties, chilly for Tallahassee, and many of the people were wearing coats and scarves. But when I delivered that line, I swear, the sun did peek out for a moment.

I pledged an administration of bipartisanship and openness. I planned to hit the ground running, I said, and govern in the open spirit that had defined my campaign. This was one Republican governor who understood he worked for all the people of the state.

When the swearing-in was over, we left the Old Capitol, and everyone paraded together through downtown Tallahassee to the Governor's Mansion. I sat on the back of a vintage red Mustang convertible, not so different from the one I'd had in college when I voted for president the first time. It was a loose, high-spirited march through downtown, leading to an old-fashioned backyard Florida barbecue.

The governor's ball had been canceled. But that didn't mean we couldn't still have a rollicking good time. We threw open the gates of the mansion and invited everyone in. It was the People's House.

Four thousand people showed up. As they were filing in, I ditched the dark suit I'd worn for my swearing-in and threw on a sweater and jeans. We didn't have a formal receiving line. Everyone mixed and mingled and stood around. People stayed for hours, and so did I. I worked the crowd slowly, shaking hands, saying hi to old friends and posing for pictures with everyone who asked. Now *this* felt like a party to me.

At one point, I jumped up onstage with the band. Bill Wharton, a blues musician and gumbo cook known as Sauce Boss, introduced me.

"I'm a happy warrior," I told the crowd spread out across the lawn. "I look forward to governing, and I look forward to serving the people of Florida."

It wasn't a long speech, and it wasn't the most eloquent I'd ever delivered. But it definitely came from the heart.

I showed up early the next morning at the Governor's Office. I couldn't wait to get to work. The office is a huge, rectangular room on the plaza level of the State Capitol with heavy draperies, a Florida seal woven into the carpet, and sufficient square footage to comfortably accommodate the ego of any Florida governor. The desk, which is flanked by a Florida flag and an American flag, looks like it was built for a giant. There are two chairs and a small table in front of the desk, and another seating area—a couch, a couple of chairs, and a coffee table—off to the side. On a credenza beside the desk is a multi-line phone. One line connects directly to the Speaker's podium in the House. The other rings on the Senate president's podium. That way, the governor can bark orders, urge cooperation, or just call to say hi, whatever the circumstances might indicate.

It's a real command station in there, although when people came in to visit, I much preferred talking in one of the seating areas. Sitting behind that desk felt a little like driving an aircraft carrier.

That first day, I didn't immediately summon the Republican leaders of the legislature to my big new office for an opening strategy meeting. I went to their offices instead. I spoke with Ken Pruitt, the seasoned Senate president, and Marco Rubio, a bright young representative from Miami who was the new Speaker of the House. Both men had a lot of power in their hands—the power to set agendas, the power to schedule votes, the power to name committee chairs. I told both Ken and Marco how much I wanted to work with them.

I paid similar calls on Alex Sink, the only Democrat in the new cabinet, and on the two top Democrats in the legislature, the House minority leader, Dan Gelber, and Senate Minority Leader Steve Geller. I don't believe a Republican governor had ever visited the Democratic leaders in *their* offices. Everyone seemed to notice.

Then I took my first official act. I ordered the creation of the Florida Office of Open Government, putting Patricia Gleason in charge. She'd been the top open-government lawyer in the attorney general's office, and she really knew her stuff. Florida had a proud tradition of open government. The state's open-records law was passed at the start of the twentieth century. The modern open-meetings law went back to 1967. But enforcement was in the hands of the governor and sometimes came down to "You'll know what we want you to know and nothing more." Now, I hoped the pretty words in the statutes would be reflected in daily actions.

"Respecting the public trust that is bestowed upon all of us who serve the people of Florida is a top priority for me and for my administration," I said in appointing Pat.

Before I completed my first month in office, I called the legislature into special session to do something about the gouging insurance rates that private insurance companies were charging Florida homeowners. All across the state, people were being pummeled by the sky-high rates at State Farm, Travelers, and other big insurers. People suspected—and for good reason—that the insurers had some quiet agreement to keep all their rates super-high, far higher than was justified by any risks the companies were taking on.

I got input from all four leaders—Ken, Marco, Steve, and Dan—
and then came up with a fresh approach for making the insurance
industry more competitive. My four partners were practical, flexible, and eager to get things done. This, I thought, was how the legislative process ought to work.

Both houses passed a bill that gave far broader authority to
the state-owned Citizens Property Insurance Corporation to compete against the private gougers. At the same time, Kevin McCarty,
our state insurance commissioner, started leaning on the private
companies to keep their rates in check. We brought real competition
and lower rates to an industry that had been behaving more like a
high-priced private cartel.

If that opening burst of activity was any indication, the job of governor wasn't nearly as difficult as I had imagined it might be. You
could bring people together. With the legislature's cooperation, you
could make new laws. Bipartisanship was paying early dividends on
issues Floridians really cared about. We hatched plans to improve
public school funding. We hammered out a balanced budget. We
reinstituted phys ed in public school. Too many of Florida's young
people, I had noticed, were out of shape and far too heavy for their
age. I was convinced—so were doctors and public health officials—
that we had to get our children running and sweating again.

As the new governor, I had some influence—not total control but
some influence—over who should be chairman of the state Republican Party. My choice was an Orlando-area businessman and self-
made millionaire named Jim Greer. Jim wasn't a longtime party
official. We'd met when I was overseeing business regulation in Jeb's
administration and Jim was helping clients comply with state liquor

and food regulations. Some people in the party wanted to keep Jeb's chairwoman, Carole Jean Jordan. But Jim had been my Seminole County campaign chairman. He'd impressed me with his energy, his organizing skills, and his obvious knack for fund-raising. "He's a new face, and I think that's an important part of it," I said when I nominated Jim at a state party meeting at Disney World's Swan and Dolphin Resort. "It's important to reach out to African Americans, to Hispanics—that's going to be incredibly important as we continue to grow as a party."

Even before the insurance bill passed, I introduced a plan to lower the soaring property taxes that Florida homeowners had to pay. This was a heavy lift. It required an amendment to the Florida state constitution. As home values had risen over the years, taxes had shot way up. Now that prices were slipping, the taxes never seemed to fall. I wanted to double the state's $25,000 homestead exemption, roll back city and county tax collections to 2003–04 levels, and make the state's Save Our Homes tax cap more flexible. My approach would save taxpayers $33.5 billion over five years, the analysts said.

"We won't let you down," I told a group of public school teachers who came to see me at the Governor's Mansion one day. "Take that message back to your friends, please. And please, if you would, call your state senators and your members of the House of Representatives. Tell them how important it is to you as an educator, how you need for these oppressive property taxes to go down. Tell them you need for them to agree on something."

Just the fact that a Republican governor was meeting at the Governor's Mansion with public school teachers—unionized public school teachers—produced some grumbles. But changing the homestead exemption with a constitutional amendment would be difficult, I knew. The amendment needed to pass the legislature and then get 60 percent of the people's vote in a referendum. I figured we needed all the support we could get.

Everyone liked the sound of lower property taxes. But the details could get awfully convoluted. Marco Rubio had a plan of his own. He wanted to eliminate all property taxes—all property taxes!—on primary residences, then add another 2.5 percent to the state's 6 percent sales tax. To me, that just seemed like a way to shift the tax burden onto poor people, who tend not to own homes and have to spend every nickel they make.

Marco's plan didn't get anywhere. But with patience and persistence, mine slowly did.

It took three sessions of the legislature and a lot of long conversations. "The House will not do this," Senate President Ken Pruitt told me after we'd failed in the second session and I was pushing to have a third. "Charlie," he said, "I think you're wasting your time here."

I was determined. "Let me carry you on this," I told Ken. "One more try. We'll get it through."

And we did. The constitutional amendment passed both houses of the legislature.

With that reluctant blessing, the people still had to vote. We set the property tax cut referendum vote for January 29, 2008, the day Floridians would be voting in the Republican and Democratic primaries for president.

I thought the idea had a strong shot.

Looking back on those early days of achievement and cooperation, I really believe they were the Golden Age of the Florida Legislature. I owed a lot to my partners in the House and Senate, Democrats and Republicans both, who had rarely been treated like partners before.

They seemed to like it. We got an awful lot done awfully fast.

The people who had elected me seemed happy too. Polls aren't the only indication of how a politician is doing. But it's definitely nicer when they're flying high. Mine were floating in the thin air up above 70 percent.

That's what happens when you're the people's governor.

As our early accomplishments piled up and Tallahassee settled into a new bipartisanship, Republicans, Democrats, and Independents could see what we were doing. I believe the people sensed we were working for them.

Chapter 6

I didn't want to go much longer without fixing our broken election system. What could be more bipartisan than that?

Ever since the debacle of 2000, Florida had been known as the place where fair and open elections went to suffer and die. It had been six years already since the US Supreme Court chose an American president, which definitely wasn't how our system was supposed to operate. And there was no real reason for confidence it wouldn't happen again.

If we couldn't run a fair and competent election, how could anyone have faith in our democracy? I never wanted to see my state embarrassed like that again.

This is basic stuff. We don't live in a monarchy or a dictatorship. We live in a representative democracy, which means we get to elect the people who lead us. What a beautiful thing that is—when it works!

But we have to make efforts to preserve this beautiful system. It does not preserve itself.

I had no idea yet how much that belief—something I thought

was universal—would put me at such odds with my own Republican Party. I certainly didn't expect that the basic process of voting could be as viciously partisan as the races themselves.

After the 2000 election, Jeb Bush promised to replace much of the state's hated voting technology, including Palm Beach County's butterfly ballots along with their notoriously dimpled, perforated, and hanging chads.

The new system the counties chose was touch-screen voting machines. Soon enough, fifteen Florida counties had signed on. But that didn't work out too well. The costs were high. The glitches were constant. And worst of all, no one seemed to trust the electronic counts. Without paper records, how did voters know their choices were being accurately recorded? How could anyone be sure some evil hacker wasn't manipulating the results? Jeb dismissed those fears as "conspiracy theories." But in the run-up to the 2004 presidential election, the Republican Party of Florida sent out fliers urging their voters to use absentee ballots because of the disturbing absence of a paper trail from the Election Day machines.

Republican leaders wanted *their* votes to be counted.

My friend Robert Wexler, the Democratic congressman whose district included parts of Palm Beach and Broward counties, was feeling extremely frustrated. Some of the worst of the 2000 drama had unfolded in Robert's district. He'd been trying to convince Jeb to give up on this touch-screen wizardry and insist on a paper trail for every Florida vote. But Robert was getting nowhere with Jeb.

Robert didn't need to convince me. I was already there.

He and I had many conversations while I was running for governor, even though he was a liberal Democratic congressman and I was the Republican gubernatorial nominee. He was a friend first, and I appreciated that. His paper trail idea, I thought, was utterly sensible.

As a first step, it seemed to me, we should dump the leap-of-faith touch-screen machines for some technology that kept a careful paper record.

At my urging and without much fuss, the legislature passed a bill requiring paper backup for all voting machines. The fact that the federal government would cover the $28 million price tag didn't hurt. The Democrats were happy. At least we were taking voting seriously. I wouldn't say the Republicans were thrilled. I'm not sure they exactly grasped my passion for the issue. The reaction among Republicans in the legislature seemed to be, "Charlie's out there on this thing. It more or less makes sense. He just got elected. Let's get out and support him."

I signed the bill on May 22 at the office of the Palm Beach County supervisor of elections in West Palm Beach, where lines of klieg lights and forests of microphones had stood for weeks during the 2000 fiasco. Robert was back for the signing.

"It just makes common sense," I said that day. "You go to an ATM machine, you get a receipt. You go to a gas station, you probably don't like the receipt you get, but you get a receipt. And with the most precious, cherished right we have in a democracy, we deserve to have a record so we can verify."

But that was just the start. If how people voted was important, *who* got to vote was even more so. The issue had come up unexpectedly in the governor's race. Three weeks before Election Day, Brendan Farrington, a political reporter with the Associated Press, asked what I thought about automatically restoring the legal rights of former felons.

"Will you support that if you win?" Brendan asked.

"*Former* felons?" I wanted to make sure I understood Brendan's question. "After they've served their time and paid their debt to society?"

Brendan nodded. To ask the question was almost to answer it.

"Yes, I will support it," I said.

Republicans like to see themselves as the tough-on-crime party. Not for nothing was I "Chain Gang Charlie." But I'd been thinking about the question of forgiveness even before Brendan asked. I'd been amazed while out campaigning by how many decent-seeming Floridians were ineligible to vote.

I'd have a friendly conversation with someone after a speech or a rally. We'd discuss a major issue or a nagging local concern. As we were trading good-byes, I would say: "I hope you'll consider voting for me."

"I'd like to," the person would answer, "but I can't."

I can't tell you how many times I got that!

A brief exchange would lead to a heartbreaking story of some long-ago mistake in life that ended in a criminal conviction. You hear enough of those stories, it's hard to keep ignoring them. I saw one statistic that said 30 percent of all black men in Florida were being denied the right to vote. No one should feel comfortable with a number like that.

Brendan's question dragged a forty-five-year-old memory out of my head. I was talking with my grandfather. I was just a little boy. Pappap was holding a pencil and looking at me.

"You see this pencil?" he asked. "What's on the end of it?"

"An eraser?" I answered, a little tentatively.

"That's right," my grandfather said. "An eraser. You know why it's there? To erase. Every pencil has an eraser because everybody makes mistakes."

Forgive and accept forgiveness.

I hadn't expected the question from Brendan. So I wasn't prepared with a carefully crafted policy or a long line of statistics. But I knew how I felt.

"It all comes down to one fundamental question," I said. "Do you believe that an individual has paid their debt to society? If they've really paid their debt to society, then why not restore their right to vote?"

Nobody's perfect.

Everyone makes mistakes.

Pencils have erasers.

People deserve a second chance.

Isn't that the very basis of our democracy and religious faith?

I quickly came to see that restoring the rights of ex-felons would be far more controversial than anything involving voting-machine technology. The basic idea of voting might sound nonpartisan, but the uproar it generated was all about politics. All my Republican friends seemed to be certain about what was waiting for us down this path: If we invited hundreds of thousands of ex-felons back onto Florida's voting rolls, the vast majority wouldn't be voting for us.

"Just look at 'em," I heard more than one Republican say. "Those are Democrats."

I wasn't sure how those new voters might end up casting their ballots. Maybe my Republican friends were right. But I didn't care about partisanship.

The laws that kept most ex-felons from voting in Florida went back 136 years. That was the Jim Crow era after the Civil War. Slavery was over. But white judges and politicians in the South were doing everything they could to make sure the newly freed slaves were still kept down.

Over the years, Florida developed a system for restoring the legal rights of some people who'd been convicted of serious crimes. But the process was so long and arduous that only a tiny, tiny percent of the state's ex-felons ever got through it. The result in modern times was that 700,000 Floridians with felony convictions—who'd served their sentences, paid their fines, and completed all restitution to their victims—still didn't have the right to vote, serve on a jury, run for office, or hold a variety of state licenses.

They had done everything that was asked of them, but they still weren't real citizens of the state.

As governor, Jeb Bush had taken the usual Republican approach to ex-felons and voting. He did what he could to make sure as few as possible ever got that right. The Florida Clemency Board kept most of its cumbersome procedures in place. In 2000 and 2004, with a sharp nudge from the Republican Party of Florida, the state elections division tried to purge tens of thousands of names off the rolls, although those efforts stumbled when the lists were found to be riddled with errors.

I knew I'd face real opposition, from my own party especially.

"Why would you want to do this?" Republicans were already asking.

"Because I believe in forgiveness," I said. "Who doesn't deserve forgiveness? Everybody makes mistakes."

I put the issue on the agenda for an April 5 special meeting of the Florida Clemency Board. That board was made up of members of the state cabinet—Attorney General Bill McCollum, Chief Financial Officer Alex Sink, Agriculture Commissioner Charles Bronson, and me. The politics on the Clemency Board were going to be challenging.

Under state rules, the members of the Clemency Board weren't allowed to communicate with one another about the issue until the meeting began. Alex Sink, a lifelong Democrat, hinted strongly she was inclined to support my proposal. Bill McCollum let it be known he was tilting exactly the opposite way. Bill had been in Congress before he became attorney general. He was part of the House Republican team that prosecuted Bill Clinton for the Monica Lewinsky affair. He definitely hadn't lost his prosecutorial zeal. "Half of those who are released from prison today will commit crimes and be back in prison within five years," he said in one premeeting interview. Restoring rights to felons, he made clear, was not the Republican way. Republicans are tough on crime. They like stiffer penalties. They do not go suddenly soft just because a felon's finally done his time.

The real unknown was the commissioner of agriculture, Charles Bronson, who was also a Republican. The way I read the lineup, he was almost certainly the swing vote. If Alex and I voted yes and Bill voted no, the future of the whole proposal rested in Charles Bronson's hands. A yes from him, 3-1, would get nonviolent felons voting. A no vote would mean a 2-2 tie, killing the measure, at least for now.

Charlie Bronson is a very conservative guy, but a really good fellow. He and I sat next to each other in the state senate. I always enjoyed talking to him. He's a big guy from a wealthy farming family, a very historic Florida family. I knew he'd been some kind of law-enforcement officer early in his life. There were indications prior to the meeting, reading between the lines, that he had a measure of forgiveness in his heart. I was encouraged by that but wasn't at all sure what it meant. When I walked into that meeting, I truly didn't know what I'd walk out with.

As the meeting began, I addressed the issue directly and tried to put it in crystal clear terms. "Justice delayed is justice denied, and people are waiting," I said. "This is about fundamental fairness."

I laid out my plan. It would apply only to nonviolent felons who had served their sentences, completed their paroles, and paid their fines and restitution. I emphasized that it wouldn't include everyone. People convicted of violent crimes—murder, rape, kidnapping, robbery, and major drug sales, as well as various habitual offenders—would not have their rights automatically restored. But the nonviolent ex-felons—drug users, check kiters, white-collar criminals of various sorts—would be able to vote, serve on a jury, run for office, and hold a state occupational license. The rights would not include owning a gun.

The debate that followed was one of the tensest hours of my life.

Alex Sink spoke on behalf of the measure. As predicted, she was on board.

I was also right about Bill. The conservative attorney general weighed in. I could tell immediately how revved he was. "Reckless and irresponsible," he called the move. "I'm just very upset about this," he said. "I think we're making a grave mistake."

I think Bob Butterworth, a Democrat who preceded both me and Bill as attorney general and had joined my administration as secretary of the Department of Children and Families, put his finger on something important when he disputed Bill's unsupported claim that the new clemency policy would put Floridians at risk. It's actually a "crime-fighting strategy," Bob said after the meeting. "It will allow for reintegration of people into law-abiding society, giving them a new set of reasons to stay clean."

With Bill a firm no, that left Charlie.

After hearing the arguments from both sides, Charlie did something unexpected. He passed me a handwritten note with his own tweaked proposal. He suggested we add a provision saying felons who regained their rights and then committed another crime would not be able to regain those rights again for ten years. "I don't mind giving people a second chance," he said. Right there, I knew we had him. "But if they blow that second chance, I don't know why we ought to give them a third chance."

Alex jumped in with her own amendment, loosening that a little. It went back and forth a bit longer. But in the end, Charlie was a yes.

Restoration of rights was approved by the Clemency Board on a historic 3–1 vote. It was a major victory for decency, a major victory for more than half a million Floridians who automatically became full citizens again. No more labyrinth of procedures.

A few days later, I got a handwritten note from Bill Clinton, thanking me for spearheading the effort.

> *Dear Governor Crist,*
>
> *Thank you for your leadership restoring voting rights to convicted felons. Once they've served their sentences, it's the right and decent thing to do. When I was Arkansas Attorney General, I convinced our Legislature to do it. Unfortunately, the problem we had was that many of the affected people didn't know they could register to vote. You might want an outreach campaign.*
>
> *Sincerely,*
> *Bill Clinton*

The next day I put in a call to the ex-president's office in Harlem. "Mr. President, I wanted to call and thank you for your handwritten note about the restoration issue," I told him. "It really moved me. And I just wanted you to know how grateful I was for your taking the time to do that."

"Well," he said, in that slow but intense way of his, "do you have a minute? I'd like to tell you a story."

Who wouldn't want to hear a story from President Clinton?

"Any time someone does something like that, I always write a note," he said. "The reason I do that is because the man who raised me, my stepfather, was a great man. Was great to me. Raised me as his own, and he was a very patriotic guy. He'd fought in the war. He'd been significantly injured in the war. And then he came back. Early in his life, he made some mistakes. And he lost his right to vote. He lost it for his whole life. It was never restored to him."

"So tough," I said.

"It was," he agreed. "I can remember every single Election Day, watching it tear the heart out of my stepfather to not be able to go and execute his democratic right to vote when he had fought for his country and gotten wounded and all the rest of it. That's why what you did meant something to me. That's why I sent you that note."

Chapter 7

These were all important good-government issues—open government, consumer fairness, voting rights. As far as I was concerned, not one of them should create any partisan division, any more than Florida's natural environment should. My commitment to the environment went all the way back to my days as a child, spending lazy weekends on Tampa Bay with my parents and my sisters. We loved what God and nature had bestowed on Florida. I couldn't imagine *not* protecting something as precious as that. And now that I was governor, I figured, I had some new tools to help the cause.

These days, it's the Democrats who are usually considered pro-environment. But I never saw any reason that Republicans had to be the Scorched Earth Party. In fact, the first person who ever mentioned climate change to me was no less a Republican than Senator John McCain. I'd heard the term before. But I'd never really focused on it. This was in 2005, just as the Arizonan was starting to think about running for president. I know this may sound odd, given how hostile many of today's Republicans are to the whole idea of climate change. But John was the one who brought up the issue—and not to debunk anything.

We had met for breakfast at the Biltmore in Coral Gables, Jeb Bush's favorite Miami-area hotel. I was still attorney general. There had been some speculation that maybe I would run for governor.

We had a nice getting-to-know-you talk. We swapped funny stories. We talked some politics. We analyzed the potential fields for his race and mine. Just as we were wrapping up, John said to me, "Charlie, there's one other thing I wanted to mention to you."

"What's that?" I asked.

"I really think you ought to pay attention to this issue of climate change," he said. "It's going to be a very important thing for our country and our planet. So kinda study up on it. Learn what you can. I'd get in front of the issue, if I were you."

The heating of the planet and the rising tides that come with that, John said, could be especially damaging to a state like Florida, with its massive coastline and crucial tourist economy. "That's one reason I felt compelled to mention it to you," he said on his way out the door. "You're at ground zero here."

I knew that was true. Florida has more than 1,300 miles of coastline and bright, sunny weather that a lot of people really, really love. The Florida economy and the Florida environment are inexorably intertwined. This industry called tourism is the real engine of the Florida economy, 85 million visitors a year generating $67 billion in spending. Tourism dwarfs the next-largest categories—agriculture, health care, construction, high tech (including the space industry), and the business-services sector. Every year, the environment propels a big part of our growth. Ruin that, and we'll never get it back.

John McCain, I knew, wasn't the first Republican politician to speak up for the environment, not even close. Al Gore was just a wide-eyed Harvard graduate applying for a cub reporter's job at the Nashville *Tennessean* when President Nixon was signing the Clean Air Act into law. The Republican president went on to create the nation's first vehicle-emission standards, sign the Clean Water Act, halt all dumping in the Great Lakes, establish the Environmental Protection Agency, and push assorted other earth-friendly policies that today's party leaders would no doubt angrily denounce.

He did all that in just a term and a half. And Nixon was far from the only green Republican.

Teddy Roosevelt really was the father of modern environmental conservation—a word, you might notice, that shares a Latin root with "conservative." He was an avid hunter and sportsman. He created our National Parks system. In 1903 he signed an executive order establishing the Pelican Island National Wildlife Refuge off the coast of Florida—the first of its kind in the nation. He showed that development and preservation don't have to be mortal enemies. Along with Abraham Lincoln, TR is one of the greatest heroes the Republican Party has, one of the reasons I'd always been proud to call myself a Republican. He's on Mount Rushmore, for crying out loud.

And this all seemed quite natural to me. I'd grown up on the water. I loved going fishing with my dad. I knew as much in junior high school about Florida marine life—manatees, dolphins, grouper, and all their friends—as I did about popular TV shows. Oddly, Flipper turned up in both.

So it pained me when I began hearing members of my own Republican Party—often, though not always, in Washington—ridiculing the whole idea of climate change. "Liberal crap," they said.

"The climate's always changing," these debunkers were saying. "The pollution's not that bad. We can't restrain the development economy."

Conservative Republicans like Dennis Baxley, the Florida House Speaker pro tempore, argued that climate change was way out of our job description. "We would be better off approaching world hunger or bringing peace to the Middle East," he said. "I'm not going to spend the state budget on global warming."

This kind of thinking was really taking hold on the Far Right. Pseudo experts were questioning well-established climate trends. That was followed by a new flurry of anti-evolution talk, as if that issue hadn't been settled by Charles Darwin. Textbooks were being rewritten to accommodate ancient prejudices—actual facts be damned. These new American know-nothings were increasingly distrusting of basic science, data, and facts, which to them always seemed to carry a liberal bias. And in some circles, at least, this stuff was catching on.

It was vitally important, I was convinced, to do what we could to reduce climate change as much as possible. Cleaning our rivers. Cutting carbon dioxide. Finding new ways to protect the wetlands. Those were all beneficial on their own terms, whether or not someone accepted the science of climate change or cared to heed its warnings. It seemed to me we should be doing all those things anyway.

I didn't only read about climate change and discuss it with my friends. I led by example. In April I ordered an energy audit at the Governor's Mansion and outfitted the place with high-efficiency lightbulbs and a Heliocol solar heater for the outdoor swimming pool. I also got a new car: an ethanol-fueled Chevy Tahoe. There was only one ethanol station in Tallahassee, but the effort was worth it, I thought.

Then, on July 12 and 13, six and a half months into my term, I convened the two-day Serve to Preserve Florida Summit on Global Climate Change. I invited Vinod Khosla, co-founder of Sun

Microsystems at Stanford University and one of the world's leading experts on clean-energy technology. Robert Kennedy Jr., the environmental lawyer and son of the late senator, came down from New York. Arnold Schwarzenegger also came. The Republican governor of California by then, he brought his own deep concern for the environment and no small amount of star power.

Arnold was a perfect example of a pro-environment Republican. We first met in 1992 on the South Lawn of the White House. He was chairman of the first President Bush's Council on Physical Fitness. I was invited by Arnold's cousin-in-law, my friend Pam Shriver, the professional tennis player who'd become president of the WTA Tour Players Association in St. Petersburg. Arnold and I just said hello that day. But we stayed in touch. He was a fellow Republican. Eventually, he put aside his action-star duties and came into my field, politics. Unfortunately, given my physique, there didn't seem to be much opportunity for me in his. But when I ran for governor, he was helpful in my campaign. As governor of California, he'd shown he was one Republican who cared about the environment. One of three keynote speakers at the summit, he gave a talk called "Strength in Numbers," explaining how much more we could accomplish on climate change if we stopped thinking of it as a partisan issue. When Arnold's there, people pay more attention. And wasn't that the whole point?

After the summit, I immediately signed three executive orders limiting greenhouse-gas emissions, setting stricter limits for cars sold in Florida, and insisting that utilities generate at least 20 percent of their electricity from renewable sources. Surprisingly, I didn't get much immediate blowback in Florida, even from my fellow Republicans. The only exception I recall was a snarky op-ed in *The Miami Herald* from Marco Rubio, then Speaker of the Florida House of Representatives. Marco said he didn't really mind my focusing on the environment, but he didn't like the way I was doing it. "We must be willing to embrace the free-market approach—not European-style, big-government mandates," he declared.

Which meant, in practice, do nothing.

I wasn't about to do that. I just kept going. I signed a law stopping pollution runoff into the Atlantic Ocean. I stood outside the Governor's Mansion with executives from Progress Energy and announced a new biomass plant in rural North Florida that would turn waste wood into electricity. And I was eager to do something to protect the Everglades.

They are our grandest natural prize, a truly unique place on the planet. The "River of Grass," Marjory Stoneman Douglas called this awesome region. "There are no other Everglades in the world," she wrote in her book by that name. "They are, they have always been, one of the unique regions of the earth; remote, never wholly known. Nothing anywhere else is like them."

The Everglades are so full of life—birds, fish, reptiles, all these wonderful and exotic creatures and plants. This is the only place on the planet where crocodiles and alligators coexist. If you take an airboat ride through the Everglades, you will see more bird life than you've ever seen anywhere.

Two and a half months after our climate change summit in Miami, I was standing on a stage in New York City with Bill Clinton when the former president shot a little grin in my direction and began to speak.

"This man is a Republican, and I'm probably about to hurt his reputation," the former president said.

Then, he ticked off some of the efforts I'd been making as the governor of Florida to fight climate change. Reducing carbon emissions. Promoting solar power. Constantly highlighting the issue in one of the most vulnerable places on Earth. "As we all know, Florida is one of the sunniest places in America," President Clinton said. "If they can prove it works, it can be done in sunny places all over the world."

The ex-president had obviously paid attention to our summit in Miami. I'm sure that's what got me invited to speak at the Clinton Global Initiative, which ran from September 25 to 28 in New York, putting me in the company of Tony Blair, Ted Turner, Brad Pitt, and a first-string list of other leaders, thinkers, and creative types. Bill Clinton, it turns out, has a really good Rolodex. But except for Arnold Schwarzenegger and me, Republican governors apparently didn't usually get invited to that sort of thing. President Clinton seemed pleased to have me there.

Together, he and I announced that Florida Power & Light would build a giant solar plant as part of a $2.4 billion clean-energy program. The seventy-five-megawatt Martin Next Generation Solar Energy Center would be the world's first hybrid solar-energy plant and the first utility-scale solar facility in Florida. It involved 180,000 mirrors over 500 acres of utility-company land and would generate enough clean power to serve 11,000 homes.

"This is a huge deal for America, and I think potentially a huge deal for people all around the world," said the former president, as the company's chief executive, Lew Hay, looked on proudly.

I gave a dinner speech to a group of people who run utility companies. I spoke about new ways of generating solar, wind, and geothermal power. That's a topic I get quickly excited about. At the dinner with the power-company people, I knew to eat light. But even though the day had been truly unforgettable, the best was yet to come.

Harry Sargeant, a Florida State fraternity buddy of mine who'd become a fighter pilot in the United States Marine Corps' Black Sheep squadron and then a hugely successful energy and shipping magnate, had set up a late dinner for me. It was at Campagnola, a world-class country-Italian restaurant on Manhattan's Upper East Side. Harry had invited a group of New Yorkers who had some connection to Florida and might be willing to help with fund-raising for the Florida Republican Party.

I came in off 1st Avenue, past the narrow bar and the pianist playing Sinatra. In the main dining room, I saw Harry sitting at a large round table with several other people. One of them was Brian Ballard. Also at the table was a very attractive woman with long dark hair, brown eyes, and a stunning smile.

I hope that's Carole, I thought.

Harry had told me about Carole Rome. Half the plan for the dinner was to meet her. Next to her was a conspicuously open seat.

After greeting everyone, I sat down.

We hit it off instantly. It was like I had known this woman my entire life. She was smart. She was funny. She seemed great.

Everyone at the table was talking politics. Carole jumped in comfortably.

At some point, like I do with most people, I turned to Carole and asked: "Where did you grow up? What was that like? Did you have a big family? Tell me what you're doing now."

She told me about growing up on Long Island in a place called Roslyn. Her family was in the Halloween business, she said. I don't think I'd ever met anyone in that field before. She had a business degree from Georgetown University. She was obviously smart. She told me that she had two daughters and that she was getting divorced. And she mentioned how much she loved Florida. She had a place, she said, on Fisher Island near Miami. She'd said she'd been coming to Boca Raton with her family since she was a little girl. We talked about how much both of us enjoyed being on the water and going to the beach.

I was paying close attention to all of it.

As much as I was enjoying getting to know Carole, I made sure to include the others in the conversation. I wanted everyone to have a good time. This was, after all, a fund-raising dinner. These people were considering writing substantial checks. After dinner, several of us went to a lounge on East 63rd Street called Club Macanudo to listen to some live music and extend the evening a bit.

I'd been single for nearly thirty years. I'd dated some very nice women. But after my brief marriage during law school, I had never said "I do" again. I'd known Carole for all of three hours. It was far too soon to be thinking long-term. But some kind of light did go off in my head.

As we separated on the sidewalk, I gave her a kiss and thought to myself as we said good night: *I definitely have to see her again.*

Being governor, I kept discovering, was a very blessed life. I spent most of the week at the Governor's Mansion in Tallahassee. Then I'd usually go home to my condo in St. Petersburg for the weekends. I got to travel around the state and occasionally outside it. I got to meet amazing people. I got to focus on things that needed improving—and actually improve them. What wasn't to like?

I was protected twenty-four hours a day by my own armed detail from the Florida Department of Law Enforcement. These talented and highly thoughtful professionals drove me around in a black SUV and always stayed near me in public. On a personal level, I didn't have to worry about very much.

The Governor's Mansion was ridiculously large for a single guy living alone, though the staff couldn't have been more warm or hospitable. The mansion had its own library, a wonderful TV room, and, for my early-morning swims, that large solar-heated outdoor pool. I wasn't a demanding resident. I just kept saying "Thank you." But I do think the staff might have been a little bored. Legislators and friends and others dropped by sometimes, and I hosted various official events. But it wasn't like I had a family living there. Many nights, I came home late, had a quiet dinner, did some reading, and went to bed.

But things were about to get even more interesting for me.

It so happened that, a few nights after I met Carole in New York, Harry was hosting a second fund-raising event, this one at his home in Gulf Stream near Palm Beach. I asked Carole if she wanted to go with me. The second night was even more magical than the first.

So comfortable, so at ease—we were in total sync with each other.

Then, we started dating.

Dating a governor is not without complication. It's a little different from dating a regular guy. There are a few extra stares in restaurants. And you have these people with guns around you all the time, everywhere you go. They are wonderful people. They're kind enough to look out for you. But their presence can be awkward on a date.

It's true, governors have a lot of official duties and responsibilities. But it's also true that governors are human beings too.

I had met this wonderful lady. Now I was falling fast.

In early November, I was going on a trade mission to South America. By then, Carole and I were speaking every day.

"I'll be down there," I said. "You know, if you want to, maybe toward the end, you could join up with me. Of course, you'll have to cover your own bill. I'm on a mission for the state. But I have to eat at night. I wouldn't mind eating with you."

I'm not sure that came out as smoothly as I would have liked it to. But Carole agreed to fly down.

We met up in Rio de Janeiro, Brazil, one of the most fun-loving cities in the world. We saw the amazing Christ statue on the hill, *Cristo Redentor* (Christ the Redeemer). After the day's meetings were done, we had a couple of fabulous meals. Then we flew to Buenos Aires, the Paris of South America. I don't know what the river is called, but we had a meal in a restaurant on the river that was just incredible. We saw the Casa Rosada, the palace where I believe Eva Perón came out and said, "Don't cry for me, Argentina." I wasn't paying too much attention to the tour book. Mostly, I was staring at Carole. Then, we wrapped up the trip in Santiago, Chile.

If a trip like that doesn't help to propel romance, I don't know what would.

I was head-over-heels smitten. By the time we left Santiago, we had known each other for a couple of months. I had been single a very long time. I wasn't going to do anything hasty. But I thought to myself, *I'd like to marry this girl.*

As soon as I got back to Tallahassee, I stumbled into an extraordinary idea.

I was in a meeting with two Tallahassee lobbyists for the giant United States Sugar Corporation, my friends Brian Ballard and Mac Stipanovich. U.S. Sugar was one of the largest landowners in Florida. My chief of staff, Eric Eikenberg, was also there. Brian and Mac were explaining to Eric and me how the company's latest backflow plan would not disrupt Lake Okeechobee, a key source of water for the Everglades. It's fair to say I wasn't yet convinced.

"I have an idea," I said, interrupting Mac midsentence. "Why don't we just buy you out?"

I told them I remembered Marjory Stoneman Douglas writing that the only way to preserve this fragile part of earth forever would be to buy it back and make it public. This purchase would allow us to restore the natural flow of water down the spine of Florida, the mighty Kissimmee River, which had nourished the Everglades for centuries—but who knew how much longer it would?

Brian and Mac seemed slightly taken aback. But they agreed to float the idea by company executives. On our way out of the meeting, I stopped in front of a portrait of Teddy Roosevelt.

"This is the type of deal that TR would love," I told Brian, who nodded back politely. I don't think he and Mac thought there was any way this would come to pass.

But discussions began about a highly ambitious possibility, that the South Florida Water Management District would purchase 187,000 acres of farmland from the company. The way I saw it, this would be an important protection for the Everglades' future, truly Florida's Yellowstone National Park.

No threats were made at all. But I think U.S. Sugar officials were concerned that in the new Crist administration, clean-water regulations weren't going to be taken quite as lightly as they were during the Jeb Bush years. And we began to explore what a fair price might be.

It didn't hurt that I had appointed Jerry Montgomery and Paul Huck to the Water Management District's governing board in April and reminded them how important I thought clean water was. The water-management board had voted to deny U.S. Sugar's back-pumping request.

It took a couple of dozen meetings in all. We negotiated the price down from the company's original suggestion of $2.5 billion to $1.75 billion. And on June 24, 2008, I announced that we had a deal.

This was a world-class, world-saving achievement.

I promised I would keep pushing my efforts on behalf of the environment. I was proud of them, and many began to take hold. But the tide of opposition kept rising slowly inside my own Republican Party, slamming against logic and moderation like they were a compromised shoreline. These relentless know-nothings even set their sights on my good West Coast Republican friend.

On June 13, 2008, I flew out to California to speak at the Ninth Annual Orange County GOP Flag Day Dinner. Orange County, a solid Republican suburb south of Los Angeles, was Nixon's old territory. The Flag Day dinner is a big event out there, bringing together donors, political activists, party leaders, elected officials, and candidates. Nine hundred people had paid $250 each to attend. This wasn't a bad gauge of how the Republican Party was feeling.

I was honored to attend.

I began my talk at the Hyatt Regency Irvine by thanking my hosts and taking a moment to praise the state's Republican governor, who was then six months into his second term.

"Your governor, Arnold Schwarzenegger," I said, "is doing a great job. I love him."

In this crowd, I expected that to be an easy applause line.

Instead, I heard a few boos. Then a few more. Then it seemed like the whole banquet room shared one long groan.

I'm sure this had to do with many things. California was being whacked by the economy, just like Florida was. Arnold, his critics on the Right were complaining, had made a sharp left turn. His pro-environment message might have gotten him some appreciation from Hollywood liberals, but he had clearly lost his grip on this crowd.

I had praised the moderate, pro-environment Republican governor to a gathering of Republicans. My praise was met with anger. Something was very, very wrong.

Chapter 8

Mitt Romney wasn't happy. Neither was Mike Huck-abee nor Ron Paul. The whole Republican presiden-tial field was taken aback. But from what I heard, it was Rudy Giuliani who was somewhere on the far side of furious. His face got red. His jaw jutted out even farther than it usually does. I'm not sure whether steam burst from his ears or not.

I was less than fourteen months into my term as governor. The polls were still strong. The media coverage was largely favorable. I had fallen in love. I was feeling confident, clearheaded, and proud of what we had already gotten done. Some Republican Party leaders found me a little too independent. But my commonsense, broad-based initiatives were popular with Republican voters and also with Democrats and Independents. I felt like I'd really found the sweet spot of Florida politics as the state was heading back into the na-tional spotlight.

It was Saturday, January 26, three days out from the 2008 Florida primary, and I had just endorsed John McCain.

On this final weekend, the candidates were spread across the state: The cheery warrior Huckabee, who'd scored an upset win in the Iowa caucuses. Methodical Mitt, who was on top of the polls in Florida and still had a huge pile of cash in the bank. The hard-charging Rudy, who hadn't won anything and absolutely needed the state. And crusty John McCain, who'd taken New Hampshire but was running out of money in Florida and watching his poll numbers evaporate. A week before the primary, John was trailing Mitt by five. The latest statewide numbers had him down by eleven. Ron Paul, God bless him, was running a parallel campaign somewhere.

John was scheduled to speak that night at the Hilton St. Petersburg Carillon Park, where the Pinellas County Republican Party was holding its annual Lincoln Day Dinner. The party people had asked me to introduce him.

I got a call from John the day before. He was campaigning in Miami with Congressman Mario Diaz-Balart.

"You could endorse me tomorrow," he joked—or half joked.

"It'll be a nice introduction," I assured him.

On Saturday afternoon, I called Arlene DiBenigno, who had worked in my administration and was running John's Florida primary campaign. "I'd like to see the senator before the dinner tonight, if he has a minute," I said to Arlene. Without hesitation, she told me to stop by John's hotel suite.

When I arrived, he met me at the door, already dressed for dinner.

"Come on in," John said with his usual gruff friendliness. "Can I get you something to drink?"

"I'm fine, thanks," I said.

We sat across a coffee table and talked for a few minutes, discussing the maneuverings of the various candidates and what kind of voter turnout to expect. I knew the Florida primary had been a struggle for him. He didn't say so, but I think he sensed the state might be slipping away. In his own steely way, he looked to me like a man who was trying to dig himself out of a hole. I'd always felt a bond with John. He had endorsed me in the primary when I ran for governor. But in his primary race, Rush Limbaugh and some of the other conservative talk hosts were bashing John for being too moderate. He was my kind of Republican—in tune with the party's basic principles but a commonsense leader and always his own man.

The first lull in the conversation, I took a deep breath. "John," I said, "I wanted to tell you I'm going to endorse you tonight."

John looked at me like he wanted to be sure he understood what I'd just said. Then, he jumped up from his chair. I got up from mine. He marched around the table and gave me a giant hug.

"I can't thank you enough," he said. "This means everything."

I told him that I had made up my mind just that afternoon and hardly anyone else knew. Just my father and Carole—I'd told her on the boat that afternoon, "I can't let my friend down"—and a couple of my closest political advisers. My friend Brian Ballard, who'd been raising money for John, had been trying to persuade me to quit staying neutral and come out at the end for McCain. "If you do this," Brian said, "you will do something very few people ever have the chance to do. You will have a genuine influence on who becomes the next president—or at least the next Republican nominee."

I didn't ask John for anything. We didn't discuss the vice presidency or any other job. We barely had time to get over to the hotel's grand ballroom and let the word out.

People were already in the ballroom as John and I walked in together. They noticed that. I could hear a steady buzz as we made our way up front. I stepped onto the stage in front of a huge American flag and called John up.

"We have a lot of good people who are running for president this year," I said. "But you have to think about, when it comes to Tuesday, who you're going to vote for and who you're going to support. And I have been thinking about it a lot."

I didn't want to waste any time up there. I got right to the point.

"After thinking about it as much as I have, I don't think anybody would do better than the man who stands next to me, Senator John McCain."

Then I added straight-out: "That's an endorsement."

It might have been the shortest endorsement speech in American history. But believe me, the point was not missed. The McCain supporters started clapping even before I got all the words out. Backers of the other candidates looked shocked and glum. John, who isn't shaken by much, sounded nearly overwhelmed.

"I am very honored," he said. "I cannot tell you, cannot describe to you the honor and privilege that I feel to be endorsed by this great governor of this great state of Florida."

All the candidates had sought my support. This time, Florida was a key, early battleground state. We'd moved the primary up to January to make sure of that. Mitt didn't expect my endorsement. But his people had been in constant contact with George LeMieux, hoping I would at least stay neutral, even hinting to George about a major campaign job if Mitt was the nominee. Until he heard otherwise, I think John expected me to stay neutral as well. But ever since early summer, Rudy had been working me hard. In June, George and I met in the Hamptons with Rudy and his campaign strategist, Tony Carbonetti. I never promised an endorsement. But we had a very friendly visit. Rudy told me how much he hoped I could support him. "Florida's make-or-break for us," he said. We agreed to stay in touch.

All along, my first choice was John. We didn't agree on every single issue. But I trusted his sound judgment, and I trusted his maverick heart. I thought he'd be the party's strongest candidate, and not just because he was a war hero. Like me, he was in—but not owned by—the Republican Party. The fact that John made Rush Limbaugh leery, that the talk show host found the senator insufficiently ardent, was a positive sign for me. Rush's daily radio attacks got so heated, Bob Dole, the 1996 nominee, even wrote him a letter, saying he should really back off. Rush's response to the uproar? He threatened to endorse Barack Obama.

At a time when extremism seemed to be rising inside the party, John was the voice of reason to me—on immigration, on the economy, on the red-meat social issues. He had the values, the grounding, and the life experience to know what he believed in and the confidence to do what he thought was right.

Way back in the summer, Rudy's people had suggested mid-November as a good time to endorse their man—late enough that voters would be paying attention, early enough to deflate the other campaigns. But I didn't see any reason to rush an endorsement for anyone. The field was too fluid. There was no way of telling who'd still be viable after the first of the year. John's campaign was having its ups and downs. When I saw John in Tallahassee in early October, he asked me to wait until after the New Hampshire primary to decide. "I'm telling you, I'm gonna win this thing," he said.

John knew I liked him and was inclined to be helpful. He was my kind of moderate Republican. But this was a complicated decision for a governor like me. John's campaign hadn't been going smoothly. Some of his top consultants had left in a huff. By the time the Florida primary arrived, who knew if he'd still be in the race? If I was going to make an endorsement and risk alienating the other candidates and their supporters, I didn't want to waste my support on someone who wasn't still a viable force.

I made no commitment to John. But I told him I wouldn't do anything hasty. And I was glad I hadn't.

The morning after I endorsed him, John and I stood outside the First Watch restaurant in downtown Tampa for a rally his people threw together overnight. I delivered my endorsement proudly. "I'm not the sort of guy who decides to support a candidate or an issue because of some deal," I said. "It's because of what I feel in my heart."

"I'd like to give you a little straight talk," John said. "This is going to give us momentum in order for us to win."

The endorsement got huge coverage. It led the papers in Florida and got hours of analysis on CNN, MSNBC, and Fox News. Immediately, John shot up in the polls. His contributions, which had really been lagging, suddenly began rolling in again. It was just the shot he needed to rise above the pack. Rudy's campaign, already struggling, really collapsed.

John won a solid victory in the January 29 Florida primary with 36 percent of the vote, a good fifteen points above where he'd been polling. Mitt Romney came in second with 31 percent. Trailing in third, with less than 15 percent, was Rudy Giuliani.

According to exit polls, 40 percent of Republican voters said my endorsement influenced their choice. It was a big day for me. Not only did John race to victory after I endorsed him, Florida voters also approved my property tax reduction amendment. It got 64 percent of the vote.

John McCain was the big winner—along with Florida. But I also felt like I was on a roll. I'd done something good for commonsense politics—and if Brian Ballard was onto something, maybe I'd even had some influence on who'd become the next president.

The next day, January 30, Rudy withdrew from the race and endorsed John McCain. He and I agreed on that much: John would make an excellent nominee.

Ever since, Rudy has grumbled to friends and reporters that I somehow double-crossed him or led him to believe that I was going to endorse him or, in some of his tellings of the story, out-and-out lied to him. None of that is true. Rudy just heard what Rudy wanted to hear. And he wasn't John McCain.

On the Democratic side, Barack Obama and Hillary Clinton went back and forth for a while, each one scoring primary victories and overcoming temporary setbacks. John Edwards burned up and burned out, trying to swat back reports that he'd fathered a child with a documentary filmmaker very much not his wife. Hillary was never able to close the deal. Obama was gaining control. America was gradually getting to know this extraordinary man. People were responding to the same thing I had when I watched him speak at the Democratic convention in 2004. He wasn't a rising star in my party. But there was something extraordinary about this young Illinois senator, and I wasn't the only one who had noticed.

As the campaign rolled on, two things were becoming apparent to me about Barack Obama. He was a tremendously gifted political figure, and some people I knew really, really loathed him.

He had the ability to attract large numbers of dedicated supporters—young people, suburbanites, minorities of course, but also many people who'd never voted before. They were putting their lives on hold to help him get elected. He was a Democrat. As a Republican, I was supposed to hate him. But it was clear to me, even then, why people loved him so much.

Obama had an awesome personal story. Left by his father. Raised by his grandparents and his single mom. Earning an Ivy League education, achieving at every turn. Rising to the heights of American politics. Now he was a first-term senator, looking like a serious contender for the big job. If that's not an inspiring American biography, I don't know what is.

He had a great wife and impressive daughters. He was a stirring orator. And as a bonus, he came from a racial group that had long been disadvantaged, providing hope and encouragement to others around the globe.

And yet quite a few conservatives seemed to positively hate him. What was that about? They didn't just disagree with his policies. They didn't simply not care for him so much. This was a hatred beyond all reason. And it seemed to justify any outlandish insult or allegation. He was a socialist, the haters were certain. No, he was a Communist. He was a terrorist. He hated white people. He was a secret Muslim. He had a radical Christian preacher as his spiritual leader. He wasn't born in America. He very well might be, some of these people suggested in all seriousness, the Antichrist.

To me, it wasn't necessary to embrace his every position. As a Republican governor of Florida, I didn't embrace them all. He was left of me on Iraq. I was right of him on guns. We were both for gay civil unions, though neither of us was pro-gay-marriage—yet. But as far as I was concerned, only someone with a screw loose could look at Barack Obama and see a terrorist or the Antichrist.

And some people did.

Back in Tallahassee, I was focused on my duties as governor and helping John McCain, my own party's candidate for president. So began the talk: whether John might return the favor of my endorsement with an offer to be his vice president. He clinched the GOP nomination on March 4 with a one-day sweep of primaries in Ohio, Texas, Rhode Island, and Vermont. He'd have to pick someone, right?

This might be hard to believe, but between the Florida primary and the end of August, John and I never discussed the vice presidency—not once. The topic was all over the media. I made the long list and the short list. That's what the newspapers and the cable shows said. I was weighed, discussed, rated, and debated— all without anyone saying anything directly to me. No one from the campaign reached out to my people. No message was delivered first- or secondhand. I would even be flown with three other potential candidates to Arizona for a rustic weekend at the McCain ranch with John and his wife, Cindy, and some of their closest friends— still without anyone explaining why.

It was the strangest dance I'd ever been part of.

Over those months, John and I spoke about all kinds of things— lighthearted and serious. But never once did we broach the topic of my being his vice president.

I had no idea if this was how things were going for the other officeholders being similarly mentioned—Minnesota Governor Tim Pawlenty, Louisiana Governor Bobby Jindal, Connecticut Senator Joe Lieberman, South Carolina Senator Lindsey Graham. All I knew was that people kept asking what I was hearing from the McCain camp, and I wasn't hearing anything.

In the second week of May, I got a call from Rick Davis, John's national campaign manager. "Senator McCain and his wife would like you and Carole to come out Memorial Day weekend to their place in Sedona, Arizona, with some other people," Rick said. He mentioned Mitt and Ann Romney, Bobby and Supriya Jindal, and Joe Lieberman. There was no special agenda for the weekend, Rick said—in fact, he suggested, no serious purpose for the visit at all. "Just to relax, to hang out, spend a couple of nights, meet some of the McCains' close friends—just be their guests."

Well, okay.

It all sounded lovely. But I thought I had some idea of what was going on. It was humbling to be invited. But it didn't sound like just an ordinary casual Memorial Day weekend visit. We hadn't done this last summer. I'd never been invited to the McCain ranch before. This couldn't be a total coincidence.

I told Rick we'd love to come.

Before the weekend, Carole got a friendly call from Cindy McCain. "I'm so excited you all are coming," the senator's wife said. "I want you to know it's very casual. I mean muddy, dirty, hiking-boots casual. We'll do some hiking, have a cookout, just have a good time. Jeans, boots, whatever—it's completely relaxed."

Carole packed her jeans and sneakers and, just in case, a casual sundress. I didn't get a similar call from John.

When we finally reached the rolling foothills outside Sedona, we couldn't help but notice several TV-satellite trucks camped right outside the McCain gate. Was this typical, for reporters in Arizona to greet travelers who fly in for a weekend of burgers and relaxation?

I didn't think so.

After a long drive down a winding dirt road, we pulled up to the living compound in our Florida Department of Law Enforcement SUV. There was a large main house and a couple of smaller guest cottages. The whole property was landscaped with rocks, cacti, and other desert vegetation.

The senior senator from Arizona greeted us near the barbecue in blue jeans, a sweatshirt, and a baseball cap that said NAVY. He had a long fork in his hand.

"Come here, Carole," he called out warmly. "Come here, Charlie. Try that! Do you like chicken? Do you like hamburgers? We got it all."

Lindsey Graham was there. He and Joe Lieberman were so tight with John, they finished one another's sentences. Besides the Jindals and the Romneys, the others included Charlie Black, the former Reagan and George H. W. Bush strategist, and his wife, Judy, and Fred Smith, the FedEx chairman, and his wife, Diane. Sharon and Oliver Harper, friends and neighbors of the McCains, were there. And three McCain children, daughters Meghan and Bridget and son Jimmy, who was just back from fighting in Iraq.

There had also been a previous gathering at the ranch, I heard. That group included Minnesota Governor Tim Pawlenty and others.

Carole and I were assigned a two-bedroom cabin that we shared with the Jindals. Bobby and Supriya were kind and friendly, though Bobby had a tendency to turn quickly serious. Several times, when the conversation veered toward lighthearted topics, he steered it back to health care reform, energy issues, or the economy.

The McCains were totally gracious hosts. Their kids were open and interested. Jimmy told us about his time in Iraq. Their home was inviting and beautiful in a cozy desert kind of way—lots of family photos, animal-skin rugs, and Native American art. The hiking trails—and especially the picnic area beside a stream out back—were glorious. This was Arizona ranch living at its finest.

We all talked and told stories into the evening. John kept barbecuing. He excitedly described the fifty-seven species of birds in the area. We had dinner down by the river one night. Carole got to wear her sundress. Lindsey and Joe and John kept ragging on one another.

We consumed some very nice wine. As well as I could figure, John and his friends were trying to size us up personally, gauging how they might get along with us should the need ever arise.

The only thing that was never discussed was the reason I still think we were there, the vice presidency.

Not a mention. Not a word. Not a syllable.

I'm not sure anyone even acknowledged that America has a vice president.

Carole and I had been keeping our relationship relatively quiet. We didn't exactly hide it. We went out frequently in Tallahassee, St. Petersburg, and Miami. But we certainly didn't broadcast the details. Our families knew. Our friends knew. Plenty of people in politics knew, including, of course, the McCains. But people we ran across pretty much respected our privacy. Florida doesn't have gossip columnists like New York, Washington, or Hollywood. I didn't put out a press release saying, "Dating a lovely lady." A picture did move on the national wires showing the two of us coming out of a hamburger restaurant in Sedona, holding hands. I'm sure some people were talking, but I didn't participate.

Back in Tallahassee, the staff at the Governor's Mansion got used to seeing Carole around. They were completely embracing. I'd been bouncing around this sprawling home, all alone. I think the staff felt the same way I did: It was much, much nicer having her there.

Carole and I were thinking more and more about our lives together. She was very aware of not inserting herself into my public duties. "The people of Florida elected you," she said one day. "They didn't elect me."

She was always friendly and personable and welcoming when she met people from my world. But it wasn't in her nature to grasp any kind of formal role.

I respected that. But some public attention came with the territory of being close to me. She understood that and accepted it. But if anything, she sidestepped the limelight. I just wanted her to be comfortable, whatever that meant.

We dated into the summer. On Wednesday, July 2, just as everything was slowing down for Independence Day, I went to the Gold & Diamond Center at the Northeast Park Shopping Center in St. Petersburg and bought a one-of-a-kind sapphire-and-diamond engagement ring designed by the store's owner, Hien Nguyen.

We went to dinner that night at Ceviche, one of our favorite neighborhood places, right across from my condo. I was planning to propose after dinner.

But in the elevator on the way up, we ran into a couple who live in the building. The Tampa Bay Rays were playing the Boston Red Sox that night. The man said: "Why don't you come up and watch the end of the Rays game with us?"

Carole seemed up for it. I didn't want to say in the elevator: "Well, um, sure, except that I was thinking about going home and asking her to marry me."

So I just said, "Sure."

We all watched the game together on TV, as the Rays came from behind with six runs in the seventh inning to win. We said good night to the neighbors and walked back to my place. It was late, too late to be popping questions.

The next morning, July 3, Carole was sitting on the couch in the living room. I sat down next to her. I had the jewelry box in my hand. She looked at the box. She looked at me. I took the lid off. And I asked her to marry me.

She said yes, thank God.

By accepting my proposal, she was taking on a lot. I had to make sure she understood that and was comfortable with it. Not only would she be marrying a guy who was an amateur at long-term romance, she was also assuming the role of First Lady of Florida.

The people might not have gotten a vote on this one. But I had.

I told her she could find her own version of what that meant. I wanted her to.

"We'll do it so you're comfortable," I said. "We'll just have to figure it out together."

How someone chooses to take on the role of First Lady, I explained to her, is really up to the individual. I didn't want her to feel put upon to take on this cause or that one. I didn't want any of it to be a burden on her. She told me she wasn't worried. To her, she said, it all sounded like a fun adventure.

I told my parents and my sisters. They were ecstatic. They could see how happy Carole had already made me. My friends all seemed to like her too. I had the press office put out a short statement, saying I was engaged to marry businesswoman Carole Rome. When the *St. Petersburg Times* called for a comment, I couldn't resist telling them, "She is special in every way. She is brilliant, beautiful, and sweet. I'm very, very lucky." I don't believe "First Fiancée" is an official title, but some people started using the phrase around Tallahassee.

Into late July I heard nothing from the McCain camp, nothing at all about the vice presidency. Was the idea dead? Had it ever existed? Had the presumptive Republican nominee settled on someone else? I didn't know what to make of the radio silence. Then, Rick Davis, John McCain's national campaign manager, called again.

"I know you've been reading in the papers some speculation about whether or not you'd be considered for the ticket," Rick said. "Let me tell you: You are being considered for the ticket. This is real. You have to decide if it's something you might want to be considered for."

That was easy.

"Listen," I said, "if you guys think it'll help, of course."

"It's a huge sacrifice," Rick cautioned. "Your life will not be your life anymore, not that it is already. But things will really explode."

"Let me talk to Carole, talk to my family, talk to my parents. But I think I'm in."

It was not a difficult decision. It was about the future of the country. It was a call to service. It was flattering. I felt comfortable with John McCain. He was a patriot of the highest order, a war hero, and a true public servant. We shared a moderate view of the world. I trusted his heart. I'd have been happy to serve as his vice president.

When I called Rick back with my final okay, he mentioned the name A. B. Culvahouse. "He's a lawyer friend of Senator McCain's who will sit with you for a day and ask you all kinds of things." The lawyer, I discovered later, had been vetting potential Republican vice presidents since 1976.

"But before we do that," Rick said, "we have to send you a lot of paperwork to fill out. I have to warn you. We're gonna ask you about everything you've ever done in your whole life and everything you've ever imagined doing. Income taxes, friends, family—everything."

That didn't bother me at all. My life was an open book already. There were a whole lot of questions. It was like writing the most detailed résumé ever—then multiplying it by ten. I listed jobs. I gave references. I detailed the sources of all my income—that didn't take long. I gave lists of my relatives and friends. I confirmed that I hadn't been arrested, convicted, or accused of official wrongdoing. I said I hadn't revealed government secrets to anyone. I sat down with my staffers Eric Eikenberg, Dane Eagle, and Erin Isaac and a couple of others and answered all the questions. It took us three grueling days.

The lawyer and his associate flew down to Florida. They wanted a discreet place to meet. That ruled out the Capitol, the Governor's Mansion, my condo building in St. Petersburg, and every Starbucks and most of the restaurants in Florida. I suggested my parents' house on Snell Isle. "Give us the address," the lawyer said. "We'll meet you there."

We set up in the living room and stayed there all day. They went over some of the same ground as the written questionnaire, then got into detailed discussions of important policy questions.

"How far would you go to capture Osama bin Laden?" Anything legal.

"Do you believe in torture?" No.

"Should Americans have a right to health care?" Absolutely.

I answered every question, and the lawyers kept coming up with more.

Then, for weeks, the McCain team slid back into silence.

The decision had to be made shortly before the Republican National Convention, which was set to begin September 1 at the Xcel Energy Center in Minneapolis–Saint Paul. We'd already been to Sedona. I'd already filled out the forms. I'd gone through the day-long interview with the Washington lawyers. I didn't know what to expect next.

I did notice that the phone didn't ring.

It was hard not to feel a little anxious. I was being considered for a job, and that job was vice president of the United States. It was like

I was living in a daily countdown. Instead of working out every morning, I was working out twice a day, just to shake off the extra energy.

Carole asked, more than once: "Did they call yet? Did you hear anything?"

I was hearing nothing.

I got one report from my lobbyist friend Brian Ballard. In a phone call with John, he asked directly what my chances were. According to Brian, John measured his words carefully.

"Well," the senator said, "I can't tell you what is going to happen. But I can tell you what Culvahouse, the lawyer, told me about Charlie: 'This guy is ready.'"

That made me feel good. At least they hadn't met and decided, "No way!"

In the final week of August, the week before the convention in Minneapolis, we all got word about the logistics of John's big announcement. The pick would be revealed that Friday, August 29, at Wright State University in Dayton, Ohio, a crucial battleground for November.

Carole was up in New York, visiting family. "Did anyone call you to make arrangements?" she asked on the phone.

Um, no.

No calls. No idling Gulfstreams at Albert Whitted Airport. No men in dark suits and earpieces in the condo lobby. All that radio silence didn't seem like a very promising sign.

At 11:30 A.M., my cell phone rang.

It was John McCain. "Listen," he said, "I wanted to touch base with you. Obviously, we are announcing this thing. I assume it's pretty obvious we decided to go in another direction."

It was very John. Direct. Straightforward. Almost matter-of-fact. "It was an honor to be considered," I said. I told John I'd do whatever I could to help him in the fall campaign.

I still didn't know who the pick was. I felt awkward asking, "Well, who's it gonna be?" So I didn't. I found out when America found out, at 12:18 P.M., that John had chosen Sarah Palin, the governor of Alaska.

I hadn't even realized she was in the running. With all the short lists and long lists, I had never heard her name mentioned at all. I don't believe she ever went to Sedona. From what I heard later, she was more of a late-hour addition to the mix.

She and I had probably run into each other at a Governors Association meeting. But I had no specific memory of it. Initially, I didn't have much of a sense of what she was like or what she believed.

She called herself a maverick.

She was clearly beloved by the staunch social conservatives.

She was obviously proud of her independence from the old Republican hierarchy.

She was definitely popular with the hard-cores, this energized band of absolutists who considered flexibility a sign of weakness and had turned the idea of "family values" into something harsh, divisive, and mean. I knew that her kind of Republican didn't much like my kind of Republican—or, I thought, John's kind of Republican.

I quickly discovered my initial impressions were right: Her idea of a maverick and John's idea of a maverick were as far apart as Arizona and Alaska. They might start with the same letter, but they really were a continent away.

I didn't know if Sarah Palin knew anything or had good judgment or was prepared, as a potential vice president, to lead the country if it ever came to that. But she was young. She was fresh. She was a woman, which was part of the consideration, I am sure. And she could fire up a crowd of conservative party activists just by saying, "You betcha!" The consultants kept saying these people were a growing force inside the party, and the rest of us had better learn in a hurry how to connect with them.

I would like to have been picked. Campaigning with John would have been an invigorating experience. I could have highlighted education, the environment, and other issues I cared about, issues that Republicans sometimes tended to ignore. John has a unique personality, but we really were compatible in a lot of ways. I believe I could have helped him on the campaign trail. Had we won, it would have been an honor to serve the country as his vice president.

But I wasn't devastated that I didn't get the nod. I understood from the start there were many considerations and many possible candidates. I never had the feeling that I deserved it somehow. I really meant what I said when I told John I was honored to have been considered. I was.

After the pick, whenever the campaign came to Florida, McCain campaign officials would ask me to join one of the nominees, whoever happened to be in the state. Out of loyalty to John, I was more than happy to help.

I never said anything negative about Sarah Palin. I even said she'd "do a great job" as president should, God forbid, something happen to John and noted that she was the "only executive in the race." I was trying to help my friend, and I didn't want to sound like I had my nose out of joint for not being chosen. But campaigning with Sarah was an unusual experience from beginning to end. She was definitely different from anyone I'd ever campaigned with. We made a bus trip together along Interstate 4 between Tampa and Orlando on October 26. She was very, very quiet. She gave the speeches she was asked to. She spoke with Sean Hannity of Fox News and Elisabeth Hasselbeck from *The View* when they showed up for get-out-the-vote rallies at the Silver Spurs Arena in Kissimmee and the Tampa Convention Center. But other than that, she talked to almost no one.

She sat by herself on the bus, read some briefing papers, and took a few notes. That's highly unusual for a political personality. People in our business tend to be outgoing and gregarious.

Maybe her reticence came from the skewering she was getting in the media. I really don't know. But commentators—and not just Democrats—were questioning her basic readiness to serve, and she was stumbling through some painfully awkward interviews.

When Katie Couric asked, "What newspapers and magazines did you regularly read?" the best Palin could manage was "Um, all of them." *Saturday Night Live* was merciless with Tina Fey's dead-on impressions. Tina/Sarah's "I can see Russia from my house" became a national punch line.

I tried to be friendly. "Anything I can do for you, just let me know," I said cheerily.

"Thank you" was all she answered, her words almost encased in ice.

That was about the extent of our friendly banter.

I know people in Florida. I'd have been happy to help her. But she never asked, and she deflected my gentle overtures.

She was campaigning a vital swing state, and still she never asked me: "What's going on in Florida? What are the local issues here?

What are people thinking about?" Even if she didn't care, why not make idle conversation?

After we'd been riding on the bus a while, she went all the way to the back to be totally alone. She seemed very uncomfortable around anyone, almost as if she didn't want to engage in conversation and reveal what she did or didn't know.

People on the bus kept asking, "Is everything okay? Is she all right? Does she need anything?"

In her speeches and in the few interviews that I heard her give, she emphasized a worldview that to me sounded almost paranoid. It wasn't just different from what the Democrats and Barack Obama were saying. It was nowhere close to the way that John McCain—or I—saw the world.

Let me speak for myself here: I wanted to protect the environment. She wanted to "drill, baby, drill."

I wanted to find a way to work with our international allies. She was more go-it-alone in the world.

I wanted to extend fresh opportunities and help people succeed. She wanted to blame the poor, the unemployed, and struggling.

I wanted to let individuals and families make their own personal life decisions. She was deeply suspicious of abortion, contraception, and alternative lifestyles.

I believed that diversity was one of our strengths in America. She seemed to consider it a threat.

She was a member of the same party John and I were, but our worldviews couldn't have been further apart. Here's the scary thing I didn't fully grasp yet: Hers was the future of the Republican Party. Ours would soon enough be looking like the past.

If this was the new guard, I'd be saying, "Please, bring the old guard back."

When John campaigned through the state, he was completely the opposite. He was Mr. Gregarious, Mr. Inclusive. He was making America sound like a country I would want to live in. He was talking and asking questions the whole way.

John and Barack Obama ran spirited campaigns that fall. They disagreed on Iraq, on health care, on business regulation—on quite a few issues. It wasn't actually that dirty a race. Both candidates generally conducted themselves with civility. But there was something in the air on our side, and I didn't like the way it smelled.

The animosity toward Obama was growing wildly on the Far Right of the Republican Party. It was getting louder. It was getting uglier. And it seemed to know no bounds. And John, to his credit, wanted no part of it.

One of his finest moments on the campaign trail, I thought, came in early October at a highly charged town hall meeting in a Lakeville, Minnesota, high school gym. I wish I'd been there. It was riveting on TV. The crowd, who'd heard months of anti-Obama scare stories, was clearly agitated. As John moved through some of his questions and answers, people were shouting insults about the Democratic nominee. "Liar!" one man yelled.

"Terrorist!" someone else said.

One man said he feared Barack Obama would "lead America to socialism."

Then John McCain took a question from a woman in the audience. He leaned in, sharing his cordless microphone with her.

"I can't trust Obama," she said. "I have read about him, and he's not, he's not, uh—he's an Arab. He's not"—before McCain pulled the microphone away.

"No, ma'am," the senator said. "He's a decent family man and citizen that I just happen to have disagreements with on fundamental issues, and that's what this campaign's all about. He's not an Arab."

That was greeted with a hearty round of boos.

Clearly, there was something out there. It was hard not to recognize it, even for a lifelong Republican like John McCain.

Even for a lifelong Republican like me.

"The people here in Minnesota want a real fight," another man called out from the crowd. These were McCain supporters. But he didn't look too comfortable standing among them.

"We want to fight, and I will fight," the senator said. "But I will be respectful. I admire Senator Obama and his accomplishments, and I will respect him."

More boos.

John pressed on.

"I have to tell you. Senator Obama is a decent person and a person you don't have to be scared of as president of the United States," John said.

"Come on, John," another called out.

"Liar . . . terrorist . . . Muslim!"

And Barack Obama wasn't even the president yet.

Chapter 9

Everyone knew Election 2008 was going to produce a massive voter turnout. An African American man was on the ballot as the Democratic nominee for president, and he had a real chance to win. Millions of new people had registered to vote, hundreds of thousands of them in Florida.

But I wasn't at all sure Florida would be ready to accommodate them.

One thing we knew for certain: Florida, as it usually is, would be one of America's most important swing states. We could go Democratic. We could go Republican. However we went, Americans often had a tendency to follow.

No one could say for certain that Florida would be picking a president again—but no one could deny it either.

We'd made some improvements in the voting mechanics. We'd dumped the touch screens, which were about as popular as rush hour traffic on I-95. We'd created a new paper trail, which was important. But the memories of 2000 still hung over the state like an embarrassing indiscretion: The ridiculous lines at the polls. Our utter incompetence running a recount. And, when it really mattered, our inability to even say who won. I certainly had no confidence that those problems were all behind us.

Late in his first term, Jeb had taken some steps to make voting less onerous and to ease the lines a bit. He ordered an expansion of early-voting hours, which was nice. Then, a year later, the expansion was reversed. Early-voting hours were reduced again and confined to election offices, city halls, and libraries.

I couldn't help but wonder: Did my fellow Republicans actually want people to vote? It didn't take a crowd-control expert to imagine that the next high-turnout election could easily turn into another fiasco.

Luckily for everyone, 2004 did not draw huge crowds. As John Kerry tried to deny George W. Bush a second term, not everything went smoothly in Florida. There were still some lines. But the race wasn't close, and the voting process was a clear improvement over the dark days of Bush versus Gore. In fact, early voting was popular enough in 2004 that the state's election supervisors asked the legislature for more of it in future elections—more polling stations, longer hours, and additional publicity.

But Republican leaders in the House and Senate would have none of that. They moved to curtail early voting instead.

Democrats objected. "They're using their power, their majority, to make it harder for people to vote," House Minority Leader Dan Gelber said. "They're grabbing every political advantage they can find." But the Republicans pressed ahead.

The early-voting schedule was cut again—from twelve hours to eight hours a day. Strict limits were placed on where the early voting could occur. No more schools or churches or community centers.

Now, the early ballots could be cast only in election offices, libraries, and city halls.

"If you're Jewish and have to go to St. Timothy's Catholic Church, people complained to us and said they're bothered by that," explained one of the bill's sponsors, Republican State Representative Kevin Ambler of Lutz.

The rollbacks sailed through the House, 82–36, on a largely party-line vote. Over the objection of Democrats and local election officials, Jeb signed the reductions into law on June 20, 2005, a year and a half before I came in.

Apparently, that's what we'd learned from the cataclysm of 2000. Do a little something but not too much, then pull back on even the tiny reforms that we'd made. Well, you can't say no one was warned.

Election 2008 was going to be different. I wanted to make sure of that. Now, I was the one in charge. Jeb had moved on, and the legislature was still the legislature. I truly believed people have a right to vote. But when it came to the issue of voting, I kept finding myself clashing with people who were supposedly on my side.

It wasn't just that I had jettisoned Jeb's touch screens, which Republicans seemed fine with. It wasn't just that I had restored voting rights to people with criminal pasts, though the Republican law-and-order crowd was still grumbling about that. It was my next stand for fair voting in Florida that became the political equivalent of an indoor nuclear bomb. The boom was louder than I ever expected, and the fallout lasted for years.

The move I sought should have been the least controversial of my whole administration. What I wanted was so basic, so unambiguously right: That our citizens be allowed to vote in a reasonably convenient manner. That people shouldn't have to wait in line for hours in the blazing Florida sun. That the state should help folks exercise this precious right of democracy—not throw up every imaginable barrier to turn them away.

What kind of person could possibly disagree? The way my fellow Republicans went nuts, you'd have thought the party's entire future was on the line. And you know what? In a way, it was.

Here's what happened that year: The voting in Florida's 2008 Democratic and Republican primaries went fairly smoothly on January 29. Hillary Clinton held back Barack Obama and John Edwards on the Democratic side. After I endorsed John McCain, he slid past the others in the Republican field. But a primary is a whole lot easier to run than a big general election—a shorter ballot, lower turnouts. So the truth is, as the historic election of 2008 was upon us—Barack Obama versus John McCain—we really didn't know how prepared we were.

We quickly found out.

As Florida's limited early voting began on October 20, I wasn't out touring polling places. I was mostly back in Tallahassee being governor and, when they were in the state, out campaigning with John McCain and Sarah Palin. But I was reading all the papers and keeping an obsessive eye on the local TV news and talking to lots of people. I could tell immediately, things were not going well out there. From the very morning that the polls opened, the lines were enormous. Soon, the waits were getting interminable. The pared-back system of early voting looked like it was being overwhelmed.

What really got to me was how hot it was in Florida in late October. We had a lot of senior citizens waiting in these lines, especially in minority sections of South Florida. My heart just bled for them.

I heard about one lady who fainted and had to be rushed to the hospital. Others were standing for four, five, and six hours in the broiling Florida sun. Friends and relatives were bringing them water, hats, sunscreen, and other supplies. Vendors were selling snow cones.

I was the governor. This was my state. And I knew immediately this was wrong. We couldn't let those people wait out there forever. Whatever the politics behind it, I wasn't comfortable with it at all.

Under Florida law, the secretary of state is responsible for overseeing elections. Reporters were asking Secretary of State Kurt Browning what he was planning to do.

Nothing, was his answer.

He said he wasn't troubled at all by the long, slow lines. "Lines are a sign of a healthy democracy, and certainly our democracy is healthy today," he said on October 21.

Kurt was a really smart guy. I had appointed Kurt to the job that Katherine Harris held during the Jeb years. Was he taken out of context? Did he really believe that? I didn't know. But he clearly wasn't springing to action. And the lines were getting longer by the day. The newspapers were weighing in with editorials, demanding something be done.

Voters were left waiting so long, Miami-Dade and Broward counties installed an Early Voting Wait Clock on their websites, listing the expected waiting times at the various polling spots. In Broward, the Florida county that includes Fort Lauderdale and has more Democratic voters than any other in the state, the wait clock on the first Friday of early voting said "4 hours" for Miramar City Hall.

Kurt did praise the clocks, calling them "an innovative idea." Apparently, it was okay to make people wait half the day as long as you told them how long they could expect to be standing there. By the end of the weekend, nearly 1.2 million people—about 10 percent of the state's voters—had inched their way to the front of those lines.

There was no count of how many got discouraged and left. And the number of Floridians who wanted to vote was growing still.

The reason for all this, I thought, was obvious. With Jeb's 2005 cutback in early voting, we simply didn't have the hours or the polling places to meet the demand. MSNBC's Rachel Maddow had a dead-on analogy, I thought, about Jeb's 2005 voting cutbacks. "Close a couple of lanes on the bridge at rush hour," Rachel said, "more people will be late for dinner—right?"

Exactly right!

Election 2008 was on the road to being 2000 again. If this was how we were handling the turnout for early voting, I could just imagine the meltdown come Election Day.

I knew I couldn't let this happen.

I was the governor. I was the chief elected official in the state. The principle of fair voting was a bedrock of our democracy. Any repeat of 2000 would be an insult to the state I loved. It would be an affront to the rule of law and the code of decency. It would be a personal embarrassment to me. There was no way I could shrug and say, "Oh, too bad!"

Monday, October 27, was the busiest day yet. A total of 43,000 votes were cast on that one day in Broward and Miami-Dade, 5,000 more than on any previous day. And there was no end in sight. When Miami-Dade's thirty-seven polling places opened at 11 A.M. Tuesday, one week out from Election Day, some of the lines wrapped around buildings. Others extended for several blocks. And some of the times on those Early Voting Wait Clocks were turning out to be wildly optimistic. Voters who saw the ninety-minute estimate at the Model City Library on Tuesday morning barely got through in twice that time. Yet every Republican leader I spoke to in Florida had the same advice:

Do nothing.

It's only temporary.

Tough out the awful pictures and ever louder complaints. It'll all be fine. Clearly, some Florida Republican leaders looked at the lessons of history differently from the way that I did.

The do-nothing excuses were being voiced by Republicans across the country, it seemed. I was hearing them on the national cable news debate shows and reading them on the op-ed pages: justifications for making voting as difficult as humanly possible, especially for those who tended to vote with the Democrats.

What was going on here? Why was the Republican Party clamoring to make it harder for citizens to vote?

Some people in the party clearly wanted to put their thumb on the scale. They wanted to make it as hard as possible for the people who tend to vote early: older people, African Americans, Latinos, other minorities—Democrats! The fewer of those people who vote, the better it is for Republicans. It was basic election math.

That kind of cynical thinking flew totally in the face of everything I believed about the sacred trust of public office. I looked at the job of governing differently from that. When you get elected governor of Florida, I believe, you're not the governor of the Republicans of Florida or the Democrats of Florida. You're the governor of the people of Florida, and you damn well ought to behave that way.

Some Republican leaders clearly did not agree with that. They had a different idea.

Don't rock the vote! Shrink the vote!

Don't promote participation! Discourage it!

Don't exercise your rights! Abandon them!

Find something—find anything!—to suppress an inhospitable sector of the electorate.

The closer we got to Election Day 2008, the worse things were looking again.

A worried crowd of Haitian Americans piled into a branch library in North Miami. These were patriotic American citizens with a perfect right to vote. The library stopped letting people queue up at 3 P.M. And even though closing time to vote was well before most people got off from work, some of them at the library that day didn't vote until 8 P.M. The people weren't making outlandish demands. They weren't asking for anything unreasonable. They just wanted to vote.

And we had this system in place that was doing everything it could to stop them. The professionals on the ground didn't like that any better than I did. Miami-Dade Supervisor of Elections Lester Sola said he didn't understand why the legislature had given county election officials so few options for early-voting stations. "Why overwhelm a library when you have a large regional park next door?" Sola asked. "We had a lot more flexibility before."

Frankly, I didn't see how we could let this go on.

"We need to expand these hours," I told my staff.

I got a call from Dan Gelber. We were from different parties, but the House minority leader and I had open lines of communication. He was typically direct on the phone.

"I'd like you to consider signing an executive order extending the early-voting hours so that these long lines don't persist," he said. "We need to give our citizens a reasonable chance to vote."

"Can I do that?" I asked. "The lawyers around here aren't so sure."

With Dan still on the phone, I called in a couple of the lawyers from the general counsel's office. "I want to look at the draft of an executive order allowing me to expand these early-voting hours," I said.

I knew there was no time to convene the legislature. And to be honest, I wasn't sure their Republican leadership was in any mood to act or even go along with what I wanted to do. They were the ones who'd made the cutbacks.

"We don't think it's constitutional," the general counsel said. "We don't think you can do this."

"What would make it constitutional?" I asked.

They thought for a moment and conferred among themselves. "Maybe if it was an emergency. Maybe then it would at least be arguably constitutional."

The TV was on with the volume down in my office. The pictures sure looked like an emergency to me.

"If people aren't able to exercise their right to vote in a democracy, you don't think that's an emergency? If that's not an emergency, what's an emergency? Voting—free, open, and fair voting—is a basic act of our form of government. It can't be denied. Let's argue it from that point of view."

The lawyers could tell I felt strongly. They still sounded reluctant.

Dan was still on the line. He remembered something I hadn't: In 2002, Jeb Bush had issued a similar order to help voters deal with the glitches of using the new voting equipment. I didn't know what the courts might ultimately say about this, but it at least gave me a hook.

"Draft the order," I told the lawyers. "I respect what you've said. But I'm gonna go ahead and issue the order anyway because I know it's the right thing to do. I work for those people who are standing in line out there. I have to act on their behalf. If somebody wants to challenge it, so be it."

The lawyers went away. They drafted an order, and they brought it back to me. The order declared that Florida was in a state of emergency. And it extended the early-voting hours across Florida from eight to twelve hours a day, from 7 A.M. to 7 P.M.—and a total of another twelve hours on Saturday and Sunday before the election.

"This should help," I said.

I signed the order. I called Dan and told him what I had done. Then I called the reporters in.

Steve Bousquet of the *St. Petersburg Times* asked if I thought this might help Barack Obama in his race with John McCain. "I don't care," I said. "That's not the point of this. It's not a political decision. It's a people decision."

Three hours later, the voting hours were expanded. The lines began to shrink. The people were able to exercise a critical right of democracy. We expanded the vote.

Now that made me proud.

I had seen a problem I could have ignored. I acted instead. The problem went away. Life actually got better for the people in the state. How many of us ever get an opportunity to make a difference like that?

Not everyone was happy that I'd acted. Marco Rubio, then Speaker of the Florida House, told reporters he wished the legislature had been allowed to weigh in first—though "time constraints" and political calculations made that impossible, he added. "The public would see the legislature as an entity that is trying to prevent people from voting," he said. Coincidentally, Marco was among those Floridians who'd been dissuaded from voting by the long lines.

Some of my Republican friends were a whole lot angrier over my decision than Marco was. When I got back to Tampa, I was riding in an SUV with Mel Martinez, one of our two US senators, and Ana Navarro, a Republican operative from Coral Gables and a sometimes TV pundit. Ana's a dedicated activist, but I wouldn't call her the sweetest person I've ever met. She's very strong-willed and at least as sharp-tongued.

"Governor," she said, "I can't believe you signed that executive order. You just handed the election to Obama."

I don't often get angry. I'm not wired that way. But that really annoyed me. I snapped back at her.

"Ana," I said, "that's all very well and good. But you're not governor. Someday, if you ever happen to be governor, you can be the person who says, 'I'm gonna suppress the people's right to vote, the rights of the citizens of the state that I work for.' You can be that person. I'm not gonna be that person."

Mel gave me a surprised double-take as if to say, "Whoa! Charlie's pissed now!"

I know Ana wasn't the only one thinking like that or seething about my executive order. That kind of thinking was becoming pervasive among Republicans. She was just saying directly what others were probably saying behind my back. But however the message was delivered and by whom, it seemed to me just as wrong.

Very few Republicans wanted to say it openly. But they could all read voter-breakdown tables, and they could see some obvious trends.

Latino, Asian, and African Americans all voted heavily Democratic. By smaller margins, women and young people tilted the same way. These were groups who tended to swing close elections. Clearly, the things that help people vote often help the Democrats.

Which puts Republicans in an uncomfortable box: Who wants

to be the party trying to get people *not* to vote? I know I never believed in that. I still don't.

Barack Obama won the election, of course, won it solidly. The turnout was huge, as predicted. Florida was close, as usual. The state's twenty-seven electoral votes helped to put Obama over the top.

Both candidates, I thought, ran impressive campaigns to the end.

John wasn't the kind of guy to wallow in regret, even though the vote didn't go his way. He advanced his issues and made his points forcefully and adeptly.

Why did Obama win and McCain lose? Several reasons, I think. Republicans were hurt by the unpopularity of George W. Bush and the war in Iraq. Sarah Palin excited a narrow part of the Republican base but alienated many, many voters who considered her ill-equipped to serve.

And Barack Obama connected very forcefully.

His inspiring biography, his powerful oratory, his message of hope and change, the sense that Republicans were slipping out of the mainstream—all of it together lifted Obama over the top. That's how elections are won in America. Obama clearly won this one.

And you know what? I was okay with that.

Sure, I had a personal closeness with John McCain. For a minute there, I even though I might play a key part in his administration. But Barack Obama was an undeniably impressive figure and a dedicated leader. Somehow, I was confident, America would be okay in his hands.

November 12 to 14, a week after the vote, the Republican Governors Association was scheduled to meet in Miami. Topic number one was the lessons learned from the 2008 election. Defeat has a way of teaching more lessons than victory ever does. Even the name of the conference reflected that: "Listen to the Voters and Serve."

Sarah Palin was there. I gave her credit for coming. As the host governor, I held a joint interview with Governor Mark Sanford of South Carolina, discussing a split in the party over how we should attract new voters.

Should we home in more tightly on the people who've always supported us? Or should we try to attract new blood? I was on the new-blood side.

Governor Sanford said our message was just fine. "There are a lot of blacks, there are a lot of Hispanics," he said, "that very much agree with the idea of limited government, less in the way of taxes."

Sure, and we're lucky to get 5 percent of them!

I was asked to speak to the group about how I thought the Republican Party should evolve. We Republicans had to look beyond our traditional constituencies, I said. The nation was changing, I said, growing ever more diverse. The Republican tent had to be bigger than it had ever been before.

"This party can no longer *hope* to reach Hispanics, African Americans, and other minority groups—we need to just do it," I said. "Embracing cultures and lifestyles will make us a better party and better leaders. This desire for inclusiveness is near and dear to my heart."

The other governors listened politely. A few even nodded along. But I would not call the response enthusiastic.

"Last week," I said, "the American people made a choice, and this week, if we choose to call ourselves leaders, if we truly endeavor to serve with a servant's heart for the people who count on us, then we too must work together, listen to one another, and learn from the leaders who made the kind of history the American people deserve."

I'm not sure I convinced anyone.

I had better luck with Carole.

She and I got married on December 12 at the stately First United Methodist Church in St. Petersburg. Carole wore a classic floor-length silk gown. Her daughters, Jessica, who was twelve, and Skylar, ten, escorted their mom down the aisle. When the Reverend David Miller asked who gave away the bride, each of the girls answered, "We do." My dad was my best man.

We had a terrific reception a few blocks away at the Vinoy Renaissance hotel, the same place I'd celebrated my victory in the governor's race. It's a grand hotel overlooking Tampa Bay with porches and gardens and a real old-Florida vibe.

For a sitting governor, drawing up the guest list can be a little challenging. Family and friends—that was the easy part. But the guests also included elected officials and committee chairpersons and generous donors and, well, the list did go on a bit. We included as many as we possibly had room for.

It wasn't a typical wedding in one other way. We had to remind guests, "No gifts, please." The state of Florida has ethics rules.

But it was a truly wonderful night near the end of an action-packed year. People came and stayed, ate and drank, and toasted our good fortune. My parents and my sisters looked so proud of me. They could see how happy Carole made me. They'd been waiting a very long while for this.

Chapter 10

I know how hard this is for you," the new president of the
United States said to me. We were standing backstage together
at the Harborside Event Center in Fort Myers, and the crowd
was already stoked.

"I know what you're risking here," Barack Obama said.

Actually, it wasn't that hard for me, this joint appearance he and
I, president and governor, Democrat and Republican, were about to
make. Frankly, I wasn't sure I was risking anything at all. The nation's economy was sinking, Florida's right along with it. The new
president had a credible economic-stimulus plan—official name, the
American Recovery and Reinvestment Act of 2009—that could
mean a fresh $13 billion for my struggling state. That's a lot of cops,
teachers, firefighters, and road-construction crews. What? I was supposed to fight him on that?

This was Tuesday, February 10, 2009, just three weeks into
Obama's first term as president. The excitement that he'd generated
in his history-making campaign hadn't begun to fade. As far as the
people in the event center were concerned, he was the rock star

president, and they were absolutely thrilled to gather in his glow. They'd waited in line for hours for the 1,500 tickets. They brought signs with them that said "Help us, Mr. President" and "Yes, we can."

As he and I made our way through the crowd toward the stage, how could anyone not feel the power of this man? The music was blasting. The people were on their feet. They were clapping, cheering, waving, and calling out both our names. We were shaking hands and slapping five—and smiling, everyone was smiling—all the way up to the front.

But this was more than a feel-good rally or some postelection victory lap. Much more. There was serious business to be done.

For Obama, the poetry of the campaign trail was now being challenged by the prose of governing at such an obviously difficult time. The US economy was stumbling badly, suffering through the roughest patch since the Great Depression. Some economists were already calling this period the Great Recession—and for good reason. The workforce had already lost 3.6 million jobs, 600,000 in just the past month. Middle-class people were losing their homes to foreclosure. And the southwest coast of Florida, which had boomed through the late 1990s and early 2000s, was one of those places where people were feeling it worst. In the final two years of the Bush administration, the unemployment rate in Lee County, which includes Fort Myers, had leapt from 3.5 to 10 percent. Solid local employers like Kraft Construction and Chico's were laying off workers. Almost 12 percent of the homes in Fort Myers were in foreclosure, the highest rate of anywhere in America.

A month before the election, George W. Bush had gotten fairly solid bipartisan support from the Congress for his TARP plan, which directed the Treasury Department to purchase up to $700 billion in troubled assets from some of America's largest banks. But when the new president took office and proposed a $787 billion economic-stimulus plan to jump-start the broader economy, that bipartisanship seemed to evaporate overnight.

A new kind of opposition was waiting for him.

While the president's supporters were still basking in the high glow of his historic victory, many of his critics across the country were seething more angrily than ever. One of the glorious strengths of our American democracy has always been how, once an election is over, most people accept the results and move on. That didn't seem to be happening for Barack Obama. The wildest charges—that he was a secret Muslim, that he wasn't born in America, that he had socialist or Marxist tendencies, that he was in league with terrorists— hadn't been quieted at all by the election results in November. If anything, as the new term began, the complaints were being re- peated more energetically than ever before.

This movement didn't have a name yet, though it would get one soon. There wasn't even formally a movement yet. But the anger from these Obama-hating fiscal hawks, social conservatives, and hard-core anti-immigrationists was definitely growing louder and more organized. They reminded me of the people John McCain had faced in that gymnasium in Minnesota—only his campaign was over, and the outrage now was squarely focused on the new African American president.

The Obama stimulus plan didn't fit their theory of what govern- ment should do at a time of economic crisis, which seemed to add up to nothing at all. The unfettered market was supposed to solve everything.

The stimulus plan was Obama's first major piece of legislation.

The debate in Congress was highly partisan and acrimonious. The bill passed the House of Representatives 244–188—without a single Republican vote. Not one. Now the president was out on the road trying to broaden the support. As he boarded Air Force One to fly to Fort Myers, the senators were assembling in Washington and preparing to vote.

If anyone needed a cheat sheet for the sharpened partisan divide, just notice who turned up at the event center in Fort Myers and who did not. Our chief financial officer, Democrat Alex Sink, came to see the president. So did quite a few members of Congress from Florida—Alan Grayson, Allen Boyd, Corrine Brown, Kathy Castor, Kendrick Meek, Ron Klein, Suzanne Kosmas, Debbie Wasserman Schultz, and Robert Wexler—all Democrats. The local Republican congressman, Connie Mack IV, son of the senator, was not on hand.

Starting to notice a pattern?

As a lifelong Republican, I always considered that kind of tribalism silly—and wrong. The president was coming to help revive our desperate economy. That's no more partisan than firefighters running into a burning house. At some point, shouldn't the good of the people come before partisan politics?

And I didn't think it made me a bad Republican to ask questions like that.

When word got around that I was planning to greet the president in Fort Myers, I started getting the look again. Some of my fellow Republicans—Florida political people, Tallahassee lobbyists, concerned friends—made their feelings known to me. No one forbid me from going. No one really could. But the grumblings I was hearing were loud and clear. Obama was a Democratic president, the partisan logic went. He was pushing Democratic plans. Republican politicians should not be giving aid and comfort to him.

So in that hall that day, except for Jim Humphrey, the mayor of Fort Myers, I believe I was the only Republican official.

I thought it was important enough to be there that I pulled out of a lunch in Tallahassee with Jeb Bush and other former governors. Jeb, of course, had also come out against the stimulus plan, calling it "a whole lot of spending and it's not very stimulative."

With the president standing at the edge of the stage, I walked out to introduce him.

"Well, Mr. President," I said, "welcome to Fort Myers, Florida."

I sketched out briefly the challenge as I saw it.

"Our budget is in balance here in Florida," I said. "We have some people that have worked very hard in our Florida Senate and our Florida House to make that possible. In fact, we've had to cut about seven billion dollars over the past two years, and we haven't raised taxes, and we're still in balance.

"But to be candid, it's getting harder every day, and we know that it's important that we pass a stimulus package. It's important."

I was interrupted there by applause.

"It is important that we do so to help education, to help our infrastructure . . ."

Applause.

". . . and to help health care for those who need it the most, the most vulnerable among us."

More applause.

"And let me finish by saying, Mr. President, we need to do it in a bipartisan way."

Even louder applause.

"This issue of helping our country is about helping our country. This is not about partisan politics. This is about rising above that, helping America, and reigniting our economy."

I could have gone on longer. But I didn't. The president was waiting to speak, and the people were eager to hear what he had to say.

"Ladies and gentlemen," I said, "please give a warm Florida welcome to President Barack Obama."

He walked out toward me.

Both of us smiled.

The applause was just about frantic. We shook hands. The new president leaned forward and gave me a hug.

Reach.

Pull.

Release.

As hugs go, it wasn't anything special. It was over in a second—less than that.

It was the kind of hug that says, "Hey, good to see you, man. Thanks for being here."

It was the kind of hug I'd exchanged with thousands and thousands of Floridians over the years.

I didn't think a thing about it as it was happening.

But that simple gesture ended my career as a viable Republican politician.

It changed the rest of my life.

Reach, pull, release—just like that.

Obama was his usual, eloquent self that day. He clearly believed in the power of his stimulus plan and the possibility that the government could actually help people. He clearly relished the possibility of bipartisanship. He had not seen much of it during his short time as president.

"The thing about governors," he said, looking over at me, "is they understand our economic crisis in a way that maybe sometimes folks a little more removed don't understand."

As he had said backstage, the president clearly appreciated that I was here with him. He was getting almost no support from Republicans in Washington. And it wasn't like he was pushing some pet Democratic scheme. He wasn't trying to turn Ronald Reagan National Airport into Ted Kennedy National Airport. He had a solid proposal to rescue the nation's faltering economy, using mainstream techniques that Republicans and Democrats had supported for more than sixty years. He was doing what almost every president since FDR had done. Now that Obama had taken office, the Republicans were playing Herbert Hoover again.

To the new president, I think, I represented a welcome glimmer of bipartisanship at a starkly divided time. He laid it on pretty thick.

"Governor Crist shares my conviction that creating jobs and turning this economy around is a mission that transcends party," he said. "And when the town is burning, you don't check party labels. Everybody needs to grab a hose, and that's what Charlie Crist is doing right here today."

He spoke like he was addressing adults.

"I'm not going to tell you that this plan is perfect—it was produced in Washington," the president said. "I also can't tell you with a hundred percent certainty that everything in this plan will work exactly as we hope. But I can tell you with complete confidence that a failure to act in the face of this crisis will only worsen our problems."

Then, he explained why, turning complex economic concepts into clean common sense.

"Last night," he said, "I addressed the nation to explain why I believe we need to put the economic recovery plan that is before Congress in motion as soon as possible. But during the day, I spent some time in Indiana, talking to folks in Elkhart.

"In Elkhart, the unemployment rate went from four-point-seven percent last year to fifteen-point-three percent this year. One year, and the unemployment rate tripled. Today, I wanted to come to Florida, and I wanted to visit all of you in Fort Myers because you have seen hardship, as well.

"We're talking about families. We're talking about some of the people in this town hall meeting today, your neighbors, your friends. We're talking about people like Steve Adkins, who joins us today with his wife, Michelle, and their son, Bailey, and daughter, Josie.

"Steve's the president of a small construction company in Fort Myers that specializes in building and repairing schools," the president said. "But work has slowed considerably, like it has across the board in the construction area. Now, he's done what he can to reduce overhead costs, but he still has been forced to lay off half his workforce, which means that many of those people may now be trying to figure out how are they going to pay their mortgage, how are they going to pay for the basic necessities of life, which puts us on a downward economic spiral.

"Steve and Michelle have made sacrifices of their own. They've sold their home and moved into a smaller one. And that's what this debate is about: folks in Fort Myers and all across the country who have lost their livelihoods and don't know what will take its place, parents who've lost their health care and lie awake at night praying their kids don't get sick, families who've lost the home that was the foundation of their American dream, young people who put that college acceptance letter back in the envelope because they can't afford it."

Not since Ronald Reagan had I heard a president turn a human anecdote into such a powerful policy point.

While Obama was taking questions from the audience, an aide walked onstage and handed him a note. The president looked up from the paper and said: "By the way, I just wanted to announce that the Senate just passed our Recovery and Reinvestment plan."

The room broke into another round of applause.

"So that's good news," Obama said. "And I want to thank all the members of the Senate who moved the process forward. We've still got to get the House bill and the Senate bill to match up before it gets sent to my desk. So we've got a little more work to do over the next couple of days. But it's a good start.

"And you know why it passed?" the president joked. "Because they knew I was coming down to Fort Myers. They didn't want to mess with folks in Fort Myers."

The crowd seemed to like that.

The 61 yes votes in the Senate (to 37 nos) included just three Republicans, I learned later. Our Republican senator, Mel Martinez, was not among them.

As the president and I walked off the stage together, Terry Moran, co-anchor of ABC's *Nightline*, was waiting backstage with a crew. He had been promised a joint interview with the Republican governor and the Democratic president about the stimulus plan and the power of bipartisanship.

"So, why?" Terry asked me. "Why are you here, governor?"

That was an easy question. "Because it's important to my state," I said, "and this stimulus package would help us with education, infrastructure, health care, and we've got a budget that's getting tighter day by day."

Terry pressed harder. "So, Governor," he said, "in Washington, not a single Republican House member voted for this bill. Only three Republican senators. What's the disconnect between you as a Republican governor here in Florida and Washington Republicans?"

I didn't want to bash Washington Republicans. Why do that? "All I can explain is my perspective," I said. "And it's really as being the CEO of Florida and how it affects my state and how it affects our people and that it will benefit them enormously and that's how I look at it. It's no more complicated than that."

Terry turned to the president.

"How do you account for the difference?" he asked.

"Well," Obama said, "I think Governor Crist described it properly. He's on the ground. He's dealing with folks every day. I think in Washington, there's a danger where the debates get very abstract. And frankly, that they're very ingrown. It becomes more of a competition between Democrats and Republicans for power or attention or who's controlling chambers than it is about what's happening on the ground. And that's a danger that both parties can fall into. It's something that I want to fight. That's why it's so useful for me to come out and be on the ground here because it reminds me of what's going on and why I was sent to Washington in the first place."

"Nothing like the voice of the people," I piped in.

"Absolutely," the president said.

It was just an uplifting moment, I thought. It gave hope to both of us. While the tone in Washington was stubbornly divided, it too could change—if the president and I just set the right example.

It was a beautiful sentiment, filled with the optimism that got me—a Republican governor—and him—a Democratic president— elected not so long before.

I didn't know it yet. But that high-spirited day in Fort Myers— meeting Obama (bad enough) and greeting him with a hug (even worse)—ended my viable life as a Republican politician. I would never have a future in my old party again. My bipartisan hopes and dreams, I would discover soon enough to my shock and disappointment, were vastly overstated and hopelessly out of date.

Chapter 11

I'm not a constant viewer of the business-news channel CNBC. When your stock portfolio is as puny as mine, you don't need minute-by-minute market updates. But on Thursday, February 19, nine days after Barack Obama came to Fort Myers, CNBC reporter Rick Santelli flew into a rage in the commodity pits of the Chicago Board of Trade.

I didn't see the segment live. But like a lot of people in and around politics, I heard about it—and saw the video—in one hot hurry. The topic was the president's latest economic-recovery effort, the Homeowner Affordability and Stability Plan, which was designed to help struggling borrowers refinance their mortgages and avoid foreclosure. The CNBC reporter was livid. In his view, this much-needed effort to assist troubled homeowners was a dangerous scheme to reward society's "losers" who couldn't or wouldn't pay their debts.

"Government is promoting bad behavior," he fumed. "Do we really want to subsidize the losers' mortgages? This is America. How many of you people want to pay for your neighbor's mortgage? President Obama, are you listening?"

The reporter was yelling into the camera. He was breathing hard and waving his arms.

"How about we all stop paying our mortgages?" he demanded. "It's a moral hazard."

What America needed, Santelli declared, was a "Chicago Tea Party" like the one in Boston Harbor in 1773 when the colonists rose against oppressive British rule.

CNBC has a niche audience. But conservative linker Matt Drudge promoted the video aggressively. So did Michelle Malkin and dozens of other hard-right bloggers. The conservative activists understood that the Obama campaign had won the digital war leading up to November's election, but they were intent on showing they knew the Internet too. The Tea Party video quickly became CNBC's most watched ever, displacing a Jim Cramer blowup from 2007.

It all sounded like heartless grandstanding to me. I knew many, many homeowners who were struggling mightily to save their homes. I didn't know anyone who was trying to be foreclosed on, although I'm sure some people were abusing the system somewhere. But the video was getting enough traction that the following day, White House Press Secretary Robert Gibbs called out Santelli by name.

"It's tremendously important," he said, "for people who rant on cable television to be responsible and understand what it is they're talking about. I feel assured Mr. Santelli doesn't understand what he's talking about."

Gibbs suggested Santelli might like to come by the White House and actually read the plan. "I would be more than happy to have him come here and read it. I would be more than happy to buy him a cup of coffee—decaf," the press secretary said.

"I'm not really big on decaf," Santelli said on CNBC. "I think I prefer tea." But he was already becoming a folk hero in the right-wing blogosphere; he wasn't about to back down. Friday afternoon, he was back on the air, waving a copy of the plan. "Guess what?" he said. "I still don't like it." Helping struggling homeowners was actually immoral, he seemed to say. "Do we want to teach our children that you can get out of a mistake and that there are do-overs? I just don't think that's American."

Within days, I saw on TV that anti-Obama activists across the country were organizing rallies against the president's economic policies and calling them "Tea Party" events. People were registering websites with names like ChicagoTeaParty.com and reTeaParty .com. Guests on Fox News were speaking approvingly about this new "Tea Party Movement." A Facebook page went up calling for "Nationwide Chicago Tea Party Protests" in forty cities across the country on February 27.

As the movement kicked into gear, I noticed, conservative bloggers played a vital role getting the anti-Obama message out. Fox News contributor Michelle Malkin, Matt Drudge protégé Andrew Breitbart, Seattle's Keli Carender, and sites with names like HotAir, RedState, the Gateway Pundit, and Townhall. Javier Manjarres had a Tea Party slant on Florida on his Shark Tank blog. Quickly, it seemed, some major conservative donors stepped up. Freedom-Works, a group run by former House leader Dick Armey, was among the earliest and most generous. But billionaire brothers David and Charles Koch also got in early through their group, Americans for Prosperity.

The presence of these big-dollar conservative contributors made me wonder just how grassroots a movement the Tea Party was. Others wondered too. "The tea parties don't represent a spontaneous outpouring of public sentiment," cautioned *New York Times* columnist Paul Krugman. "They're AstroTurf (fake grass roots) events, manufactured by the usual suspects."

But this much was undeniable. There was genuine anger and outrage in some pockets of America, and these people sprung to action with lightning speed.

They had no governing body. They had no central membership roll. They were splintered into hundreds of independent groups, many, though not all, of which had "Tea Party" in their names. They had no national hierarchy, written platform, or general bylaws. They didn't agree on everything, but they pretty much all agreed on this: Government is bad, especially the Internal Revenue Service. Still, many of these same groups had managed to obtain tax-exempt status under the theory that they were nonpolitical "civic leagues" or "social welfare organizations." To sidestep federal taxes, the groups had to assert that their money was used for charitable, recreational, or entertainment purpose—not primarily for political campaigning.

As someone who would come to feel their sting quite directly, let me say this much: They sure felt political to me.

Carole got the best piece of real estate in American politics, at the left elbow of the leader of the free world.

This was twelve days after the president's swing through Fort Myers, three after Rick Santelli's eruption on CNBC. She and I were in Washington for the annual conference of the National Governors Association. There had already been some grumbling in the conservative media about my embrace—literal and figurative—of the president and his economic-stimulus plan. Several of the bloggers had pointedly mentioned that I had physically hugged the president. To them, this seemed like an especially distasteful act—that I, a

Republican governor, would hug the Democratic president, this *particular* Democratic president. The very thought of it seemed to make their skin crawl.

The highlight of the three-day gathering in Washington was the Governors' Ball at the White House. It wasn't an official state dinner. I guess you have to be a king or a president or someone else more important than a governor to get one of those. But it was definitely a dress-up affair, the first formal dinner of the month-old Obama administration. This was the same night as the Academy Awards. Though Hollywood might have had us beat on glamour, we were at least as dressed-up. The president and the male guests all wore tuxedos. Most of the women, including Carole, were in designer evening wear. Hers was a chocolate-brown ABS gown, which stands for Allen B. Schwartz, she explained patiently to me.

Almost all of the fifty governors were there, including my climate-change ally Arnold Schwarzenegger and Pennsylvania's Democratic governor, Ed Rendell, who were two of my favorites. One no-show was Sarah Palin, arguably our party's biggest star. I'm not sure if the Alaska governor and Republican vice presidential nominee had pressing business in Juneau or lingering hard feelings from the campaign trail.

The White House staff really knows how to throw a party. The evening started promisingly with cocktails and passed hors d'oeuvres in the Red Room with music by a Marine Corps combo. The governors and their dates or spouses—in Tim Pawlenty's case, his sixteen-year-old daughter—seemed almost giddy to be there. Much of the conversation involved marveling at how dressed up everybody was. It's funny, isn't it? All these grown-up politicians at the White House and the talk wasn't so different from our high school proms.

Then, it was time to move into the State Dining Room for a

welcoming toast and a lavish dinner, followed by dancing to one of the president's all-time favorite bands, Earth, Wind & Fire.

I could only imagine what kind of dance moves some of these governors would have, including the notoriously rhythm-challenged governor from Florida.

After a quick trip to the powder room for Carole—okay, a not-so-quick trip—we were one of the last couples to collect our place cards from a White House steward. Carole had been with me at the White House for the last Governors' Dinner in our early dating days, when George W. Bush was president. That time, the couples were assigned to different tables. That wasn't a social custom either of us liked too much. I figured, I decided to marry her. I wouldn't mind dining with her too.

The cards said we were both at Table 11. As we were led to our seats, we quickly discovered that Table 11 was all the way up front, just to the right of the room's elaborate fireplace. Already seated, facing us, with an empty seat to his left, was the president of the United States.

Carole was seated there. I was next to her. Also at the table were Ed Rendell and Democrat Deval Patrick of Massachusetts and their wives.

Hmm, I thought to myself. *So this is the president's way of saying, "Thanks for Fort Myers."*

I was keenly aware of the power and allure of proximity. On a smaller scale back home, I'd seen people jockeying to sit next to me. All politicians experience this. But Carole and I hadn't jockeyed at all.

"This is my Forrest Gump moment," Carole whispered to me.

The president joked with Carole that he had no idea how to run a formal White House dinner. A couple of times, a waiter whispered instructions to him. He spoke with the rest of us about his efforts to get the economy moving and the importance of everyone working together.

"Mr. President," I said, "I hope you won't give up on these bipartisan efforts. That's very important, I think."

"As you know," he said, "finding the partners isn't always easy. But don't worry. I'm not giving up."

He was loose, open, and friendly, the opposite of pretentious. It really did feel like we were just a few couples out for a nice dinner. A really, really nice dinner.

The president excused himself from the table and went up to the podium to welcome the guests. "Even Axelrod has cleaned up pretty well," he joked. David Axelrod, chief strategist for the Obama campaign and now a senior White House adviser, had never been known for his crisp attire. But the president turned quickly to his central message—the need for everyone to work together in a time of crisis, regardless of party or politics.

"We are going through some tough times," he told the governors. "I don't need to tell you—you're seeing it in your own budgets, you're seeing it in your own states. There are going to be some differences, both within your state and in the country, in terms of how we address these problems."

But those differences don't have to be paralyzing, the president said. "I want you to know that regardless of our occasional differences, and in this very difficult time, my hope is that we can all work together. And I'm confident that we can."

All I could think was: *Good luck with* that, *Mr. President!*

He'd been in office four weeks. I'm not sure he fully appreciated yet what bitter opponents some of today's Republicans could be. Words like "working together" and "compromise" were nowhere in their vocabulary. He could reach out all he wanted to. That didn't mean anyone would ever reach back. The long campaign was over, but I suspected that the divisive politics had only begun.

I knew. I'd been out there. No one in his party had been slamming *him* for hugging *me*.

The food, the service, and the setting were spectacular enough to melt the hearts of even the staunchest partisans—at least for a couple of hours. The menu, our waiter explained, was designed to reflect the season and represent the American spirit. It included red dragon carrots from Ohio, beef from Nebraska, watermelon radishes grown in the Washington suburbs, and sea scallops from Massachusetts. The dessert was a cobbler with huckleberries from Idaho.

The president was right about Earth, Wind & Fire. Even after four decades on the road together, their no-boundaries mix of R&B, soul, funk, disco, jazz, and rock was sizzlingly hot.

By the time they got to "Shining Star" and "September," a couple of dozen governors were on their feet, hoping that no one was shooting cell phone video. Carole covered for me as well as she could.

The governors were all back in the same room the next morning, minus the spouses and White House china. My suspicions were quickly borne out. In short remarks, President Obama told the governors he welcomed "healthy debate" over economic policies or anything else. But he urged the state leaders not to let partisanship wreck the recovery.

"If we agree on ninety percent of this stuff and are spending all our time on television arguing about one, two, three percent of the spending, that starts sounding more like politics," he said.

The president didn't mention Bobby Jindal by name. But on Friday, the Louisiana governor, who had just been tapped to deliver the Republican response to the State of the Union address, had announced that he would reject $100 million in federal unemployment compensation for his out-of-work residents. And on Sunday, the Louisiana governor and I had appeared together on NBC's *Meet the Press*, where Jindal declared his disdain for the president's $787 billion economic-stimulus plan.

My guess was the president was watching, that he hadn't yet switched the family-quarters TV to sports for the afternoon.

He took questions from the governors for the better part of an hour. Some of it was constructive enough. But many of my fellow Republicans didn't seem to have heard a word President Obama said—or they came in with their minds so locked down, he was only wasting his breath.

"Don't you have any concern about the deficit?" one governor asked incredulously.

"These theories of yours," another governor spat out. "A bunch of liberal spending, right?"

"You claim . . . ," I heard someone else say quite dismissively, as if the president had invented the millions of Americans who were struggling to find work.

It wasn't that reasonable people couldn't exchange insights on these important issues. It was that the loudmouths in the room seemed far more intent on lecturing the president. To me, it sounded more like barroom finger-pointing—five or six beers in—than any give-and-take between the nation's governors and the leader of the free world.

It wasn't everyone. But it was enough of them. And for a while there, they all but commandeered the room.

I hadn't said anything. In settings like this one, I don't usually feel the need to hear myself talk. In a room packed with politicians, there are always plenty of blowhards to fill the air. But I could feel the president was getting ready to wrap up the sessions, and I was seething in my seat. *How two-faced,* I thought. *Most of them score their cheap political points—then end up taking money in the end! You'll see them at the ribbon-cuttings for the projects they're denouncing now!*

I decided I had to speak. I motioned to the president, and he called on me.

"Mr. President," I said, "I've sat here for about an hour."

People seemed to be paying attention. There must have been something in my tone of voice.

"I've listened to my colleagues give you a bunch of garbage"—I kind of spat that word out—"about the stimulus. I've taken a lot of grief from these guys and others in my party for having been with you a couple of weeks ago in Fort Myers. I went there because I was raised by my mother and father and taught how to behave. Taught to be decent to other people. Taught to treat them respectfully—especially if that person happens to be the president of the United States of America."

I noticed a few people shifting uncomfortably in their seats, though no one interrupted me.

"What I see here," I said, "is a lack of respect that is unattractive and inappropriate, and I am sick of it. It is not the way we ought to be behaving toward one another. It is not the way we ought to be treating you. We ought to be treating each other as we're told in the Bible—'do unto others.'

"I just had to say that because I'm tired of watching this shit"—actually, I didn't use the expletive. That's what I was thinking. I said "watching this stuff."

The room burst out in applause, probably because more of the governors in the room were Democrats than Republicans.

Not everyone appreciated the sentiment, of course. I got a few glares and a few cold shoulders from the governors in my party. But after the meeting broke up, Donald Carcieri, the Republican governor of Rhode Island, patted me on the back.

"Wow," he said. "That was incredible."

"It's just how I felt," I said. "I had to get it off my chest."

Joe Manchin, a moderate Democrat from West Virginia, came over too. "You gotta tell that more often, how you were raised, your values, and why that is important," he said. "That was powerful to watch."

Then Valerie Jarrett, senior adviser to the president and one of his closest friends, came up to me, as well.

"That's exactly what he needed to hear," she said. "That's exactly what *we all* need to hear."

As Valerie spoke, I could see tears were running down her cheeks. "Thank you for saying that," she said.

Chapter 12

I was fortunate when it came to my appointments to the Florida Supreme Court. I got to make four of them, filling a majority of the seats on the seven-judge court. My first three went through without much controversy, two conservative white men and a moderate Hispanic man. But in March of 2009, as the forces of intolerance were tightening their grip on the Republican Party in Florida and across the country, Supreme Court Justice Charles Wells was reaching the mandatory retirement age of seventy. So I had a chance to put a fourth judge on the court. This time I found myself swept up by an ideological tornado.

Nothing gets under the skin of conservative activists like the specter of liberal activist judges. The judges don't even have to be all that liberal to cause an uproar on the Right—or all that activist. Even moderate judges can fall under intense suspicion, and "judicial activist" is often just another way of saying "too liberal." Conservative "activists" are perfectly welcome, of course.

James Perry taught me all that.

All the usual procedures were followed. Seven judges and lawyers applied for the open seat. The Florida Supreme Court Judicial Nominating Commission considered the applicants and sent four finalists to me, all of whom were deemed qualified for the state's highest court. One of the finalists was James Perry, a judge on Florida's Eighteenth Judicial Circuit Court in Sanford. Clearly, he was no far-out liberal. He'd been appointed to the position by Jeb Bush. And he had a personal story in the same league as Barack Obama's.

He grew up in eastern North Carolina, overcoming rural poverty and the South's Jim Crow laws. He was obviously bright. He'd gone from St. Augustine's University, a historically black Episcopal college in Raleigh, to New York City and the top-ranked Columbia Law School. He decided to go to law school the night Martin Luther King Jr. got killed. He'd been serving with distinction in his current judgeship, the first African American judge ever to sit on that court. He rose to chief judge, and he never forgot where he came from. He was founder and president of the Jackie Robinson Sports Association, a baseball league for 650 at-risk boys and girls that had been widely praised as an innovative program. His coaches were not just expected to teach bat, ball, and glove skills. They served as mentors and tutors to the young players as well. "A kid who steals second base," he liked to say, "usually isn't stealing anything else."

The nominee certainly looked great on paper. But during our interview in the governor's office at the Capitol, I realized what I'd heard and read was just a start. He had a calm demeanor and quiet humility that I hadn't expected from someone who had achieved so much. He was a big man. He'd been a first lieutenant in the army, winning a top marksman's award. But to me, he seemed like a gentle giant.

As we began talking, I said something to him that I often say when I'm interviewing people for positions like this: "Please relax. Don't be nervous. This is going to be a piece of cake."

Most of the time, the people I'm interviewing look at me like, "Yeah, right." High-profile job interviews can be nerve-wracking experiences.

But not for Judge Perry.

"I'm the most relaxed guy you are ever going to meet," he said.

"Why's that?" I asked.

He had what I thought was the perfect answer. "Because I just try to do what's right."

That was profound to me. It said volumes.

We discussed his love and respect for the law. He explained how he felt a strong responsibility to balance competing values in his work as a judge. He said he recognized how powerful the law could be and also its limits. He spoke about God, what an important part his faith played in his life.

As our conversation continued, I could detect a real sweetness in Judge Perry, a quality I always tried to find in people who would be on the bench, especially the state's Supreme Court. We invest huge power and authority in these judges. I always tried to be mindful of how these men and women can impact the lives of everyday Floridians. Judge Perry obviously cared about people. He understood the difficulties and challenges of life and still had a very cheerful heart.

Just talking to him, I could tell he'd be an excellent addition to the Florida Supreme Court. I was so impressed by the man that I pretty much concluded by the time our interview was over that I was going to pick him. Plus, I believed the highest court in a state as diverse as Florida could use a little more diversity. The retiring Justice Wells was one of four white males on the Supreme Court.

I don't know how it became widely known that I was giving Judge Perry such serious consideration. But it must have. I started getting very strong signals from my Republican friends in Florida.

The message was loud and uniform: Do not appoint this man.

Republican politicians and conservative lobbyists weren't just opposed to the appointment. They erupted as if I'd just planted a bomb in the basement of the Capitol.

I felt like I was with John McCain with the hostile crowd in that Minnesota gymnasium. And all the people were bellowing at us.

Too liberal. Not qualified. A poor fit for the court. They mustn't have read his résumé. He was a man of extraordinary personal achievement. He cared about others. He had a strong sense of social responsibility. But he'd worked his whole life inside the system. He was far from a wild-eyed liberal. But when his opponents got going, they did not stop.

I got a phone call from Kathleen Shanahan, a very well-connected Republican friend of mine. Kathleen had been Jeb Bush's chief of staff as governor. She'd also been Dick Cheney's chief of staff in the 2000 campaign.

She was very direct with me. "Governor," she said, "if you appoint this man, it's over. It's over for you. For a Republican, this is like throwing down the gauntlet."

I went and looked up what Jeb had said back in 2000 when he appointed Judge Perry to the Eighteenth Circuit Court. Jeb could have been quoting me: "James brings a high level of professionalism, knowledge, and skill to the bench. His community service and commitment to the Jackie Robinson Little League demonstrates his dedication to the community. I am confident that his expertise, strong commitment, and dedication will continue to be an asset to the 18th Judicial Circuit and the state."

Sounds like the man would make a pretty good judge, right?

When I got off the phone with Kathleen, I couldn't help but

think, *Don't you even realize who appointed this guy?* The irony of it was just absurd.

I didn't really understand the passion behind the onslaught of complaints. Was it racial? As with Obama, it was always hard to tell. There was nothing in Judge Perry's record that screamed "liberal" or put him outside the judicial mainstream. His temperament was certainly measured. His biography was awe-inspiring. And the court could use greater diversity.

By then, the e-mails, faxes, calls, and letters were pouring into my office, 27,000 of them in all, denouncing Judge Perry and the idea of him on the court. Many were from Florida, but many others were not. The complaints about the judge seemed to have gotten into the bloodstream of Tea Party America. Pretty soon, the outrage was coming from people thousands of miles away who I'll bet had never in their lives given a moment's thought to the Florida Supreme Court. Conservative groups were sending out press releases by the hour, calling the judge a dangerous liberal, warning that he would tip the court's balance in scary ways. Some of this began to creep into the media coverage, even when the reporters were careful to attribute the upset to those who were expressing it. None of the critics seemed to have many particulars. As far as I could tell, they just didn't like the guy.

The National Rifle Association was concerned. So were anti-abortion groups. I was "missing a real opportunity . . . to bring the court back into ideological balance," said John Stemberger of the staunchly pro-life Florida Family Policy Council.

Here's a rule of thumb I've learned from twenty-something years in Florida politics: When the Family Policy Council starts talking about balance—run like hell the other way!

The pressure kept building. It was coming at me from every which way.

I went on a fund-raising trip to New York for the Florida Republican Party. We had a dinner at the 21 Club hosted by Paul Singer, a wealthy hedge fund chief who'd been very generous to us.

After the dinner, one of the party leaders told me what our host had told him: "If Governor Crist puts that man Perry on the court, I will never help him again in any political campaign." The hedge fund man was used to writing large checks. This wasn't a small threat.

All I could think was: *Wow, what's that about?*

I got a call from a former member of the Florida Supreme Court.

"It would just be awful to appoint Perry," he said. "He's really not up to the task of being a justice of the Florida Supreme Court."

Of course, Judge Perry had better credentials—on paper and in his heart—than many of the judges who'd preceded him. And no one could point to anything specific that made him unqualified. No issue or case or whiff of corruption. It was all just, "Why are you putting this liberal guy on the court?"

Part of the uproar, no doubt about it, came from how important these judgeships are and how long these judges can hang around. When a governor appoints the secretary of an agency or even a chief of staff, those people keep their jobs only as long as the governor serves. When the governor's gone, they are too. But Supreme Court justices can stay until they turn seventy. They are a gift that keeps on giving to the people of the state.

So special interest groups pay extra-special attention to them. Justices rule on decisions that will live long after them and will affect entire industries. They change how taxes are collected, how regulations are applied, how the state constitution is interpreted. Significant policies come before the court every year. Tip the balance on the court, and you're tipping the balance of the state.

But in Judge Perry's case, I did have to wonder: *Is part of the problem that he is black?* No one ever discussed race with me directly. I didn't expect anyone to. Did people just figure that a new black judge would have to be a liberal activist? I thought I was appointing a highly qualified jurist. They thought I should be limiting my choices to down-the-line conservatives.

Early 2009 was an especially dicey period. Republicans were feeling battered by the election of Barack Obama. Not only was the new president the candidate of the other party, people were calling him illegitimate also. The intolerance was noticeably rising. The reaction to anything faintly liberal was growing ever-more intense. And here I was, the Republican governor of Florida, choosing someone other than a rigid conservative for the state's highest court. That was unacceptable.

Some of the reaction was cumulative too, I believe. The Perry nomination came after I'd done many other things that struck some Republicans as just too darn independent. Clearly, Judge Perry became a lightning rod for a lot of pent-up Republican frustration with me.

It was as if people were saying: "This is it. We've had enough of your crap. We've let you appoint a lot of Democrats. We've let you be an environmentalist. We've let you get along with the unions. We've let you help public school teachers. We've let you stand up for women. We haven't really bucked you on all these things. We've tolerated your independent streak. But this is it, pal. Enough's enough. You do this, we're done with you."

I did it, of course.

All the push-back didn't work. Political pressure was never something that swayed me. In fact, with this appointment, it almost got to the point where the more push-back I was getting from these so-called conservatives, the more I said to myself: "Screw it. I'm gonna do what's right." The more pressure I got, the stronger I held on, the more determined I became. And the madder they got.

It's not that I'm such a tough guy. I just knew that there were people counting on me, people who would be affected by the court's future rulings, everyday Floridians, the people I had sworn to serve. I wasn't about to let some rigid, intolerant Republican enforcers tell me who to put on the Florida Supreme Court.

We held a small ceremony when I announced the appointment. Judge Perry, who had stayed entirely quiet during the controversy, was there.

"We have a very diverse state, and I think it's important that our court understand all the different perspectives that make Florida a great place to live," I said. I then turned to Justice Perry and said: "I'm grateful that you said yes."

I am especially pleased personally and for the state of Florida that I appointed such a fine man to the court, despite the roar of opposition, because of what came next. I didn't know it yet, but soon enough Florida would get a governor who was way out there and a legislature that was off the right cliff too. The only effective counterforce, the only institution that would hold things back and keep the balance a little more moderate, was the judiciary.

Supreme Court Justice James Perry would play an important part in that. I'm so proud I appointed him.

Chapter 13

I know what you're thinking. You're thinking I should have left well enough alone. I should have just kept doing what I was doing, basked in the support of the people of Florida, fought the rising tide of wackiness, run again for governor, and lived the nonpartisan dream.

I loved being governor, and the people seemed to like me back. My approval ratings, which had topped 70 percent in my first year in office, were still up around 60 percent. I had a record I was justifiably proud of. We'd cut property taxes by doubling the homestead exemption. We'd pushed back insurance rates. We'd restored voting rights for nonviolent former felons. We'd made some actual strides on education reform. I'd appointed four justices to the Florida Supreme Court—Charles Canady, Ricky Polston, and Jorge Labarga, along with Justice Perry—a majority of the state's highest court. I'd conducted groundbreaking climate-change summits and a successful trade mission to Israel, the first Florida governor to do any of that. We'd made real progress on protecting the Everglades. Those first two especially—the property taxes and the insurance rates—were key promises I'd made in the campaign. I know plenty of people were surprised during my first few months in office when I actually achieved them.

And just as important—*no, more so*—we were changing the way Tallahassee worked. Democrats and Republicans were talking to one another, civilly. Lots of people who had been excluded from Florida state government—teachers, minorities, union members, women, Democrats—were in the game now. The governor was Republican. Republicans had a majority in both chambers of the legislature. But we weren't locking ourselves into rigid ideologies or trading insults with the other side. Heck, most of the time we didn't even consider them the "other side." We were solving problems for the people and doing it cooperatively. This sounds almost impossible, given what's happened since. But we truly had an almost nonpartisan government in Florida—more so, I'll bet, than in any of the other forty-nine states. And compared to the harsh dysfunction in Washington? We were Peter, Paul and Mary singing "Kumbaya."

That was very important to me.

So I began to think: What if I could take these Florida values—this nonpartisan approach of just working for the people—and carry that to Washington? Could I in some small way change the crazy way things were being done up there? If I could achieve that, I reasoned, it would be good for the country. More selfishly, it would be good for Florida too. Tough stuff was still coming at us. We knew that. And whatever help we'd get would be coming from Washington.

Barack Obama, I noticed, could probably use some assistance. He'd won a rousing victory in the 2008 election. But the bitter fight over the stimulus was giving way to a series of other bitter fights. Republicans, it seemed, were dead set against almost anything the new Democratic president might propose. Barely four months into his term, Washington was more divided than ever. It wasn't from lack of trying by the president. His temperament, I could tell, was similar to mine. He was a natural coalition builder. He liked finding common ground. Whatever the issue, he had a natural instinct for bridging differences and working respectfully. Still, from the moment John McCain was defeated, Washington Republicans were on a relentless campaign to make sure the new president failed. The guiding strategy: Fight him on everything—everything!—whether it was a good idea or a bad idea. Fight him even if it was originally a Republican idea, as his new health-reform plan was. It was modeled after Mitt Romney's program in Massachusetts. How Republican can you get? Didn't matter. If the Democratic president wanted it, just say no—on health care or any other issue. Use whatever tactics were available for the fight. Filibuster. Demonize. Refuse to vote on the president's nominees. Weather bad polls. Do whatever it takes— just try to stop this man at every turn. And if that means the government becomes paralyzed and the people have to wait longer for their problems to be solved? Well, that's just the cost of achieving the larger goal—defeating Barack Obama every single day.

This was an explicit strategy, and it went far beyond the usual party rivalries of Washington. Karl Rove, who was the political brains behind George W. Bush even when he wasn't calling to ream me out, was a key proponent of this just-fight-'em approach. But it didn't stop with the bare-knuckle operatives like Rove. Even Mitch McConnell, the genteel Republican leader in the Senate, was now a proponent of this constant combativeness. When I'd met him in the past, the senior senator from Kentucky always struck me as a gracious and reasonable man. But clearly, there was something in the air in Republican Washington, and McConnell had gulped a lungful.

His number-one priority, as he made clear in an interview, was not passing important legislation. Not bringing people together. Not finding ways to work effectively across the aisle. "The single most important thing we want to achieve," he told the *National Journal*, "is for President Obama to be a one-term president."

Really?

That certainly wasn't the approach that was serving us so well in Florida. It wasn't my idea of how to get things done in government. Some in my own party were telling me I didn't have to be so coopera-tive. Republicans held all the marbles in Tallahassee, they said. Who needed Democrats? Jeb Bush hadn't worried too much about the Democrats' morale. He was from the our-marbles school of govern-ment. He happily cold-shouldered teachers, union members, women's groups, and anyone else who smelled faintly Democratic. Especially the Democratic leaders in the Florida House and Senate. Who needs 'em? Spoken and unspoken, that was the organizing principle during Jeb's eight years—and before him too. Sorry, the people on the outs were told. Nothing personal. That's just politics.

I took great pains to reach out to the Democratic leader in the Senate, Steve Geller, who I'd known since our days at Florida State. I did the same with House Minority Leader Dan Gelber, who I re-ally had great respect for and whose company I enjoyed. They didn't take the Rove-and-McConnell approach. They were willing to work with me. And we had the results to show for it.

As all this was happening, Florida politics was unfolding unpredict-ably, as it almost always does.

Soon after the 2008 election, one of our US senators, Mel Mar-tinez, called to tell me he had decided not to run for reelection in

2010. The call came as a surprise. There was no reason to think Mel couldn't have been reelected, and not too many senators voluntarily leave Washington after just one term. Mel said he wanted to spend more time with his family in Orlando. I certainly had to respect his explanation, although I had a strong feeling that his reasons were a little more complicated than that. I knew that Mel had grown extremely frustrated with Washington's failure to adopt comprehensive immigration reform.

That was an issue Mel cared deeply about—and not just because he represented Florida in the US Senate. Mel had his own amazing immigrant story. Born in Sagua La Grande, Cuba, he was fifteen years old and spoke virtually no English when he was brought to America in a humanitarian effort called Operation Peter Pan. He lived in youth facilities and foster homes for four years before being reunited with his family in Orlando. He finished college and law school and became a successful lawyer. He then went from Orange County chairman to Florida co-chair of the 2000 George W. Bush campaign for president to Bush's secretary of housing and urban development, the first Cuban American to serve in any president's cabinet. President Bush loved Mel. When Mel ran for Bob Graham's old Senate seat in 2004 and won, he became the only immigrant in the US Senate and its first-ever Cuban American. No one had to tell Mel Martinez how broken America's immigration policy was.

Mel was happy to work with anyone to achieve an important goal. His two chief immigration allies in the Senate were Republican John McCain and Democrat Ted Kennedy. Just thinking about that makes me smile.

But his biggest opponents, Mel came to discover, were some of his own fellow Republicans. Conservative talk radio hosts were seething with anger at immigrant "lawbreakers storming the borders."

Militias were forming from Arizona to Michigan. The so-called Minutemen and other vigilante groups were vowing to take the law into their own hands. Even these real extremists were getting support on Capitol Hill from Republican officeholders like Jeff Flake, the congressman, then senator from Arizona, and South Carolina Senator Jim DeMint. And many moderate Republicans, who were probably inclined to be more open, were scared to death of getting tagged "pro-amnesty."

"You wouldn't believe some of the people up here," Mel told me on the phone one day from Washington. "Some real knuckle-draggers."

Over the months that followed, I began giving real thought to the idea of not running for reelection but running for Mel's US Senate seat instead. I took seriously everything Mel had told me about the acrimony he had faced in Washington. I knew his dismal portrayals were real. But once Mel mentioned he was leaving, I had trouble shaking the idea out of my head.

The argument for going to Washington, I believed, was fairly compelling. *Maybe now,* I thought, *I can turn that bipartisan dream of mine—Tallahassee values in Washington—into reality.* Who knew when I'd ever have that chance again?

Most of my advisers were not convinced. "Why would you leave all this?" they asked me. "You're accomplishing stuff. People like you. You get to run the joint. The governor has a lot of jobs to give out. Why do you want to go to the Senate?"

Brian Ballard, my lobbyist friend in Tallahassee, called one day and said, "Can I come over to the mansion and talk about this before you make a final decision?"

Brian had been a great friend and financial supporter. Without a doubt, he had my best interest at heart.

"I really think you should run for reelection," he said. "Things are going well. You'll probably get reelected. It's good for Florida. It's good for you."

"Of course, I'll think about it," I told him. "You're a dear friend, and you've asked me to. But this is where I'm leaning." He knew that.

Before I appointed George LeMieux to the Senate seat, he also told me the same thing. He said, "I'd like you to stay as governor because, in a way, I get to fulfill my dream."

He made many of the same arguments Brian had. I didn't doubt the motives of either man. Brian and George cared about me and my future. But you have to understand. It's nice for these guys in Tallahassee to have their friend as the governor. Even if I don't do a thing for them, there's still a perception. They can get retained by clients because their friend is the governor. Perhaps they can influence him. Proximity is power in a place like Tallahassee. Or Washington.

People imagined all kinds of reasons I was thinking of running for the Senate. That I doubted I could be reelected as governor. Not true. No one was talking about running against me in a Republican primary. As far as I knew, no major Democrat was planning to run. I didn't have any reason to doubt I could be reelected.

Some people speculated I'd grown tired of the grunt work of running the state—maintaining a prison system, supervising a motor vehicles department, keeping state highways paved. Also not true. That kind of stuff didn't bother me at all. It was endlessly fun. I could really make things happen as governor.

When I asked Bob Graham for his advice, that's exactly what he told me. He had been governor and then senator, so he'd experienced both.

"You'll understand it in football terms," he told me. "Being governor is like being the quarterback. You're calling the plays. You're appointing the secretaries of the agencies. You're putting the players on the field in different positions. As a senator, you are more of a spectator. You are sorta in the stands, watching things. The president is the field general."

They all made good points. I know they all had my best interest at heart. But I was growing more and more convinced I should take what I'd done in Florida and try to carry it to Washington.

I was worried about our country. It was in a major storm. All the Republicans were trying to stop the president. I had an opportunity to work with him. I had confidence in the fact that he was the real deal. This was not some BS. He really wanted to have people cooperate for the betterment of America. I knew that would also help Florida, which I love and care deeply about. I could do those things with him in a symbolic way as governor, like we had with the stimulus. But I was convinced there was a more concrete, day-to-day way, and that meant going to Washington.

Carole seemed game. My mom and dad's attitude was, "If you think this is the right thing to do, we'll support you, of course." As I spoke excitedly about the broad, national impact I thought I could have, they got excited too.

I announced I was running on May 12.

"What's important to bear in mind," I told the reporters who came to hear why, "is that we do things a little bit differently here in Florida. We work together to solve problems and do what's right for the people of our state. The people are the boss. And I think regardless of party, we have to work together to get things done. And that's what I'd like to take to Washington, DC."

It sounded so easy.

In the end, Mel didn't even serve out his full Senate term. He called me again in August of 2009 to say he couldn't imagine spending another sixteen months in Washington. He was ready to come home to Florida immediately. He'd give up his Senate seat, he told me, as soon as I could appoint an interim successor.

"I can't do this anymore," he told me. "My heart's just not in it."

I understood Mel's decision, even though I hated to see him go. He was just the kind of person—smart, decent, dedicated, sane— the Republican Party needed more of. I thought to myself when he told me he was leaving: *Why do we want to drive away fine public servants like Mel?*

He sounded wistful as he said good-bye to his Senate colleagues on September 9. Immigration reform, he said, was "something that I felt very strongly about. And being the only immigrant in this body, I felt I was duty-bound to try to advance that cause."

I appointed my former campaign chairman and chief of staff, George LeMieux, to fill out the balance of Mel's Senate term. I had confidence in George. He was smart and focused and amazingly or- ganized. He was a highly capable lawyer who was my chief of staff when I was attorney general. When I ran for governor, he was really the maestro of my campaign. Then, he ran the staff in the governor's office when we won. I knew him and was comfortable sending him to fill out the final sixteen months of Mel's term.

The appointment was received fairly well. There was some

grumbling in the media that he was too close to me. A few people had advised me not to pick him. They said, "It'll look like you're sending your crony to Washington."

That advice didn't make much sense to me. What? Was I supposed to pick somebody who's my enemy? I liked George and I trusted him and I thought he would work diligently for Florida.

In fact, when George got to Washington, he was anything but my crony. He was there for five minutes and was already doing things I didn't necessarily like. He certainly didn't carry Mel's torch on immigration reform. He promptly aligned himself with the party's build-high-fences-and-evict-the-immigrants wing. Until the borders were fully secured, he said, there could be no path to citizenship for the 10 to 12 million undocumented men, women, and children who were already here, including an estimated 1 million in Florida.

So much for cronyism.

Chapter 14

Marco Rubio was already in the race when I showed up. How tough could he be?

I knew Marco well. He'd been Speaker of the Florida House of Representatives since November of 2006. We'd worked comfortably together on quite a few issues, including tax cuts for seniors and lower property tax rates. He was a Cuban American from Miami. In two weeks, he'd be thirty-eight years old. He was bright and energetic—conservative, for sure. But I wouldn't call him an inflexible ideologue, not back then. We'd differed on some things. There was the time he wanted to totally eliminate property taxes. And the time he'd written an op-ed about what he considered my excessive environmentalism. He had griped when I expanded voting hours. He sued me over a gambling deal with the Seminole Tribe. And we definitely clashed when I vetoed a bill that would have helped a friend of his get a contract for service stations along Florida's Turnpike. But those were normal Tallahassee tussles. No big deal. We had a friendly, usually productive relationship. In his office, he displayed a small wooden cross I'd brought to him from my trade mission to Israel. He'd invited me over to watch the 2007 NFL draft. We were disappointed together when the Miami Dolphins failed to grab Notre Dame quarterback Brady Quinn.

There'd been a couple of stories in the papers hinting at a rift between us. "I think some of that's overstated," he told the *South Florida Sun Sentinel*. "I hope he's reelected."

That was the Marco I knew. That was before he was being called "the crown prince of the Tea Party movement." Before Mitt Romney was vetting him as a possible vice president. Before he was invited to give the Republican response to President Obama's 2013 State of the Union address. It was long before he came out in favor of immigration reform, turning his staunchest conservative backers angrily against him. But that's another story, years down the road. In early 2009, he was just an ambitious young pol, term-limited out of the Florida House, not gunning for anyone or anything in particular— just looking for a way to advance himself.

Back when Mel first said he was leaving Washington, there'd been some media speculation that I might like to run. If I ran, Marco made clear, he wouldn't. "Everyone on the Republican side that's talking about running would step aside and acknowledge that Charlie Crist would be the best candidate," he said in a January interview with the *St. Petersburg Times*.

Marco made a different decision, of course. He quietly formed an exploratory committee in February. That leaked to the media in early March. He made his formal announcement on May 5, exactly a week before I made mine.

I'd been around long enough to know that anything can happen in any race. But I wasn't too worried about running in the 2010 Republican primary against Marco Rubio for what everyone still thought of as Mel Martinez's Senate seat. In fact, Mel and former

Florida senator Connie Mack had already signed on as co-chairs of my campaign. Marco had never run outside his small Miami district. He'd gotten a little coverage as House Speaker but not a lot. People in Tallahassee knew who he was. But he'd never raised big campaign dollars, and he didn't have much statewide name recognition. I'd been the governor for three years by then, attorney general for four years before that. I had sky-high approval ratings. I had a strong record of bipartisan achievement. And the campaign contributions were already pouring in.

Our two announcements could not have been more different. I emphasized my ability to work with Republicans and Democrats and my get-it-done ethic. "We do things a little bit differently here in Florida," I told reporters in Tallahassee the day I formally got into the race. "We work together to solve problems and do what's right for the people of our state. The people are the boss. And I think regardless of party, we have to work together to get things done. And that's what I'd like to take to Washington, DC."

In his announcement, Marco promised he'd be an unswerving conservative. "The more Republicans become less distinguishable from Democrats, the less people will vote for Republicans," he said. "I don't agree with the notion that to grow our party we need to become more like Democrats." And he mentioned he wasn't too high on Barack Obama. Even before his formal announcement, Marco had been staking out that turf, taking a little shot at me for supporting the president's stimulus plan as a big help to Florida. "If it's bad for America, it can't possibly be good for Florida," he said. "And the bailout was bad for America." He did add, however: "Now that it's passed, if there are funds available for Florida, that's fine."

The visions Marco and I staked out for ourselves were clear from day one. I was the moderate. He was the conservative. I was the uniter. He was the divider. I was a certain kind of Republican. He was a different kind. It's just that neither of us had any inkling yet how life-changing the distinction would turn out to be—for him, for me, and for the party we uncomfortably shared. Marco's rhetoric would get considerably more personal over the next eighteen months. Our race would fly in directions no one could possibly have anticipated, least of all me. Our matchup would come to symbolize a major rift inside the national Republican Party as energized Tea Party activists tried to wrestle control from a more moderate Republican establishment. A whole new breed of Republican—adamant, ideological, divisive, more interested in stopping government than making it work—would gain control. And I'd discover that the party I'd always felt comfortable in was in the grip of forces I considered deeply damaging to the state and the nation I loved.

You could trace a line from Terri Schiavo to Sarah Palin to that panicked lady in the gym with John McCain calling Barack Obama an Arab to Judge Perry to where this Senate campaign was heading next. The forces of intolerance and extremism threatened to wreck everything I treasured and believed in.

In the sweep of American politics, that all happened very quickly. The initial polling had me up by wide double digits. The first Mason-Dixon survey in May said I was leading Marco by a whopping thirty-five points, 53 to 18 percent. The state and national Republican parties were on my side from the start. Precisely fourteen minutes after I announced my candidacy, the National Republican Senatorial Committee endorsed me in the primary. "I believe Marco Rubio has a very bright future within the Republican Party," said John Cornyn, the senator from Texas who chaired the Senate campaign committee. But "Charlie Crist is the best candidate in 2010 to ensure that we maintain the checks and balances that Floridians deserve in the United States Senate."

Marco jumped onto Twitter immediately and typed: "Disappointed GOP senate comm endorses Crist on day 1. Remember that reform must always come from the outside."

But for Republican leaders in Washington, the 2010 election cycle was a gut-wrenching time. The Democrats were on the verge of clinching a filibuster-proof majority in the Senate. I got that early support, I believe, mostly because the party's top leaders thought I could win. I was never a party darling. I had that maddening independent streak. But I was popular in Florida. And my last three statewide races, I'd won. Who could take chances at a time like this? The Republican leaders wanted a brand-name Florida candidate— not a rising outsider—to defend the Martinez seat.

The Washington endorsement caused agitation among conservative bloggers and activists. Some of them sounded downright steamed. At 8:30 the next morning, Erick Erickson used his Red-State blog to declare: "Getting behind Crist in the Florida primary is wholly unacceptable." The Tea Party blogger launched a Facebook group protesting the National Republican Senatorial Committee, comparing me to two other hated Republican moderates in the Senate. "First they supported [Lincoln] Chafee. Then they supported [Arlen] Specter. Now they support Crist. I pledge to give no money, no support, no aid, and no help at all to the efforts of the NRSC."

These pugnacious blogs were becoming a key vehicle—maybe *the* key vehicle—for focusing, organizing, and, in many cases, telling people on the Tea Party right what to think. RedState was one of many.

Glenn Beck didn't even wait until daybreak. His tweet went out at 3 A.M. "Charlie Crist, just what we need, a 'soft,' 'friendly,' moderate GOP member," the talk radio and Fox News host snapped sarcastically. "BARF."

But the angry loudmouths were off on the margin somewhere, unlikely to influence too many Florida voters. Or so I thought.

Marco wasn't ceding anything. To his credit, he got in his car, and he went campaigning. With his House colleague and close friend David Rivera, he started showing up at local Republican clubs and committees from Miami to Pensacola. He was getting to know people. He was expressing his anti-Washington obsession. He was explaining how much he distrusted the Democratic president.

At almost every stop, he announced: "I will stand up to Obama."

He didn't get too many big endorsements at first. Former Arkansas governor Mike Huckabee signed on, as did Jeb Bush Jr. Not his dad, but it did make my campaign staffers wonder: What was the former governor's take on the Senate race?

The statewide polls still showed massive leads for me. But at a lot of those Republican groups Marco was visiting, little straw polls were being held: "Who do you support in the US Senate race?" I couldn't help but notice how well Marco was doing in those.

Shockingly well.

In Pasco County, north of Tampa Bay, Marco won the straw poll by a vote of 73–9. In Lee County, home of Fort Myers, he won by a 7–1 margin. In Highlands County, south central Florida lake country, the vote was 75–1. In Bay County, around Panama City, 23–2.

I was getting creamed out there!

There was no straw poll in Volusia County, the area around Daytona Beach. But the executive committee of the county Republican Party voted to censure me for a whole laundry list of alleged infractions—everything from supporting the president's economic stimulus to making unwelcome judicial nominations to choosing the wrong replacement for a vacancy on the Southeast Volusia Hospital District board. I narrowly avoided a similar fate in Palm Beach County. The vote on that censure motion failed on a 65–65 tie.

That was better than actually being censured, I guess, which in itself would have a been a fairly meaningless gesture. But it didn't make me want to celebrate. I barely dodged trouble with the Broward County Republican Executive Committee, whose leaders had always been big backers of mine. Rubio supporters demanded a straw-poll vote. Chairman Chip LaMarca refused, calling the process divisive. As the meeting finally broke up, the Rubio people were still screaming at him.

Some of these little straw polls were getting covered in the local papers. I was getting calls from friends around the state. My campaign people were also hearing reports.

I was a little taken aback as I heard about those gaping margins. "This can't be good," I said to my campaign manager, Eric Eikenberg, who'd been my chief of staff in the governor's office and was a seasoned Florida Republican strategist.

Eric didn't sound too concerned. "Don't panic over a few straw polls," he said. "We'll be fine once we get out there." And as Eric pointed out, a lot of those Republican clubs weren't exactly cross sections of the Florida electorate. They were tiny organizations, the hard core of the hard core, populated by the kinds of people who would be most easily susceptible to the anti-Washington zeal of a new face like Marco Rubio.

Generally speaking, we were all fairly dismissive—which wasn't too smart.

My finance director, Dane Eagle, said the contributions were still flowing in. Andrea Saul, a Washington media pro who'd come down to be our communications director, told the reporters we weren't overly concerned. "The activists aren't the electorate," Eric said.

That was true, of course. But being out there, in county after county, night after night—while I was back in Tallahassee being governor—was definitely an advantage for Marco. It allowed him to hone his message in front of small Republican audiences and let people see him up close. And from what I was hearing in phone calls with friends around the state and tiny reports in the media, it wasn't my record as governor that Marco was running against. It wasn't the policies I had pursued. The vast majority of those he'd agreed with me on.

He was really pushing the anti-Obama stuff hard.

And I was the guy who'd had kind words for the president's economic stimulus plan. I'd even embraced the president onstage in Fort Myers.

The hug!

That famous and dreadful hug!

"I won't be hugging Obama," Marco's point seemed to be. "I'll be standing up to him—adamantly."

There was clearly a Republican audience for this anti-Obama talk, especially when it was mixed with a healthy dose of complaints about Washington elitism and the liberal media. And not just in Florida. This stuff was a full-time staple on talk radio. Sean Hannity. Michael Savage. Laura Ingraham. Mark Levin. Rush Limbaugh, of course. On cable news shows, the same was often true. *Glenn Beck*. *Hannity*, which now featured Sean alone without his liberal counterpart, Alan Colmes. And if you thought the conservative media comments were hostile, you should check out some of the blogs! The particulars might change from hour to hour or day to day, from immigration to health care to the economy, from the president's birthplace to his religion to his supposedly radical friends. But the basic theme hardly varied at all.

Obama is bad.

Very bad.

Even worse than you thought.

And I'd said nice things about the Democratic president. What kind of Republican was I?

Clearly, a lot of Republicans didn't like the president's economic-stimulus plan, even if it was George W. Bush who had bailed out the banks and laid the groundwork. And once the president began pushing his Affordable Care Act, conservative audiences from Tamarac to Tacoma would boo reflexively at the very mention of the word "Obamacare."

I didn't agree with everything Barack Obama did. I didn't *love* the president's health-care plan. I thought it was too big, too complicated, and too bureaucratic. I didn't like the way it had inched through Congress, twisted and turned by so many special-interest groups. But I wasn't a crazy zealot on the topic. I wasn't shouting that Obamacare was about to wreck America. I actually liked many of its planks—covering people with previous medical conditions, eliminating lifetime benefit caps, and helping millions of people afford health insurance. Once the act became law, I was far more interested in making the new system work for people than endlessly trashing it and stirring up the base.

There I was, being moderate again!

But the anti-Obama sentiment went deeper than any one issue. This wasn't just a policy discussion. This was ideological disdain and personal attack.

Marco Rubio didn't invent the strategy. He didn't create the growing Tea Party anger or the fiery rhetoric or the frustration about health care, immigration, or the economy. He wasn't the first to bash Obama. But he definitely rode that train.

Sometimes, the public's feelings seemed partly racial. Sometimes, I'm sure they were not. But Barack Obama was the first African American in the White House. Florida had helped to put him there. And it was impossible to imagine an equal measure of virulence for any politician whose skin was white.

I wasn't at those county meetings. So what I was getting was secondhand. But I followed the media closely. I had friends across the state. From everything I was seeing and hearing, I could tell things were getting ugly out there.

The bloggers were getting increasingly revved, and their numbers were constantly growing. Tea Party rallies were really picking up steam. The media were giving more and more attention to the movement. Politicians were trying to figure out how to react. A new phrase was popping up at many of the Tea Party events: "We have to take our country back."

That single pungent sentiment kept being expressed: "We have to take our country back."

That phrase was very disturbing to me. Almost every word seemed packed with hostile implications. It sounded so divisive. Who's this "our"? What does "our country" mean? Who should the country be taken back from? Aren't we all Americans? Doesn't the country belong to all of us?

But as the campaign rolled on in Florida, I was seen more and more as a surrogate for the president of the United States. With a beleaguered economy and Marco's Obama-bashing, the Republican campaign for Senate was starting to look like a proxy for a much larger struggle that reached far beyond Florida, far beyond Marco and me. It really was a fight for the soul of the Republican Party. It was no less significant than that. Who would define who we were and what we believed in? Would it be Tea Party activists or the commonsense Republicans I'd grown up around? Would it be the hard conservatives or the moderates? Were we the Republican Party of Abraham Lincoln, Teddy Roosevelt, Dwight Eisenhower, Richard Nixon, George H. W. Bush, Bob Dole, Connie Mack, Mel Martinez, Jeb Bush, and Charlie Crist? Or were we fully in the hands of a new breed of unbending conservatives—true-believing, high-passion Tea Party zealots?

Both the country and I would soon find out.

Oddly, Ronald Reagan was claimed by both sides. He was the inspiration of the new-breed conservatives, a man who could attract moderate Democrats on the strength of his clarity and his likeable charm—even though some of his policies could easily have gotten him tossed off the stage at a Tea Party rally today as an unacceptable RINO, Republican In Name Only. He raised taxes along with lowering them. He shared beers and made deals with Tip O'Neill, the liberal Massachusetts congressman who was Speaker of the House. He ushered in immigration reform, for goodness' sake.

But where was the Reagan of today?

On November 3, the Rubio campaign launched a new website, www.charlieandobama.com. The home page featured a photo of me welcoming the president in Fort Myers, leaning in for our brief grab-and-go.

"Get the picture?" the caption read.

There was also a handy link to donate to the Rubio campaign.

Chapter 15

Laura Ingraham set the tone for the evening. She opened with a Nancy Pelosi Botox joke.

"She declared Tuesday was a win for the Democrats," the fiery talk radio host said of the Democratic House Speaker, contorting her face like a maniacal paralysis victim. "'A-a-a-a-as the Speaker of the House, I am so happy that we were victorious last night. I need another injection.'"

This was November 5, 2009. Republicans had just snatched what had been Democratic governorships in New Jersey (Chris Christie) and Virginia (Bob McDonnell), although Dems did flip a Republican congressional district in upstate New York. Ingraham had flown down to Gainesville to host the Seventh Annual Ronald Reagan Black Tie and Blue Jeans BBQ, a fund-raiser for the Alachua County Republican Party. The event featured a rare joint appearance by the two Republican candidates for US Senate, Marco Rubio and me.

I was busy being governor. So I wasn't able to make too many local party events. Unfortunately for me, Marco was showing up everywhere. This one was a short ride from the Governor's Mansion and seemed like a good chance to take the temperature of Republican primary voters.

More than eight hundred Republicans turned out on that night in boots or sneakers, T-shirts and blue jeans—a few jackets and ties but no tuxedos that I saw—at the Canterbury Showplace Equestrian Center on Newberry Road west of town.

The University of Florida College Republicans line-danced to the Rednex version of "Cotton-Eyed Joe," which blared from large speakers. Red meat was on the menu all evening, with or without gobs of barbecue sauce. The basic format—food, music, speeches—was like hundreds of other Republican events I'd attended over the years. The tone was not.

"I am extremely proud to be a member of the Fox News team because all of the right people hate us," Ingraham said at one point, further revving up the crowd. "People come up to me saying, 'Does it bother you that so many people really hate you?' I say, 'I love it. It makes me feel great.'"

Carole and I sat for dinner with the Alachua County party chairman, Stafford Jones. He was very gracious to us. He asked Marco to deliver the invocation, which he did, diving right into his familiar attack on me, questioning my credentials as a true conservative and saying I wasn't sufficiently anti-Obama.

"It's very simple," he said. "We already have a Democratic Party in America. We do not need two Democratic parties in America."

Marco's rhetoric was a couple of notches more aggressive than I remembered it. He must have found it was working for him, though I wasn't there to trade punches with him. Then Stafford gave me a nice introduction and I got up to speak.

I talked about what we had done in the administration, how we'd held down insurance rates and kept taxes low, how we'd beefed up education and gotten people in Tallahassee to cooperate. I knew I could never out–Tea Party Marco Rubio. I was definitely the more moderate candidate, in politics and temperament. But I did what I could to buff up my conservative cred without claiming I was something that I wasn't.

"Ladies and gentlemen," I said, "I am pro-life. I am pro-gun. I am pro-family, and I am anti-tax, and that is what the Republican Party stands for, and that's what we need to be about."

This was a Republican crowd. These were some of the touchstones of Republican politics. My opinions on each of those issues—then and now—were a little more nuanced than a fast recitation of pro-, pro-, pro-, and anti-. But this was a political rally, not a detailed policy talk. The point of a political rally is to rev up the faithful and draw in potential converts. I can't deny I might have shaded my feelings a little and emphasized the parts I knew the voters wanted to hear. Looking back at those days, I do cringe a little. I wasn't as free as I would have liked to be. I was trying to do my best with the changing reality.

I didn't say anything critical of Marco.

People were responding okay.

I wouldn't call it enthusiastic. It wasn't the warmest I'd ever been received. But as I made my points in a crowd I knew wouldn't be easy, I was happy enough with the reaction I was receiving.

Until right near the end of my talk.

The sun had gone down by then. Most of the people were sitting at large round tables. The stage was elevated. I noticed a man standing toward the back of the crowd. He looked to be in his forties. He was wearing jeans, like most people were that night. He had longish hair.

"WHY DON'T YOU GO HUG OBAMA AGAIN?" he yelled up at me, interrupting my speech.

He had a loud, rough-sounding voice. I have to say, it caught me completely off guard.

And the reaction in the crowd was kind of positive.

"Yeah," I heard someone else say.

"Hug him."

"Go back and do it again."

It wasn't a large number of people who were yelling like that. Marco was just looking on. I wouldn't call it heckling. But I'm pretty good at reading crowds, and I could tell this one wasn't with me at all.

I didn't answer the man in the back. I pressed forward with what I had to say.

I finished my speech. I don't think I seemed rattled. I got some decent applause. But as I came off the stage, I had the unshakable sense that something had just happened there. Something real. Something disquieting. Something I wouldn't be able to ignore—no one would.

I didn't know yet exactly what that sour force was. But I definitely had the sense that it was strong and it was rising and it wasn't likely to fade away on its own. And it was more widespread inside my party, the Republican Party, than I had previously realized.

I found it disheartening and disappointing. But as I came to see, it was only a forecast of what was going on—in the race that I was in and the party I had long been part of.

If anything, I underestimated how powerful that element was.

"Go hug Obama . . . Go back and do that again."

The "hug" comment that night didn't seem to register with everyone. It was never quoted in the Gainesville media. But at least one young reporter noticed the rumbles. "When Crist took the stage," Matt Harrington wrote in a long piece for *The Alligator*, the student paper from the University of Florida, "the audience also stood and cheered, but jeers about his support for Obama could be heard in the crowd."

And political people were definitely talking about the outburst, even though it wasn't detailed in the first-day coverage.

Eleven days later, *The New York Times* picked up on the significance of that night. "Hecklers with Rubio bumper stickers on their backs called out, 'Go hug Obama!'" Kate Zernike wrote. Rubio bumper stickers? I hadn't known that.

The Quinnipiac University poll still had me ahead in the Republican primary race. But it showed Marco Rubio narrowing my lead. I was now up by fifteen points—50 percent to 35 percent. Still a solid lead, but not an insurmountable one. That margin was half as large as it had been in August. Something was definitely happening out there, and it wasn't good.

I knew this went way beyond Florida. There was a lot of radical right-wing talk in the air the second half of the year. The Tea Party rallies were really getting going. The fervor had started to take hold. In town hall meetings across the country, people were shouting at members of Congress about a lot of things but Obamacare especially. And mailers had been circulating in our campaign—from the Rubio campaign, I presumed—with a photo of me from that day in Fort Myers, hugging the president.

The whole thing was out of another, darker era, that old we-don't-like-your-kind-here sentiment that some people used to express in the segregation days. That's how it felt to me, anyway. Gainesville is a university town with all that implies. But I don't know that the Republican community in Alachua County is necessarily active in the university. Clearly the Democrats in Gainesville are a fairly progressive group just like they are in Leon County, where Florida State is. But the Republicans there, not necessarily so. They're mostly pretty conservative. You're in the country, really.

It was shocking to me that someone would behave like that at an official Republican Party event and take on a sitting Republican governor in such a hostile manner. It was Marco's tone. It was the outbursts from the crowd. There was a real edge hanging in the air. I had been raised in a civil household. I'm sure most of the people at the barbecue had been raised the same way. This overt incivility about hugging the President—it just stunned me. It made me think about this party and this Senate race in a different way.

Like, *What the hell is going on here?*

Clearly, something was.

The new year started off with an ugly dustup inside the Florida Republican Party. Jim Greer, the state chairman I had supported, turned out to be great at raising money—and even better at spending it. But he wasn't a natural coalition builder, and he alienated many longtime party officials. They considered him headstrong and uninterested in what others had to say. They also said he was far too free with the party credit cards. Jim complained to me that the old guard was resisting his new ideas. Whatever the truth of that, he'd clearly lost support inside the party and resigned as chairman on January 5. He was replaced by State Senator John Thrasher, who had the backing of both Jeb and me.

All across America, the year was starting cheerily for the Tea Party movement and newly activated hard core. On January 19, Scott Brown, a relatively obscure Republican state senator, won a special election in Massachusetts to fill what for nearly forty-seven years had been Ted Kennedy's US Senate seat. He whizzed past a far better-known Democrat, Attorney General Martha Coakley.

Brown wasn't a hard-core conservative by national standards. He couldn't afford to be in a state as Democratic as Massachusetts. But the Greater Boston Tea Party hosted a fund-raising breakfast for him. He was endorsed by the Tea Party Express, which bought ads for him on national cable TV. And when he won? Well, that brought a flash of confidence to Republican long shots everywhere.

As the weeks and months rolled on and I began to make more frequent campaign appearances, I could tell the animosity on the ground was spreading. Not all the Republican audiences were as hostile as that man in Alachua County. But an undeniable nastiness was seeping through the crowds. More muttering than I was used to hearing. Less politeness and respect. Maybe it was as simple as the individuals turning out for certain events. But people seemed noticeably grumpier out there. The difficult economy no doubt played a role, and it wasn't limited to Florida. People were feeling displaced and agitated. Middle-class families were getting squeezed. In the rising agitation, I believe, many people were looking for someone to blame. Government made an easy target. In fact, most of these problems were not caused by Washington or Tallahassee. They were primarily the result of excesses on Wall Street and in the banking business—and the new realities of global business. Manufacturing was declining. Big companies kept shifting American jobs to lower-wage countries overseas. Technology also played a role in putting people out of work. Government wasn't blameless. It rarely is. But the Obama administration—and, yes, my administration too— had achieved some actual progress in easing the worst of the pain.

It would have been nice if this anger could have been channeled into something productive, like helping those in need and strategizing the nation back to prosperity. But there was very little of that amid the blame, the finger-pointing, and the outrage.

All across the country, hyped-up bloggers, hard-right-wingers, and Tea Party activists were banging hard. TARP. The stimulus. Mortgage relief. Obamacare. These were the rallying cries, and the slogan was the usual one: "Take our country back," though still never specifying from whom.

As the New Year began, conservative activists and Tea Party leaders were already focusing on Florida. To them, I represented all the evils of squishy, moderate, flexible, compromising, get-along Republicanism. The only person almost as bad as me, it seemed, was Texas Senator John Cornyn, head of the National Republican Senatorial Committee, who had so quickly endorsed my candidacy. He was getting banged up with me in many of the blogs.

Defeating me and electing Marco Rubio, Erick Erickson declared in a RedState blog post, was one of his top priorities for the year. To get at me, he decided he'd make life miserable for Senator Cornyn. He urged his followers to barrage Cornyn's office with phone calls and deluge the senator's Facebook page with angry messages.

The Texas Republican finally phoned Erickson at home in Georgia, beseeching him to call off the RedState dogs. The blogger didn't see any need to back off.

"When we're confronted by a guy who is a Republican but not a conservative versus one who is, I think we should support the conservative," he said.

The Republican primary was still eight months off. Mostly, we were raising money, gathering staff, and preparing ourselves. But the story line had been established, and it was going to be told.

David Brooks, the conservative-leaning *New York Times* columnist, described the Tea Party as both "amateurish" and "a major force," and he named Marco Rubio the top contender "to become its de facto leader." But the real national discussion started on January 10, when *The New York Times Magazine* published a story that everyone in Florida seemed to notice. Marco was on the cover. The headline ended with a question mark: "The First Senator from the Tea Party?"

But the entire piece shouted, "Yes!"

The article's subtitle declared: "2010 will be a year of Republican civil war, and Florida is where the fighting is now fiercest."

Just my luck! The poster boy for this rapidly expanding extremism was my own primary opponent in the US Senate race! The writer, Mark Leibovich, had followed Marco to some Tea Party gatherings, where the candidate seemed to be harnessing a lot of energy for his campaign. "My parents lost their country to a government!" the *Times* writer quoted the Cuban American candidate as saying at a rally in West Palm Beach. "I will not lose mine to a government!"

In the piece, Marco called the Tea Party "an important part of a bigger movement in America united behind the idea that you don't have to get rid of everything that's right about America to fix what is wrong about our country."

What empty platitudes! I remember thinking when I read that. I wasn't exactly sure what those soaring words meant. But I knew if you said them fast enough, a lot of people would probably nod along.

Knowing Marco from Tallahassee, I couldn't help but wonder just how motivated he was by all this true-believing ideology and how much he had just found a convenient wave to ride. In our days together, with me as governor and Marco as Speaker of the House, "rigid" wasn't the word I would have used for him. He'd grown up as the son of hardworking immigrant parents, struggling to achieve in America. His mother's father, Pedro Victor Garcia, got caught in the squeeze of US immigration policy in the 1960s. For four years, his grandfather was here illegally, the Associated Press concluded, until US immigration authorities gave him a visa and granted him amnesty. The Rubios were dreamers. They were not ideologues.

Marco's own life was not without struggles or controversy. When he got out of law school, he had said, he was carrying $100,000 in student-loan debt, which he was still paying off during the Senate campaign. During his time as Speaker of the Florida House of Representatives, he and fellow Republican David Rivera co-owned a home in Tallahassee that fell into foreclosure after months of deferred mortgage payments. As the Senate race was heating up, the IRS was investigating Marco for using his Republican Party credit card to charge personal expenses. The matter was settled after he reimbursed the party $16,000 of the $100,000 he had charged.

Personally, I didn't begrudge Marco any of this stuff, although our campaign took some shots at him over some of it. He had worked diligently to put most of the questions behind him. These were the hard knocks of real life.

But now things were different. Whatever his personal motivations, he and his friends were gunning at me. Their leading pitch to Republican primary voters: Crist likes Obama.

Senator Jim DeMint, former House majority leader Dick Armey, and other Tea Party favorites began endorsing Marco. On January 25, Armey's group, FreedomWorks, declared me one of its "Enemies of Liberty."

Really? An enemy of liberty?

FreedomWorks announced a multimillion-dollar national war

chest to defeat me and the other enemies, who included Arlen Specter and Harry Reid.

"It's hot in Florida, and Charlie Crist is on the run," said Tom Gaitens, a Florida field coordinator for FreedomWorks.

Clearly, the ground was shifting around me. The party that had always been my home was feeling alien now. The passion and the power were moving into different hands. The things that I believed in—practical problem-solving, bringing people together, open bipartisanship—still had a constituency, I was convinced. But that constituency was getting mighty scarce inside the Republican Party.

These new people were angry—at everyone and everything—including, or maybe especially, at me.

I'd gotten a startling view of it at the "go hug Obama" barbecue. If anything, the anger had grown more intense since then. And I wasn't the only one noticing.

"You have to show some anger," my old friend Mitch Bainwol said to me on the phone one day. Mitch had a keen instinct for Florida politics, especially on the Republican side. He was the Connie Mack campaign manager who'd first recruited me.

"People are angry out there," he said. "You've gotta show you're as mad as they are."

"They're angry," I said. "That's for sure."

"You've gotta channel and vent their anger," he said. "You've gotta show them you are angry yourself."

"But I'm not angry," I said. "I'm not an angry person."

"They're angry," he said.

"Well, I just can't do that," I told him. "It's just not who I am."

Mitch was speaking out of concern for me and my political success. I know he was. In this Republican war zone, he was giving me the right political advice. From a political point of view, he was spot on. But I just couldn't accept it. I couldn't carry out the mission he was describing to me. It just wasn't consistent with what I was or who I was. If that's what it took to win in this environment, that was too high a price to pay.

I'd seen other Republicans pretend to be angry in a way I knew was just a show for the voters and not at all a reflection of their true feelings. To me that seemed cynical and totally wrong.

"I'll be myself," I said.

But would that be enough? Would Republican primary voters— *this year's* Republican primary voters—be willing to support a candidate like me who was known as a moderate and didn't feel angry at all? I was starting to wonder. It wasn't Floridians in general I needed to convince. It was a relative sliver of them—those active Republican voters who would turn out for the party primary on August 24. I had to convince *them*.

At the end of January, Republican pollster Tony Fabrizio found that 44 percent of Republican-primary voters were supporting Marco, compared to 30 percent for me. In that same survey, Tony asked a second question that some political people in Florida had already started whispering about. What would happen if I decided to skip the Republican primary for Senate and ran instead in the general election in November as an independent candidate, not affiliated with any party at all?

It wasn't anything I was planning to do—or was even seriously considering yet. But it was the kind of hypothetical that political consultants like to toss around. A race like that, Tony found, would be considerably tighter: 31 percent for Marco, 26 percent for me, and 24 percent for Kendrick Meek, a South Florida congressman who was the likely Democratic candidate.

That idea—me running as an independent—got some wider

notice on February 1, when Chris Cillizza wrote a piece for *The Washington Post*, quoting Tony's survey and headlined: "Should Charlie Crist Run as an Independent in Florida's Senate Race?" An independent run is "not entirely out of the realm of possibility," Chris wrote.

The day that piece appeared, the Rubio campaign announced a new fund-raising gimmick to mark the upcoming one-year anniversary of President Obama's trip to Fort Myers and to skewer me for supporting the $787 billion stimulus plan. The money-raising goal? $787,000 in ten days. Donations were being taken at www.stimulusbomb.com.

This anti-Obama message was right in tune with the mood of many Republicans. The Democratic president had won the 2008 election over that Republican moderate—say it with a sneer—John McCain. But that didn't mean the conservative activists needed to like the president or support anything that he did. Marco was riding that train, and it was picking up speed. He was being thoroughly embraced by the Republican Party's reawakening activist wing, an assemblage that included politicized evangelicals, ardent bloggers, anti-abortion advocates, deficit hawks, Tea Party wing nuts, and a handful of really rich guys with very loose checkbooks.

On February 18, Marco got one of the prime podiums this new conservatism had to offer, the opening speaker spot at CPAC, the Conservative Political Action Conference, at the Marriott Wardman Park in Washington. According to the coverage, he strode onto the stage to the first standing ovation of the morning. Marco was greeted like a button-down rock star. His speech was filled with Tea Party touchstones—lower taxes, defunding Obamacare. He didn't mention immigration reform.

"A few weeks ago," he told the adoring crowd, "I wasn't sure I could make it here." Washington had just pulled itself out of a crippling snowstorm—with the help of government snowplows, district sanitation workers, and a giant transfer of taxpayer dollars into the overtime budget. "Congress couldn't even meet to work on business," he said. "The president couldn't find anywhere to set up his teleprompter to announce new taxes!"

The teleprompter joke got a huge round of applause.

He accused Obama of using the economic crisis "not to fix America, but to change America." The American people, he said, had "figured it out": "From Tea Parties to the election in Massachusetts, we are witnessing the single greatest political push-back in American history."

He drew rousing applause and shouts of "Amen!" when he condemned Obama's record on national security and took a thinly veiled poke at moderate Republicans like me. "The US Senate already has one Arlen Specter too many. America already has a Democratic Party. We don't need two Democratic Parties."

It was that line again from the first nasty barbecue.

On February 23, Jeb Bush put some brand-name polish on the message, calling my support for the president's economic stimulus "unforgivable." Speaking with the pugnacious conservative website Newsmax, Jeb started sweetly. I was "a talented guy," he said, "about the nicest guy I've ever met in politics." Then he let loose.

"There's one thing that he has done that I just find unforgivable. He is the only statewide political leader, that I'm aware of, that embraced the stimulus package when Republicans were fighting to suggest an alternative."

Now, I do believe that some things in life are unforgiveable. But accepting money from Washington to save the jobs of teachers, police officers, and firefighters and help revive our economy? No, that's not one of them. Besides, almost every governor ended up taking some or all of the money. I was just the only Republican who was so up-front about it.

Jeb, like Marco, kept pounding on the stimulus, which he termed "a massive spending bill that is not related to stimulus. It is related to trying to carry out a liberal agenda."

It was strange hearing that kind of rhetoric coming from Jeb. Jeb and I didn't see eye to eye on everything. We'd had our disagreement on Terri Schiavo and the voting procedures. But the harsher tone of the Tea Party was obviously spreading to more mainstream Republicans, many of whom felt they needed to give voice to the anger in order to keep their supporters happy and stay in office.

That was clearly what some Republican voters were itching to hear. Not how we'd solve our problems together. Not how to get America working again. But about what a radical, manipulative, disloyal, elitist, and downright un-American president we had.

On March 28, Marco and I faced off in an hour-long debate that was being carried live by *Fox News Sunday*. It was rare that a candidate debate in a Senate primary would be aired on a national broadcast network, and still more than five months before primary day. But the race kept gathering more national attention. It was being described as an epic battle for the heart and the head of the modern Republican Party.

We were both Republicans, but we clashed on everything, the president's stimulus plan most of all. Marco brought up the issue again and again, and it just made me angrier and angrier.

With so many suffering Floridians, it would have been reckless to turn down Washington's help, I said. "We utilized those monies just like Haley Barbour did in Mississippi, just like Sonny Perdue in Georgia, some of these wild-eyed liberals," I said, referring to two of America's most conservative governors who accepted the stimulus money just like I had. "If we'd taken the Speaker's approach, we would have had 87,000 more people on top of that 12 percent that would be unemployed in Florida today, 20,000 of those, as you indicated, schoolteachers who are teaching the children."

I was reacting to the same criticism I'd received from Jeb Bush, and it was just as wrong this time. Virtually every governor, Democrat and Republican, would eventually take at least some stimulus money. Their people needed it, whatever ideological lip service the politicians chose to give.

I was a "commonsense, practical conservative," I said, prepared to "work to make sure that I stand with people who will help the people of my state and my country." That sounded sensible to me. I thought it drew a nice contrast to Marco.

"You can't just be off on some limb, you know, rattling the cage and saying you're going to do great things and stand on principle or politics above the people of your state that you're supposed to serve."

I was pleased with my answer. I didn't mind running on that, even in a Republican primary, even in a year like this.

The stimulus hadn't lowered the unemployment rate, Marco argued. It was still 9.7 percent nationally, two points higher than when the stimulus was passed, 12.2 percent in Florida.

"The stimulus is a failure," he declared straight-out. "I would've voted against the stimulus."

I couldn't help but wonder: How much higher would the unemployment rate have gone if the stimulus hadn't been enacted and all those teachers, cops, and firefighters were booted out of work?

On the issue of illegal immigration, Marco wasn't yet ready to come out for comprehensive reform, a topic he would later take such grief about from some of his very same Tea Party supporters. He got to the right of me on immigration, attacking John McCain's plan to offer illegal immigrants a path to citizenship if they paid a fine, learned English, and paid back taxes.

"He would have voted for the McCain plan," the son of Cuban immigrants said of the Greek immigrant's grandson. "I think that plan is wrong, and the reason why I think it's wrong is that if you grant amnesty, as the governor proposes that we do, in any form, whether it's back of the line or so forth, you will destroy any chance we will ever have of having a legal immigration system that works here in America."

And he got in a few kind words about the Tea Party movement. "It's a lot of people from all walks of life who are fed up with our country," he said.

I delivered my message the way I like to—simple, straightforward, and clear. "I am running for the Senate," I said, "because I know our country needs help."

But I couldn't shake the feeling that the great middle of the Republican Party had somehow evaporated; that the people I had been speaking to weren't there anymore; that these decent, solid, middle-of-the-road Republicans had somehow been replaced by a new breed—narrower, more rigid, less generous, and more extreme. I didn't like what it meant for my prospects. Even worse, I didn't like what it meant for where my party, my state, and my nation were headed next.

Chapter 16

My early confidence of victory in the Senate race was being shaken. The unfortunate straw polls were beginning to be reflected in broader surveys of the Republican electorate. I didn't feel doomed yet, but Marco had clearly closed much of the gap with me. His allies were looking for opportunities to finish off whatever lingering Republican hopes I might have had.

When Republicans in the legislature began crafting a proposal to reform how Florida treated its teachers, the initial idea wasn't bad at all. Greater accountability for Florida's public school teachers. A new system of merit pay. Rewarding talented teachers for their success in the classroom. I had no problem voicing my support.

"This is a bill that really focuses on trying to help children and encouraging better teachers," I said. "That just seems like the right thing to do."

But even the most promising ideas can turn quickly sour when the reasonable people are badly outnumbered by the ideologues. Nothing illustrates this any better than the hijacking of Senate

Bill 6. As the bill moved from one committee to another, it was loaded down with amendments from extreme-conservative legislators who didn't seem to like the whole idea of public schools. The tone of the bill began to shift. It went from rewarding teachers to punishing them.

The Republican legislators probably should have just renamed it the Teacher Punishment Act. That would have been a whole lot closer to what the bill's conservative backers really had in mind.

I got an early heads-up from Alex Villalobos, a Republican state senator from Miami who had a strong interest in education issues. His wife was a schoolteacher. I'm sure he was hearing about Senate Bill 6 at home.

"This is moving in a very bad direction," he warned me. "I know earlier you had voiced your support. But I would encourage you to start reviewing what's happened to the bill."

Alex wasn't the only Republican senator with concerns. I got a similar call from Rudy Garcia of Miami, and a third moderate Republican confided bluntly to me: "Some of the lug nuts in our party have taken control of this bill. This thing is going off the rails."

Not only did the amended proposal link as much as half a teacher's pay to student test scores, but it did so in ways that were awfully subjective and ridiculously vague. Who would do the testing? What exactly would they test? No one seemed quite sure.

Newer teachers could be fired for any cause or no cause at all. Local school systems were forbidden from paying teachers based on their experience or advanced degrees. The bill took away a teacher's incentive to earn National Board Certification, which is an advanced teaching credential widely recognized across the country. And it raised a rash of extra complications for special-ed teachers, who were some of the most dedicated teachers we had.

The bill was starting to look like a Christmas tree with only red ornaments. If I didn't know any better, I'd have thought it was dreamed up by someone who spent too much time in after-school detention—and still resented his teachers for it. It certainly wasn't my idea of education reform. Two of my three sisters are teachers. I didn't think they needed to be punished for pursuing education careers.

There was one other wrinkle that seemed relevant to me. The people who really stood to make out here were the for-profit, national testing firms. If Senate Bill 6 became law, they could expect some fat new Florida contracts, the same way heavy-construction companies get all excited when new roads are about to be built.

As the amended bill neared a vote in the Senate, Florida teachers were holding "Nix Six" rallies across the state. Their union leaders were writing scathing op-ed pieces and coming to Tallahassee, looking for friends. You can imagine how far they got with that. Some Republican legislators would happily support a bill just because the National Education Association was against it.

The outcry from the teachers might have tightened the voting a little, but it didn't change the result. On March 24, the revved-up proposal was approved by the Florida Senate, 21–17, without a single Democratic vote. Four moderate Republicans joined the Senate's thirteen Democrats in voting no. The House took up an identical version of the bill the very next day, passing it fifteen days later, 64–55, also with no Democratic support. This time, the forty-four House Democrats were joined by eleven moderate Republicans.

Even with the handful of Republican defections, the punish-the-teachers bill had solid-enough support among the party's conservatives to get through.

And that's when the real drama began. I had to decide if I would use my veto. I was certainly inclined to, though I knew it would cause steaming outrage among the teacher-bashers inside my own party.

The teachers stayed strong, warning they wouldn't be the only ones who suffered. A big part of Florida's curriculum, they pointed out, would be put in the hands of the out-of-state testing firms. A far-larger percentage of class time would be spent on test prep rather than actually learning. You knew it would be. Teachers' careers were on the line.

Messages were pouring into the governor's office, 120,000 in all. Of those the staff had a chance to log, 65,000 messages opposed the bill. Just 3,000 supported the bill.

Conservative groups also lobbied hard, with added muscle from the testing companies. I wished we could have had a sensible debate about the best way to reward good teachers. But in this overheated environment, that never occurred.

Even some of the proposal's strongest proponents admitted that Senate Bill 6 had some unresolved issues. "This is not a perfect bill," conceded Don Gaetz, a Republican senator from Niceville and former head of Okaloosa County schools. "There are things in this bill that will change. It's a framework for going forward."

I couldn't tell if that was a promise or a threat.

The bill's chief sponsor, Republican State Senator John Thrasher of St. Augustine, said legislators could pass a follow-up "glitch bill" to settle some of the lingering details. I think John was making his final effort to convince me not to veto the bill.

Every day, individual teachers were writing and calling with personal appeals. They kept telling me how worried they were, for themselves and for their students. They were concerned about their job security. They felt like they were being portrayed as villains. They couldn't help but feel like political pawns. They were genuinely upset. And it was hard not to feel for them, especially given my family background.

The last straw for me came Easter weekend. Carole and I were on Useppa Island off Fort Myers. It's one of our favorite getaway spots when we need some private time. It's where we went on our honeymoon. The island has no cars or bridges. You can only get there by boat. They do have cell phone service, which can be a mixed blessing, I suppose. I spent part of our honeymoon on the phone with officials from the South Florida Water Management District, lobbying them to buy 150,000 acres of the Everglades from U.S. Sugar Corporation.

Good cause, bad timing. Thankfully, it was just a few short calls.

This weekend on Useppa, I got a call from Mike Lusignan, who'd gone to St. Petersburg High School with me. Mike wanted to express his concerns about Senate Bill 6. I knew that he and his wife have a son who is severely disabled and was attending Nina Harris School in Pinellas County. Nina Harris is an amazing place for special-needs children, with a dedicated staff and heavy family involvement. I'd visited the school and was awestruck by the level of deep commitment I saw there.

Mike said he had just gotten off the phone with his son's favorite teacher. "She was in tears," Mike said. "She knew that I was friends with you and asked if I could possibly call and talk to you about vetoing this bill."

Mike said he thought this was important enough to call about. "This is going to be a mess for special-ed teachers," he said. "With this bill, their pay is supposed to be set by how the students improve from one year to the next year. It can be very difficult for special-ed students to show such overt improvement.

"Believe me. I know," Mike said. "It just seems fundamentally unfair."

I talked to him for a while. His call really touched my heart. When we hung up, I turned to Carole, who was in the next room, and told her: "Honey, that does it. I am going to veto this thing. It's a good concept gone very bad."

I hadn't announced my intention yet. But the time for me to act was running short. I would have to sign the bill, veto it, or let it become law without my signature. A couple of days later, I was back at the Governor's Mansion when my phone rang at about 7 A.M. I always get up early and had already worked out. I was drinking my first cup of coffee and reading the morning paper. I saw the call was from my campaign co-chair, former senator Connie Mack. I answered, of course.

"Hey, Senator," I said. "How are you doing?"

"Fine," he said.

"Good."

"You have a minute? I want to talk to you about this Senate Bill 6."

"Sure," I said.

Connie got right to the point.

"I hear you are contemplating vetoing the bill," he said.

"Yeah," I said. "It's a bill that I think started out in a good situation with good intent. I just think it's gotten to the point where it's not there anymore."

He didn't debate the matter with me. He didn't even discuss the particulars of the bill.

He just said: "Well, I want you to know that if you veto this bill, I will resign as your campaign co-chair in this election."

"You gotta be kiddin'," I said.

"No, I'm not," he said. "I'm not kidding."

I was stunned.

"Well," I said, making my intentions clear, "I'm sorry you feel that way, Senator. But I'm gonna veto it."

I felt badly about that. I thought the world of Connie Mack. I always have. Frankly, I still do. I've seen him subsequently. It's been very good. But for that one moment, it kind of broke my heart that he would feel so strongly about this one issue that he would resign from my campaign. Sometimes, there are pressures beyond our understanding. I don't know what brought that to bear.

Connie's resignation didn't have much day-to-day impact on my campaign. His role was largely symbolic. It was a statement of confidence that someone of his stature would sign on as chairman. But his abrupt departure carried just as much symbolism in the opposite direction. Now, a Florida political legend was saying, "I'm cutting ties here."

Why did he decide to do that? Why was the teacher bill so important to him? In the end, it didn't really matter what Connie's or anyone's individual motives or concerns might be. There was nothing to negotiate. There was no argument anyone was open to. There is no way to change a closed mind. It seemed to me that the forces of extremism were aligned against our teachers. And the teachers' final hope this time was me.

I knew the veto would further damage my Republican primary prospects. But could I really turn our teachers into the latest Republican scapegoats?

My Senate race kept getting more and more challenging. My strong lead against Marco was ancient history now. A major piece of the

Republican primary electorate seemed simply beyond my reach. They didn't want to hear about balance, reaching out, or common sense. The Tea Party rallies were still mainly ragtag affairs. But the protesters and their Internet backers were coalescing into a well-financed national machine. Barack Obama was easily their number-one villain, but I was solidly positioned on the rung beneath him. I was an insufficiently conservative, out-there Republican. That was almost as bad as being a Democrat.

I was running for Senate, but I was still the governor of America's fourth-largest state, wrestling with a difficult economy, confronting a Republican legislature under the increasing sway of these very same Tea Party activists. By and large, the members of the House and Senate tried to do the right thing as they saw it, I believe. But not too many of them were eager to stand in the way of any political tidal waves. If the politics called for anger and intolerance, they could deliver anger and intolerance without breaking a sweat. I didn't know how much further I could continue along the path I was on. I was running for the nomination of a party I didn't belong in anymore.

Then an underwater oil well blew out in the Gulf of Mexico. Apparently, I wasn't busy enough already.

On April 21, I was with Carole at her place on Fisher Island. I got an early-morning call on my cell phone from Rear Admiral Mary Landry of the United States Coast Guard. She was calling to alert me about an explosion the night before on the Deepwater Horizon, an oil-drilling rig in the Gulf of Mexico off the coast of Louisiana. She was the federal on-scene coordinator, Admiral Landry said. Eleven crewmen were killed. Seventeen others were injured. And the admiral used a term I had not heard before.

"There's a disruption in the riser," she said.

"Admiral." I stopped her. "I don't know what a riser is."

The riser, she explained, was a mile-long pipe that connected the well at the bottom of the Gulf to a drilling platform at the water's surface. Initial attempts to stop the oil flow failed when a safety device called a blowout preventer could not be activated by the rig's crew. Over the next eighty-six days, I learned an awful lot about risers and blowout preventers and kink leaks and wellbores and British Petroleum and Halliburton and how dangerous—to people and the natural environment—deepwater oil drilling can be. But that expertise developed gradually.

"It means the pipe is disconnected, and there is the potential that it could be spewing oil into the Gulf of Mexico," Admiral Landry said.

She gave me a few other preliminary details.

The potential environmental threat, she said, was significant: 700,000 gallons of diesel on board the drilling platform and an estimated potential of 8,000 barrels a day of crude oil spewing into the Gulf if the well suffered a total blowout.

"None of that sounds good at all," I said to the admiral.

It wasn't long until the whole world knew about the BP spill. By midday, environmental experts described "surface sheening"—that was the phrase—on the water. And a whole lot more was certainly on the way. Live video from the bottom of the Gulf showed oil shooting out of that busted riser. All day and night, CNN and MSNBC and Fox—and all the local stations—kept those terrible pictures in the corner of the screen.

The rupture was more than three hundred miles off the Panhandle of Florida. But with a spill this size and with the Gulf's powerful currents, no one could say how soon that slimy black crude would be lapping against the sugar-white beaches of Pensacola, Destin, Fort Walton, and on down the Florida coast. The experts on television were using phrases like "environmental catastrophe."

As oil was gushing into the Gulf, I learned quite a bit more about our former party chairman, Jim Greer, and also announced my veto of SB 6. Even in an environmental disaster, politics and government had to go on. As of April 23, Jim wasn't only the ex-chairman. He was thrown out of the party entirely by his replacement, John Thrasher. It was starting to look like Jim's behavior as chairman—especially his spending habits—hadn't only been alienating to other party officials. What he'd been doing was also potentially criminal. I asked federal prosecutors to launch an official investigation. I hadn't been aware of anything improper that Jim was doing. But he'd been my choice as chairman, and I felt terribly let down by him.

Barely five weeks later, Jim would be arrested on six felony fraud charges. Prosecutors would allege that he had funneled more than $100,000 into a fund-raising company he created, Victory Strategies, then used the money for his personal expenses. He would ultimately plead guilty to theft and money-laundering charges and head off to prison on an eighteen-month term.

In my time in government, I have been extremely fortunate with the people I have appointed to positions of trust. Jim was a glaring and painful exception to that.

At the same time some of that was unfolding, I declared my

intentions on the teacher-tenure bill. "We must start over," I said on April 25. This punitive legislation was "significantly flawed" and "contrary to the best interests of the people of Florida."

This twisted version of school reform had "deeply and negatively affected the morale of our teachers, our parents, and our students," I said. "They are not confident in our system because they do not believe their voices were heard."

The Republicans in Washington were complaining loudly that the Democratic president had rushed Obamacare through Congress. How different was the attempted ram-through of Senate Bill 6? "The very same thing happens here," I said. Even while admitting the bill was still flawed, Florida's Republican legislators had shoved it along to my desk.

Republican leaders in the legislature were beside themselves. "I am disappointed that today Governor Crist chose to reverse direction and veto SB 6," Senate President Jeff Atwater said.

"This bill and the many hours of hard work and debate that went into it represent a heroic commitment to take education reform in Florida to the next level," said House Speaker Larry Cretul.

I can see the politics from their perspective.

This was an issue that for so many years was dominated by Democrats. Finally, Republicans found a way to control some of the conversation on education. The term "merit pay" polled well. Nobody could be against the idea of merit pay. The Republicans were able to ram this bill through the legislature. And here I was, a Republican governor who had liked the bill in its original form, now tanking it. They were like, "What the—?"

If all this additional testing had been imposed in Florida, the testing companies could have taken our model and their experience and sold it not just in Florida but also in Texas, New York,

Pennsylvania, California—anywhere they could get this kind of legislation passed.

If you own the testing company, you could plan on a huge increase in testing. You just got an A-plus in the bank.

Jeb Bush, who'd lobbied hard for the bill, put in a plug for his own version of education reform. "By taking this action, Governor Crist has jeopardized the ability of Florida to build on the progress of the last decade," the former governor said in a written statement, writing as chairman of the Foundation for Florida's Future, a group the press used to jokingly call "the Foundation for Jeb's Future" because it gave him a ready-made platform after he left office. The foundation's stated mission? "To make Florida's education system a model for the nation." Back when Jeb and I were closer, I was even on the board. Clearly, we were seeing things differently now.

Some of the criticism over the teacher bill was turning downright personal. Senator Mike Haridopolos, a Republican from Merritt Island, said I'd gone back on my solemn word. "In this business, trust is everything," he said. "Every time you make a pledge or a promise and then you go against that, everything falls apart."

Mike knew that was silly. If the legislature had passed the initial bill, I'd have stood right there with him. But what came out of the sausage factory in the Capitol was something I could barely recognize. I knew I'd done the right thing, even if I also knew it might alienate some Republican voters.

The Democrats were pleased with me, although they knew their victory might be short-lived. Democrat Dan Gelber, who'd been a leading voice against the bill in the Senate, said he was reluctant to gloat. "Obviously, it's a victory," he said. "But I'm not uncorking champagne because, frankly, it's really a sad statement that we had to fight this hard to stop something so wrongheaded."

As for those who would have been most directly affected by Senate Bill 6, they spoke to the media as if they'd just tiptoed around a loudly ticking bomb. Parents, teachers, administrators, even some students—they breathed a giant sigh of relief.

"The governor has exercised foresight, leadership, and wisdom in vetoing SB 6," said Broward County Public Schools Superintendent James Notter.

"It was the right decision," said Mark Castellano, president of the Teachers' Association of Lee County. "If they want to propose this kind of thing again, they need to do it collaboratively with us, not to us."

Soon after the veto was announced, the people who'd been most upset about the bill came outside one last time at many places across the state. In small demonstrations, they wanted to express their relief and their gratitude.

In Pasco County, teachers and parents gathered on three street corners with "thank you" signs. "How could you say in education you wouldn't reward people for advanced degrees?" asked Jan McHollan, a guidance counselor at Land O' Lakes High School.

In Cape Coral, they crowded a median strip at Veterans Parkway and Santa Barbara Boulevard. "We just thank Governor Crist for what he's done," said Mary Marken, a kindergarten teacher at Manatee Elementary School in Fort Myers. "I'm glad he put educators and education first for once."

As she spoke, others held up signs that said "Thank you, Charlie" and "Honk if you love education."

From what I heard, there was a lot of honking on Veterans Parkway that afternoon.

Chapter 17

The oil spill was looking more severe by the day. I was getting briefings from Valerie Jarrett at the White House, who began conducting frequent conference calls with the five Republican governors of the Gulf Coast states—Rick Perry of Texas, Bobby Jindal of Louisiana, Haley Barbour of Mississippi, Bob Riley of Alabama, and me. The crisis was all-consuming.

On April 27, I flew over the Gulf in a huge Florida National Guard C-144 transport aircraft. The plane looked like a flying garage. With me strapped into a seat facing backward, the crew threw open the rear of the plane so I could get a wide-angle view of what was already an 80-by-42-mile dark blob on the Gulf.

I was very happy to be strapped in.

"Unless you actually see it," I said on the flight back to Tallahassee, "I don't know how you could comprehend and appreciate the sheer magnitude of that thing. It's frightening." The spill had already made me rethink my openness to offshore oil drilling for Florida, I said.

How could it not?

As soon as I returned to the Capitol, I called Florida National Guard Major General Douglas Burnett and Emergency Management Director David Halstead. I asked them to coordinate with my environmental secretary, Michael Sole, and the Coast Guard. "Do whatever you can to keep that oil spill from coming up on the beaches of the Panhandle," I told David and the others. "It's ginormous."

I had to figure out what I was going to do about the US Senate race. It wasn't going well at all.

I saw several options. I could remain a candidate in the Republican primary, an increasingly uphill climb. I could drop out of the race entirely—perhaps even jump back into the governor's race. Or I could leave the Republican Party and continue my Senate campaign as an Independent.

The media was filled with speculation on what I should and what I could do. A Mike Thomas blog in the *Orlando Sentinel* gave ten reasons I would run as an Independent. A CBS News's piece asked: "What kind of electorate would Crist be up against if he does?" Andrea Saul, the campaign communications director, tried to beat back the rumors. But I knew I had to weigh my options as carefully as I could.

Staying in the Republican race seemed pointless. Pulling out entirely felt like quitting, and I really didn't want to do that. I never seriously considered jumping back into the governor's race. In my own heart and head, I was leaning toward the Independent route. It sounded promising, even if I didn't understand exactly what a move like that might mean.

Most of the political pros I spoke with told me I was crazy even to consider running as an unaffiliated candidate. People on both sides would hate me, they said. It would be really hard out there without a party behind me. And I'd almost certainly lose the Senate race. But if I was going to stay true to the things I believed in, I suspected I had no choice.

I sought advice from several of the people I trusted most. One of them was Stuart Stevens. Stuart is a very smart media consultant who'd worked on four of my campaigns, including this one. He's also a good guy and a close friend. He knew me, and he knew Florida politics. "You know," he said, "if you do this, I think you ruin your future politically forever."

Stuart wasn't pulling any punches, and I didn't expect him to. "I appreciate your advice," I told him. "I know that's what you believe."

I put in a call to Joe Lieberman. I'd gotten to know Joe on the 2008 John McCain campaign. I knew he'd had some experience with this sort of thing. A longtime Democratic senator from Connecticut, Joe had run for reelection as an Independent and then backed a Republican for president. Who better to seek counsel from?

When Joe called back, Carole and I had just finished lunch at Fish Tales, a great casual seafood joint with its own dock on Tampa Bay. We were out on my boat *Freedom*, a twenty-five-foot Trophy open fisherman, a perfect place to reflect on my future.

"If you decide to do it," the senator said, "you will find it incredibly liberating. You will find a new sense of freedom that you have never experienced in politics before."

It was a very encouraging call.

"From time to time," Joe said, "the parties get out of whack." He'd found that to be his experience, he said. "Clearly, that is what you're going through now."

I didn't let on to either Joe or Stuart which way I was leaning, just that I was thinking seriously about making the leap. But with each conversation, the decision was becoming clearer in my mind. I had to leave this poisonous Republican primary, whether I ultimately won as an Independent or not. I couldn't stick around anymore. The party had grown so intolerant, at least in a primary campaign, there was no place for a message like mine. The wrong things were working. The right things were not. Being decent to other people, working across the aisle, trying to get things done for the people you served—those concepts weren't connecting with Republican voters at all. What was connecting was being divisive, being intolerant, being mean. We were in the most difficult economic recession since the Great Depression. Yet today's Republicans seemed opposed to the very idea of helping people in a time of need. That didn't sit right with my values and what I'd been brought up to believe.

In this new Republican view, you needed to bash the crap out of Barack Obama. You needed to attack his health care plan. You needed to oppose anything he stood for—really, anything the Democrats proposed. It didn't matter whether the idea was a good one or a bad one. The base was hungry for juicy red meat, and you'd better serve up platters full of it. The long-term strategy, as well I could discern one, went something like this: Republicans had to hurt the president. We had to cripple government. We had to make sure that nothing the Democrats tried would succeed. That way, people would get frustrated with the current administration, and our party would ultimately benefit.

It was as cynical a strategy as I had ever heard. It was the new Republican way. But it wasn't my way.

That wasn't why I got into politics, and it wasn't a path I was willing to take now. Truly, I would rather lose than win like that. But even as I was contemplating my political future, Republicans in the legislature were doing everything they could think of to turn up the heat on me.

Disappointed that I'd blocked their attempt to squeeze Florida schoolteachers, my colleagues in the legislature kept coming back with more. Now, it was abortion they decided to throw at me.

Why is it always abortion? Can't anyone find another hot button to push?

Just before noon on April 28—a week after the oil well blowout, three days after the teacher-bill veto—my chief of staff, Shane Strum, walked into my office at the State Capitol. I would describe Shane as a very moderate Republican and a levelheaded guy. He was my chief of staff for the final eighteen months of my term.

"Governor," he said, "there's something that's come up in the Senate. Andy Gardiner is sponsoring it."

Andy was a Republican from Orlando, a tall, thin, friendly man and a fairly ardent social conservative. He and I loved to talk fishing.

"What's Andy got now?" I asked Shane.

It was late in the session. I thought I knew about all the little stink bombs my Republican colleagues had planted for me.

"It's an ultrasound bill for women," he said. "Any woman in Florida would have to get an ultrasound before she'd be allowed to terminate a pregnancy. It would be mandatory, even in the first trimester."

Ugh!

That's how I felt hearing Shane's description. Just *ugh!*

"So now we're legislating the medical tests that women receive?" I asked Shane.

"Mandatory ultrasounds," Shane repeated. "Oh, and here's the other thing," he added. "Under Senator Gardiner's measure, the woman has to pay for it, whether she can afford it or not." That could cost anywhere from $400 to $1,500.

I tend to be a cheery person. But requiring unnecessary ultrasounds and making low-income women pay for the procedures—that just felt deflating to me.

There was even more to it, as things turned out. A woman would also be required to review the ultrasound's vivid pictures of her fetus and have her doctor explain the details. Only if she could prove she'd been raped or was a victim of incest or domestic violence could she avoid the experience.

I asked Shane why I hadn't heard about any of this before. The sixty-day session was in its last few days. Wasn't this late to be scheduling committee hearings and taking witness testimony? Certainly, the legislators would need to hear from medical experts on ultrasound testing. They'd want the insurance industry and the medical profession to weigh in. Women's groups would want to be heard, of course, and so would the anti-abortion activists.

"None of that," Shane said, shaking his head.

The ultrasound proposal was a last-minute amendment tacked onto a package of nursing home reforms. There would be no hearings. There would be no experts. There would be no testimony. Republican Senate leaders were hoping for a vote in twenty-four hours.

Twenty-four hours? For something as serious as this?

What an unconscionable requirement to impose on a woman just as she is making one of the most incredibly difficult decisions of her life! This was more than partisan politics. These rigid ideologues would not stop. Their intent wasn't hard to figure out: to try to make a woman with an unwanted pregnancy feel even more terrible than she already did, or make the decision impossible for her if she didn't have the money to pay for an unnecessary ultrasound.

"What are these guys doing?" I asked Shane.

"Well," he told me, "thankfully, I think they are giving you another opportunity to look reasonable."

I didn't question Andy's motivations. I'm sure he was doing what he thought was right. When it comes to abortion, people have strong beliefs—personal and religious. I get that. Andy and his wife, Camille, have a son with Down syndrome. He's talked about that openly. But in government, don't we have to balance our personal beliefs with an understanding that other people have a right to theirs?

The timing of this couldn't have been an accident. Clearly, the legislators weren't happy with my veto of the teacher bill. Now they were raising the heat another notch. It was like someone had said: "Hey, you enjoyed Senate Bill 6? Here's another chance for you to piss off the conservatives. Let's see how the evangelicals like that." Clearly, some kind of split was coming. Sending me a highly emotional abortion bill was the Republicans' way of spurring it along. No one said that directly, but the message was clear: "Charlie has left the building. He's not one of us anymore. Let's kick him a couple of times on the way out. Let this be a lesson to other Republicans who aren't sufficiently right-wing."

I had made my decision. I flew home to St. Petersburg the next day, Thursday, April 29, and announced I was exiting the Republican primary, leaving the Republican Party, and continuing my race for the US Senate as an Independent.

It was very late to be doing this—not quite three months before the primary, barely six months until Election Day. But I couldn't wait any longer. The last day to file as an Independent was April 30.

I laid out my thinking as clearly as I knew how.

"Our political system is broken," I told a rally of 250 people at Straub Park on Tampa Bay. "I believe in democracy and the right to choose."

The voters, I said, have "had enough of political fighting. They're tired of the games and name-calling and the politics of destruction.

"I was never one who sought to hold elective office to demagogue or point fingers," I said, sounding the same theme of inclusiveness I'd been sounding for years. "For me, public service has always been about putting the needs of our state and our people first, and every single day, as your servant, I have tried to do exactly that."

If the party I'd grown up in was no longer open to a message like that, I said—well, I'd just have to take my message to a broader audience. The Republicans might be in the grip of these extremist forces. But I refused to believe all of America, all of Florida, was too.

I said we needed a fresh political tone, one that recognizes that neither party has a monopoly on wisdom. "I haven't supported an idea because it's a Republican idea or it's a Democratic idea," I said. "I support ideas that I believe are good ideas for the people—for the people. And I've always found that's exactly what the people believe too."

Howard Dean immediately grasped the reason behind my decision and the significance of it. "They've driven another moderate out of the Republican Party," the former Vermont governor, 2004 presidential candidate, and then chairman of the Democratic National Committee said on MSNBC. "There just apparently is no place in the Republican Party for moderate, thoughtful people anymore."

In practical terms, I really didn't know what being an

Independent candidate for the US Senate would mean. I'm not sure anyone did. Other people in other states had left the Republican Party—Connecticut's Lowell Weicker, Rhode Island's Lincoln Chafee, Pennsylvania's Arlen Specter. But none of them had done it at such a moment of high drama so late in a major campaign. I was, however, happy to see that all of them still had political careers after their leaps.

"We're in uncharted territory," I had said during my announcement in St. Petersburg, and that was certainly true. I didn't know if my supporters would still support me, if my donors would still give to my campaign, or if my hopeful message would ever get heard amid the uproar. But I knew this much: The conservative wave that had swept through my party made it all but impossible for a moderate Republican candidate like me. I was never going to out-Obama-bash Marco Rubio. I couldn't play to people's prejudices and fears.

Steven Schale, who ran Barack Obama's 2008 Florida campaign and wrote a smart Florida-politics blog, took a hard look at the numbers in the three-way race. I had "a hard row to hoe," he concluded. "Assuming a win number of 35-36% (I doubt we will see a 34-33-33 race), he needs to get roughly 50% of the independents and 30-35% of the vote in both parties, a very difficult challenge."

I could just imagine Steve at home in Tallahassee, crunching his numbers late into the night.

"He has to make the case to 1/3rd of all partisans that vote in an off-year election that they are better off with an independent than one of their own," he wrote. "Plus he has to figure out how to raise the cash without a party apparatus, and put together a team talented enough to win statewide in a place like Florida. Neither are easy tasks."

But Steve didn't call my Independent candidacy hopeless. "If anyone is up to the task, it's Crist," he wrote. "At the top of his game, Charlie is as good as anyone who plays it."

That was nice to hear.

As soon as I announced my decision, my entire campaign staff promptly resigned: my campaign manager, Eric Eikenberg; my media consultants, Russ Schriefer and Stuart Stevens; my pollster, Public Opinion Strategies; my communications director, Andrea Saul; and my press secretary, Amanda Henneberg. Most of them didn't hang around long enough to clean out their desks. They were just gone.

Andrea put out a boilerplate statement to the media, something to the effect of "It has been an honor to work for Governor Crist, and I wish him all of the best"—blah, blah, blah.

American politics can be an awfully tribal business. There are Republicans, and there are Democrats. The candidate who declares "I'm an Independent" had better be ready to say good-bye to a lot of supporters and friends. And staff too.

I understood the mass defections. These were Republican strategists and operatives. All of them cared about their careers. They were fearful that if they stuck it out through the general election, they might be labeled disloyal to the party and never get hired by a Republican campaign again.

Stuart and I kept talking. At the suggestion of my old friend Mike Hamby, I asked Eric to consider staying on. "Probably not as manager," Mike said, "but to help with outreach to Republicans. You'll need to reach out to both parties now."

I think Eric gave it a passing thought. He did what he needed to do. He had a family to take care of.

High-profile Republicans—people who had rushed to praise me what seemed like minutes ago—popped up immediately on TV and in the papers condemning what I had just done. Mitt Romney, the Republican presidential front-runner for 2012, pronounced himself "deeply disappointed." Bill McCollum, the Republican attorney general who was already running to replace me as governor, called my decision a "shortsighted maneuver."

Others who'd been frustrated with me for years, like Senator John Thrasher, now had another reason to complain. "He's been gone a long time in my opinion," snapped John, who doubled as chairman of the Republican Party of Florida. "This just makes it official."

Jeb Bush, who hadn't endorsed anyone in the primary, immediately threw his support behind Marco and encouraged his donors to do the same. "I hope all Floridians will ask themselves whether they want their next senator to be a rubber stamp for the Obama agenda or to stand up to it and offer a clear conservative alternative," Jeb said. He must have been reading the same talking points—or were they punching points?—that Marco was.

I'm sure there was some snarky conservative blogger somewhere who threw up a vulgar version of "Hey, jerk, don't let the door hit you on the way out!" But I didn't have time to keep up with the snarky bloggers. I had an oil spill to help with. I had an abortion bill to tussle over. I had a Senate race to run. And I had to replace a whole campaign staff.

On the same day as my big announcement, the state senate took up the ultrasound bill. The floor debate lasted barely three hours. In all my time around Tallahassee, I don't believe I'd ever seen the Senate spring into action as swiftly as that. Andy Gardiner described the mandatory ultrasounds as perfectly reasonable. Senator Ronda Storms, a Republican from Valrico, claimed the look-at-the-pictures rules weren't so strict at all. "I get to decide if I want an abortion after I look at those little toes, that little nose, that little bottom, that little baby," she said.

Democrats were calling it one of the strictest anti-abortion bills in the nation and an unjustified attack on women's rights. "You are going to put in Florida law a provision that requires a victim of a rape to actually tell someone she was raped, to get proof of the rape?" Senator Dan Gelber asked. "How wrong is that? Shame on the state of Florida."

The vote came very much like the one of Senate Bill 6. This time the count was 22–17. Ronda Storms was the only woman in the chamber to vote yes.

The House took up the bill—debated it and voted on it—the very next day, truly lightning speed for the Florida Legislature.

During the debate, the back-and-forth grew so heated and so graphic, House Republican leaders ordered teenage pages off the House floor and cleared all the children from the galleries. Two Democrats openly wept as they spoke to their colleagues against the ultrasound mandate.

Alan Hays, a Republican from Umatilla, invoked the Holocaust. "What are we as a society going to say years from now about the killing of fifty million babies since Roe v. Wade? How can you find the Holocaust so objectionable and be opposed to this bill?"

"Stand down if you don't have ovaries," Tampa Democrat Janet Long told her male colleagues.

Democrat Adam Fetterman of Port St. Lucie slammed the ultrasound requirement as "red meat" to appeal to religious fundamentalists in an election year. "It is designed to coerce a woman into changing her mind, if not scare her away from the doctor's office in the first place," he said.

Scott Randolph, a Democrat from Orlando, wept on the House floor as he described his wife having to abort a fetus that was dying inside her womb due to medical complications. After the third ultrasound, his wife could no longer look at the images on the screen and had the doctors turn it away. Scott said he wanted legislators who voted for the bill to feel his wife's pain as they tried to tell other women how to run their lives.

The Democrats' pleas had no noticeable impact. On April 30, the bill sailed through the Republican-controlled House.

The free-flowing oil wasn't waiting for gotcha politics, and I more or less moved to the Panhandle to coordinate Florida's response. I canceled campaign speeches and fund-raising events. The couple of events that did go ahead—one in Fort Myers at the home of my law school friend Liz Kagan—I called in on a speakerphone. The people understood. These were personal relationships, mostly—not the big Republican donors who had once supported me. Night after night, I stayed in little hotels. I gave interviews from the backs of little stores with scores of Florida journalists and others from around the world. I did a live shot from the coast with Bob Schieffer for his CBS Sunday show, *Face the Nation*. This was major, and everyone could see that.

I was on the phone with FEMA officials. I coordinated the county-by-county responses. I met many, many residents and business owners. This was a potentially catastrophic emergency. The governor had to be there and engaged. We visited the emergency operations centers, the EOCs, in all the affected counties—Escambia, Santa Rosa, Okaloosa, Bay—halfway down the state's west coast. The first responders were starting to float booms on the water—long, balloon-like contraptions that would act as barriers before the oil hit the shore.

It was all spill, all the time, for all of us.

We were lucky that, in 2009, President Obama had appointed Craig Fugate as administrator of the Federal Emergency Management Agency. Craig had run the Florida Division of Emergency Management for me. I hated to see him go. But he was a total pro. He knew Florida intimately. And having him on the scene made a huge difference for us. FEMA had obviously come a long way since Hurricane Katrina, when President George W. Bush caused so much eye-rolling by lavishly praising Craig's hapless predecessor, Michael Brown, saying: "Brownie, you're doing a heck of a job!"

Craig actually was.

To me, this was government doing exactly what government ought to do in a crisis. Assessing the dangers. Coordinating the response. Figuring out who was responsible and making them pay. Ensuring the right lessons were learned for the future. I was proud to be part of that. It was my idea of public service.

The other Gulf-state governors and I kept getting updates from Valerie at the White House, letting us know what new information Washington had, how federal environmental officials were coordinating with the states, and what new efforts were being made by BP and assorted other companies to seal the hole. The Obama administration was totally engaged. The other governors and I, along with other state and local officials, met with the president on May 28 at a Coast Guard station near the mouth of the Mississippi River in Grand Isle, Louisiana. We met with him again on June 4. The president and I walked Casino Beach in Pensacola. Vice President Joe Biden also showed up on the Panhandle, as did Janet Napolitano, the homeland security secretary. We had joint press conferences about all our efforts.

But as I came to see in a hurry, the other governors were reacting to all this far differently from the way I was. Despite the Obama administration's impressive efforts, my four Republican colleagues seemed to see the spill as a wonderful opportunity to pummel the president. Never mind that the administration had reacted swiftly, aggressively, and helpfully. Never mind that the federal government didn't cause the spill—private industry did. Never mind that all these Republican governors had fought vehemently against tighter safety and environmental regulations on the oil companies. Something bad had happened. Why not try to blame Barack Obama and the Democrats in Washington?

Haley Barbour, Bob Riley, and Rick Perry—they all took their shots. Complaining about the response from the Obama administration. Blaming not the companies that let this happen but the Democrats in Washington. Not one of them sounded remotely appreciative for the help from Washington. But it was Bobby Jindal, the young conservative governor of Louisiana who I'd shared a cabin with just a few years ago, who really came blazing at the president.

During the White House conference with the Gulf Coast governors and in at least two face-to-face meetings, Governor Jindal complained bitterly to the president, almost berating him.

"You're not doing enough," the Louisiana governor objected.

"You've gotta do more."

"This is just not acceptable."

"You come down and you visit, and you go away. And we're stuck here."

It was as if the commander in chief had personally swum down in fins and a scuba mask and disconnected the riser himself. Ideology and party politics, it seemed to me, were overwhelming reality again.

What else should the president be doing? It was hard to know, and none of the critics ever quite said. For his part, President Obama completely kept his cool. He didn't turn angry or defensive. He listened intently. He asked for our input. He shared specific ideas. He assured us he was deploying every imaginable resource and would keep doing so. He stayed focused. He acknowledged the governors' frustration and impatience, without ever once saying "You're right"—because they weren't. He remained the levelheaded leader from beginning to end.

Calm, I have found, is usually contagious. But Jindal at least seemed inoculated from it.

That Grand Isle meeting on May 28 was attended by quite a few other Louisiana officials, including the state's two US senators, Democrat Mary Landrieu and Republican David Vitter. Most of them pronounced themselves impressed by the president's focus and resources. Even Billy Nungesser, the Plaquemines Parish president, a notably plainspoken Republican who'd been all over national TV blasting the president, sounded unexpectedly impressed: "I feel like he really cares, and he's listening to us."

But Jindal just kept at it, trashing the president in public too. His favorite expression for the feds seemed to be "too little, too late." He said his state would take matters into its own hands, sending Wildlife and Fisheries agents out to patrol the coast. Exactly what they were looking for or what they would do once they found it— that wasn't entirely clear. But he kept complaining about what

Washington hadn't done. "We've been fighting this oil for over a month now," he said. "Too often, we've found the response to be too little, too late."

He demanded that the Army Corps of Engineers approve his $350 million plan to use dredged sand to rebuild the state's barrier islands as a natural buffer against the advancing oil, an idea environmental experts were calling harebrained.

I'm not sure if Governor Jindal knew or cared about one technical response or another. He just found something new to blame the president for.

I can empathize with the pressure he was under. The spill happened off his coast. He was closely aligned to the oil-and-gas industry. He had some political exposure, to say the least. And his citizens seemed receptive to his blame-the-president strategy. His poll numbers, which had been lagging, got a nice boost. I suppose I shouldn't have been surprised when he played the bash-Obama card. In this new political environment, attacking the Democratic president was the default position whenever anything went wrong, including environment disasters caused by a British oil-and-gas company headquartered in London.

It all just seemed so cynical to me, and the explanation was obvious.

The governors didn't want to get blamed themselves for not protecting their states. But they couldn't attack the oil companies, which had been big supporters of theirs, in Louisiana and Texas especially.

After one especially heated barrage at President Obama, Admiral Landry motioned me over to her.

"When I see these people argue with the president," she said quietly, "it makes me worry about my country. It is obvious President Obama is trying to do everything he can."

The admiral, who had been all-business, tough-as-nails for weeks, seemed to tear up momentarily. The emotion and the venom that she had just witnessed had obviously shaken her. Then, she regained her composure and returned immediately to work.

Chapter 18

The oil spill was a priority, but I was still in a Senate race—only now as an Independent with a much smaller campaign staff. To make TV commercials, I hired Josh Isay, a talented media consultant who had worked for Mayor Mike Bloomberg in New York. Bloomberg certainly had an independent streak. I admired him greatly. Josh brought in a terrific press secretary, Danny Kanner, whose media and political instincts I came to rely on heavily. Danny was totally engaged and utterly unwavering. But I still had to find someone to manage the campaign. I needed a person who was smart and loyal—someone I could really trust. And I couldn't go looking in the usual places, the networks of seasoned Republican or Democratic pros. The only obvious person who came to mind was my older sister, Margaret.

Margaret had been an elementary school teacher in Pinellas County. Lately, she'd been managing her husband's law office, the business and administrative aspects. She is very intelligent and very efficient. I was confident she wouldn't let any of our money be wasted. This was crucial because I wasn't sure what kind of resources we would have. I knew she loved me to death and would take good care of me. But it's fair to say that "campaign manager" wasn't exactly on my sister's lifelong to-do list.

"Let's be honest," I said to Margaret. "I'm in a bind."

"I've never done this before," she said. She said that several times, actually.

"Don't worry about it," I said. "I've never run as an Independent before either."

"I don't know," she said.

"We're in this together," I told her. "We're both gonna make mistakes, and that's okay. I trust you to watch my back. That's more important to me than any prior experience. No one anywhere has ever done this."

Margaret threw herself into the job immediately, working tirelessly, handling a thousand details at once. She kept apologizing to me. "I'm afraid I'm not gonna be able to do this well enough for you to succeed," she said.

"Just do the best you can," I told her. "We're all flying blind here."

And we were. Sometimes without a pilot or working radar. This was definitely shaping up as much more of a friends-and-family affair than your typical high-profile Senate run. We headed off on our ragtag campaign.

It was fascinating to see who hung around—volunteers, donors, and supporters. Quite a few of them did. Quite a few didn't. This being politics, I also got some "We'll sees" from folks who tried to walk a middle line. Some of my old friends and solid allies never thought of bailing out: They included Palm Beach County Commissioner Burt Aaronson, Democratic consultant Bernie Campbell, Republican State Senator Mike Fasano, Democratic State Representatives Luis Garcia and Darryl Rouson, and Democratic consultant

Kevin Cate. Michelle Todd didn't run for the hills like so many other Republican staffers from the governor's office. She stepped up as our political director. Tampa attorney Jeff Lieser was terrific. So was Eric Johnson, Robert Wexler's chief of staff. So were law school pals like Scott Weinstein, Liz Kagan, and Mike Hamby. At a time like this, you definitely discover who your friends are. These were real friends. My mom and dad and all three sisters stayed right by my side, as did Carole. She was the best cheerleader I had. Like me, she was a lifelong Republican who'd been growing disenchanted with the party's hard slide right. Growing up in New York and spending time in Florida, she was never *that* kind of Republican.

One group that was unwavering—thank you very much—was Florida's public school teachers. "We are a very loyal bunch of people," Andy Ford, president of the Florida Education Association, the state's largest teachers' union, told reporters after my announcement. Bob Butterworth, the former Democratic attorney general who then served in my administration, endorsed me at a teachers rally.

And I was just me. "I'm Charlie Crist, Independent candidate for the US Senate," I said when I'd meet new people. I liked the way that sounded, and I got the impression that other people liked it too.

But running as an Independent, as I kept discovering, is nothing like being the candidate of a major party—even a major-party candidate running in a primary. There's no built-in infrastructure. Nobody quite knows what to make of you. You wake up in the morning, and you're not really sure what to do. When you're the Republican or the Democratic candidate, all that stuff is laid out for you. You know who to call for money. You know what groups you can speak to. When you show up somewhere, the local party will help out. I swear I never truly appreciated it until it suddenly disappeared.

We had invitations. We were treated like a major campaign. We had offices in Broward, Palm Beach, and Leon counties, strong Democratic areas—and a headquarters in Tampa Bay because it was home. Given some of the bloodcurdling displays I'd seen in the primary, we figured we'd be stronger in Democratic precincts than in the heavily Republican parts of the state. I knew there'd also be a Democrat in the race, most likely Miami Congressman Kendrick Meek. I'd known Kendrick for years. I liked and admired him. I understood we'd be competing for some of the same Democratic votes, in South Florida especially. And I was still competing for the votes of Republicans. This was going to be very interesting—and very complicated too.

As Marco was looking stronger, money was pouring in to his campaign from deep-pocketed conservative donors across the country. These were the people who were fueling this new hard-edged Republicanism. They'd found all kinds of ways around federal campaign-finance limits, thanks in large part to the Citizens United decision from the US Supreme Court in January of 2010. The Koch brothers, Karl Rove, Dick Armey, and others—they were sending boatloads of money to Marco's campaign. In him they saw a perfect vessel for their bleak vision of a conservative America.

For us, money was obviously an issue. The campaign wasn't broke. We still had $7.6 million in the bank. But to run a first-rate statewide race, I knew, would probably take $20 million, and I had no idea how we would get there. A few of the Republican donors, not many, asked for their money back. John Cornyn, the Texas senator who'd needed all of fourteen minutes to throw the weight of the National Republican Senatorial Committee behind me when I first announced, demanded a $20,000 refund. "I know from my conversations with a number of Republican fund-raisers and donors that

that process is already well under way," he said. "I expect that will continue."

I don't think the Texas senator really needed the reimbursement. That was just his way of poking at my decision to go Independent. Actually, the money was already spent. The whole point, I believe, was to try to embarrass me and hurt me going forward. It wasn't working, but the shots were sure coming at me fast. Tom Grady, a Naples Republican, and John Rood, a retired ambassador to the Bahamas who lived in Jacksonville, rushed into a Naples court, demanding I return $7.5 million in contributions. My friend Scott Weinstein persuaded Circuit Judge Jack Schoonover that their class-action suit had no legal merit, and the judge tossed it out. The Republican Party isn't La Cosa Nostra! People are allowed to leave!

I was the same guy I'd always been. My values and my policies had hardly shifted an inch. But in the tribal world of politics, especially on the donor side, the party flag I was flying meant everything. Republican donors gave to Republicans. Democratic donors gave to Democrats. If you ever meet an Independent donor, please let me know.

Regular people don't think like this. I know they don't. But to the professionals in the game of politics, Charlie Crist, Republican, was a totally different animal from Charlie Crist, Independent. And funny, I didn't feel any different at all.

There was a positive side to all this. The Obama connection that had caused such grief for me in front of ginned-up Republican audiences was actually starting to work in my favor. Even as an Independent, I could now attract some Democratic support. According to an AP analysis—the data some reporters can find is amazing—contributors who'd given both to President Obama's 2008 campaign and to me suddenly increased fourfold.

We went all over the state, Carole and I and a few others, delivering my independent message, reminding folks that I'd always been for the people. I was never the rigid party guy. I was still Charlie, under whatever flag.

Margaret and the others were back at headquarters, keeping things more or less on track. Everyone stayed focused and upbeat, even knowing the odds. And for a minute, those odds didn't even seem impossible.

On June 9, five weeks after my switch to Independent, two new polls showed Marco and me in a tight general election race—and neither of the leading Democratic candidates able to break 20 percent. Quinnipiac had me at 37, Marco at 33, and Democratic front-runner Kendrick Meek at 17. The Rasmussen poll had Marco and me tied at 37 percent with Kendrick at 15 percent.

No one could say where this crazy race was heading. But my declaration of independence had certainly upended it. I know I was thrilled at the liberation I was already feeling. I could say what I wanted without getting "the look" from Republicans. I didn't have to explain myself to party officials, knowing I could expect cold shoulders and furrowed brows.

Requiring ultrasounds was cruel to women. That was obvious to me from the beginning. And I was sure the timing was no accident: to jam another wedge between me and conservative Republican voters. The legislative session was over, but I still had their messes to clean up. Just to be sure I was considering everything, I discussed it with the five women who were closest to me in the world: my wife, my mom, and my three sisters. "How dare they insert the state into a decision like that?" Carole asked one late afternoon. "This isn't something government has any business going near. You really want a bunch of politicians in the middle of a decision like that?"

Carole looked right at her politician husband as she said that. "Most politicians." She smiled. "You're my husband."

Like my mom and sisters, Carole isn't a feminist firebrand. She falls somewhere in the middle in her political views. Not one of the women in my life thought the leaders of the Florida Legislature should be deciding such personal issues.

Personally, I have always been pro-life. I believe life is precious and should be treasured. I like being alive. I don't think abortion is desirable. But that doesn't mean I always know what's right for everyone. Isn't that how mature people think? I've always been cautious about imposing my point of view on others when it comes to a decision as personal as this.

What's the point of that? It certainly isn't rooted in traditional conservative principles, one of which is "Stay out of other people's lives." If the thought is less government and more freedom, where's the freedom part? Seriously! Instead of trying to tell other people how to live their lives, just go and live yours!

Isn't that obvious? To me it is.

And what could be more important—or more personal—than a woman and her own body? Abortion has been legal since 1973 when the US Supreme Court decided Roe v. Wade. I understand not everyone agrees with the court's decision. Still, it is the established law of the land.

But zealots rarely give up. They keep finding other ways to fight. Abortion opponents, having failed to get the ruling overturned or to pass a constitutional amendment, have been trying to chip away at abortion, adding one onerous restriction at a time. Requiring unnecessary ultrasounds, I was learning, was the latest step down that twisted road. The game isn't hard to figure out: keep adding restrictions to this legal health procedure to make it more expensive, more invasive, more difficult, and more humiliating for any woman who dares to have an abortion.

The funny thing was, I knew that plenty of other Republican politicians agreed with me. But they were willing to say whatever it took to fire up the base. I get agitated thinking about this, even now. It's like the extremists in the party were becoming the party leaders, telling the rest of the people what to do every minute of every day. "And by the way," they inevitably add, "it's gotta be what I think is right—not you."

Extremism is infectious that way. Left unchecked, it'll eat us all alive.

Sadly, this overreaching moralism doesn't stop with abortion. I can extrapolate from the ultrasound debate to the treatment of so many other people who seem like "others" somehow. We've witnessed the rise of the antis in the Republican Party. Anti-minority. Anti-women. Anti-gay. Anti-immigrant. Anti right down the line.

"We have this certain view of the world," the antis say. "We're going to force you to think it too."

Well, I have another "anti" for them. That's almost anti-American.

On June 11, I vetoed the ultrasound bill.

"Individuals hold strong personal views on the issue of life, as do I," I wrote in my veto message. "However, personal views should not result in laws that unwisely expand the role of government and coerce people to obtain medical tests or procedures that are not medically necessary."

I preferred changing hearts to changing laws.

"Such measures," I wrote, "do not change hearts, which is the only true and effective way to ensure that a new life coming into the world is loved, cherished and receives the care that is deserved."

By the time the Deepwater Horizon well was capped on July 15, nearly 5 million barrels of oil had spilled into the waters of the Gulf of Mexico at a rate that at some points topped 25,000 barrels a day. It was the most massive oil spill ever in US waters. By comparison, the 1989 wreck of the *Exxon Valdez* released about 262,000 barrels into Alaska's Prince William Sound.

Indeed, some of that gloppy black oil washed onto Pensacola Beach—not as much as some experts had worried about but enough to wreck the Panhandle's heavy summer tourist season. As oil washed ashore, the crews who were out there cleaning did an exceptional job. Every morning before the sun came up, these men and women were out at the water's edge. They looked like miners with their headlights on, cleaning up the gook before people got up and saw it.

Three separate times, I declared a state of emergency for three increasingly large sections of Florida's Gulf Coast. Families were canceling their reservations and going to East Coast beaches or the mountains instead. It was a real punch in the gut to Florida's tourism economy. I asked BP chairman Tony Hayward to help pay for an advertising campaign telling potential visitors that the Florida Gulf Coast was inviting and safe. The oil giant coughed up $25 million in tourism-promotion grants, plus an additional $15 million each for Alabama, Mississippi, and Louisiana. I wasn't shy about asking, and BP seemed willing to pay. The scope of the long-term environmental damage remained a matter of intense debate. Some businesses never recovered. The lawsuits went on and on. Enormous damages were paid.

Out on the Senate campaign trail, Marco was still finding opportunities to blame the Democrats in Washington for the spill. "The federal government took its time responding to this early on," Rubio told Wolf Blitzer on CNN. "They weren't quick enough. I think that the bureaucracy continues to be in place."

Florida is facing "tragic" consequences, he contended, "because of the lack of response from the federal government."

Again, not a peep about how easing up on oil-company regulations in the name of free enterprise, as Marco had been pushing, would make Floridians and Americans any *more* safe. Like Governor Jindal, Marco had been an unquestioning booster of the oil industry his entire career. After his first session in Tallahassee, the Florida Petroleum Marketers Association even named him their Freshman Legislator of the Year.

In the end, I was proud to say, we protected the coast of Florida far more effectively than anyone ever expected us to. That's what can happen when federal, state, and local officials work effectively together. We got fair compensation for the damage that was done. We left the people of the Panhandle knowing that their state and federal governments were taking the threat seriously.

I was the governor, and in a spirit of true bipartisanship, I stood with the people in their time of great need.

Chapter 19

They were loud. They were proud. And they were chanting.
"*END CHARLIE'S BAILOUT!*"
"*END CHARLIE'S BAILOUT!*"
About a hundred Tea Party protesters turned up on July 15 on Gun Club Road in West Palm Beach at the headquarters of the South Florida Water Management District, a regional state agency responsible for protecting the state's clean water supply. Many of the protesters were carrying black-and-gold signs.

"END CHARLIE'S BAILOUT," the signs said.

Somewhere Barack Obama must have been breathing a sigh of relief. He wasn't being bashed for bailing something out.

I was the culprit here.

The agitated Tea Partiers were objecting to one of my proudest accomplishments as governor so far, the deal I'd announced in 2008 to purchase a huge swath of land from U.S. Sugar to improve the flow of surface water through the Everglades.

The protesters had a unique way of looking at what I considered a monumental environmental achievement. To them, it wasn't a once-in-a-lifetime chance to rescue a vital piece of our precious natural heritage. The $536 million for 730,000 prime Florida acres was an enormous corporate handout, just the latest in a long line of budget-busting boondoggles benefitting banks, car companies, transit systems, unionized government workers—and now, it seemed, thirsty alligators and crocodiles.

"We are tired of taxes without representation," Cindy Lucas, chairwoman of the Martin County 9/12 Tea Party Committee, told reporters. "People are suffering here in Florida, and we are going to go out and spend this money. No more bailouts."

"This is not going to stand," said a man named Edward Bender. "We know what's going on, and we're here to make sure the board members know." Meanwhile, inside the meeting room, another protester was handing each board member a box of cookies made with U.S. Sugar's product.

Their critique made no sense to me at all. The environmental benefits here were enormous. Buying the land was far cheaper and far more effective than any other imaginable approach. We'd negotiated what most experts termed an amazingly favorable price from U.S. Sugar. And according to officials at the Water Management District, the deal wouldn't require a tax increase.

Governors get protested every day over something or other. That just comes with the job. This gathering would hardly be worth mentioning except for one thing: This small knot of ill-informed protesters—and others like them—was about to have a huge impact on who Florida's next senator would be. It's amazing how much impact a small, motivated group can have. These revved-up extremists and their Washington backers really were redefining the Republican Party and altering the balance of political power everywhere.

As for the local gathering, Drew Martin of the Sierra Club

understood the practical politics immediately. "This is just an attempt to influence the election in favor of Marco Rubio," he said.

As the summer settled in, I was running ahead of Marco in most of the polls—but just barely. Marc Caputo's piece in *The Miami Herald* was headlined "Fragile lead for Crist in center." Marc laid out exactly what the challenge was for me: I had "a slight edge in the US Senate race—but to keep the lead, he must keep Democrats in his corner." And that wasn't proving easy. Marco's name recognition was growing. The Tea Party events were turning out real crowds. Now, the narrow gap between Marco and me was getting even narrower.

Marco wasn't the only candidate the Florida Tea Partiers were rallying around. Some of them were also talking up a wealthy businessman who had announced he would challenge Attorney General Bill McCollum for the Republican nomination for governor. His name was Rick Scott.

Rick was a dramatic-looking man with a shaved head and a slightly awkward manner. He had never held public office before. He'd built his fortune in the hospital and investment businesses, making his first splash in the political world by founding and helping to finance a group called Conservatives for Patients' Rights. Its mission: bringing "free-market principles" to health-care reform. What that seemed to mean in practice was, beginning in February of 2009, buying millions of dollars in TV ads attacking President Obama's Affordable Care Act and showing up on cable news to say how awful Obamacare would be. Rick Scott's broader political views were not entirely clear, but some things about him were unmistakable. He was staunchly conservative, though he wasn't a traditional party figure like Bill McCollum. And he had plenty of money to spend on the Florida governor's race. His personal fortune was estimated on the high side of $200 million.

As Marco and Rick were finding their campaign footing in Florida, Republicans in Washington were certainly taking notice of all the Tea Party activity around the country. In mid-July, Republicans in the House of Representatives formed a Tea Party Caucus with twenty-nine founding members, all Republicans, none of them minorities. Chairing the caucus was an especially strident congresswoman from Minnesota, Michele Bachmann. The lineup included the people you'd expect—hard-right Republicans from safe rural and suburban districts. But it wasn't all backbenchers. The caucus also included three of the seven members of the Republican House leadership—Republican Conference Chair Mike Pence of Indiana, National Republican Congressional Committee Chair Pete Sessions of Texas, and Republican Conference Secretary John Carter, also from Texas. There was one other notable caucus member—and a powerful Tea Party fund-raiser in his own right: Joe Wilson, the South Carolina Republican best known for screaming "You lie" at Barack Obama while the president was addressing a joint session of Congress.

In fact, all the caucus members seemed screaming mad at the president. Increasingly, they were the Republican base. They had the passion. They had the people. They had some wealthy donors and blog support. Now they even had a nice slice of the Washington leadership. Why get on their bad side?

It was a little tricky explaining exactly what the Tea Party Caucus was or what it would do. "We're not the mouthpiece," cautioned

Bachmann. "We are not taking the Tea Party and controlling it from Washington, DC. We are also not here to vouch for the Tea Party or to vouch for any Tea Party organizations or to vouch for any individual people or actions, or billboards or signs or anything of the Tea Party."

She sure seemed to be distancing the new caucus from the very people it supposedly represented. It sounded to me like she was trying to inoculate the group against some indefensible comment down the line.

"We are the receptacle," she explained.

She did not say what she was expecting to receive, although campaign funds and cable TV bookings seemed like a good guess.

But for staunchly conservative candidates like Marco Rubio, the Tea Partiers were a highly receptive audience. On August 14, two weeks before primary day, Marco made an appearance at the Sean Hannity Freedom Concert in Orlando. Sean, a conservative Fox News personality and talk radio veteran, frequently hosted Tea Party candidates and had publicly endorsed several of them. The night was a lively mix of politics and music. The musical highlight was Hannity singing "The Devil Went Down to Georgia" with the Charlie Daniels Band. When Sean got to the song's most famous line, he altered the lyrics to suit the audience: "I done told you once, you liberal son of a bitch, I'm the best there's ever been."

There was near pandemonium.

Not a bad opening act for Marco and his jab-Obama lines. "You know," he told the crowd, "people ask me all the time, 'Why are you running for the US Senate?' And the reason is simple. I want to win the Nobel Peace Prize. I'm just kidding. You have to be there two weeks to do that."

The president had been awarded the 2009 Peace Prize less than nine months after taking office. The Norwegian Nobel Committee cited his "extraordinary efforts" to strength international diplomacy, his commitment to nuclear nonproliferation, and a "new climate" in reaching out to the Muslim world.

On August 24, Rick Scott's anti-Obama ads, his Tea Party backing, and his hefty bankroll were enough to win him the Republican nomination for governor against Bill McCollum. The race wasn't even that close. The super-conservative businessman beat the establishment-conservative attorney general 47 to 43 percent. That same day, the official field for our US Senate race was formally set. Marco won the Republican nomination over token opposition. Kendrick Meek would be the Democrat. I was running as an Independent. There were a bunch of other minor candidates. As an Independent, I would not have a prominent spot on the ballot. My name would be listed ninth. The election would, as usual, be on the first Tuesday in November, which this year fell on November 2.

We banged our independent message as hard as we could. In the first week of September, the first full week after the parties' primaries, Josh Isay produced a powerfully clear TV commercial for me. In the ad, I am walking between two sets of giant block letters—red "REPUBLICAN" on my right, blue "DEMOCRAT" on my left.

"The way to get results for Florida and improve the economy," I say, "is by putting aside our differences and putting people ahead of politics."

All the while, I am rearranging the letters as I walk. "As an Independent, I will take the best ideas of Democrats and Republicans to get things done," I say. "Because at the end of the day, there's only one party I work for."

The camera pulls out to reveal that the letters now spell out "AMERICANS."

And then: "I'm Charlie Crist, an Independent, and I approve this message."

Across the country, the Tea Party train kept picking up speed. And the rhetoric was turning increasingly religious. On August 28, the forty-seventh anniversary of Martin Luther King Jr. "I Have a Dream" speech, conservative media star Glenn Beck came to Washington and held his own mass gathering at the Lincoln Memorial on the National Mall.

"Restoring Honor," Beck's rally was called, another version of "take our country back."

Tea Party activists came on charter buses and in family cars from everywhere, including Florida, for a long weekend of events. The crowd wasn't King-size, but it was massive, stretching all the way to the Washington Monument. Some media estimates said 500,000. The focus of the rally was more explicitly religious than political. Several of the warm-up speakers talked in considerable detail about their personal Christian faith, mixing in heavy dollops of American patriotism. Sarah Palin delivered the keynote address, honoring US military heroes and speaking in almost apocalyptic terms. "We must not fundamentally transform America as some would want," she said, never detailing who the dangerous "some" were. "We must restore America and restore her honor."

But this was Washington. Even with the religious overtones, politics was never far away. Hundreds at the rally sported stickers that read, "I can see November from my House too!"

After the national anthem and "Amazing Grace," Beck finally took the stage. This time, Beck sounded as much like a clergyman as a political prognosticator.

"Something beyond imagination is happening," he told the crowd. "America today begins to turn back to God."

Unlike Dr. King, Beck wore a bulletproof vest on stage.

As the race moved into the home stretch, Marco's crowds were growing larger and more enthusiastic. My poll numbers were slipping hard. And Steve Schale, the numbers-focused blogger and Obama Florida guy, took a fresh look at the mathematics of the race. His headline on August 31 wasn't encouraging at all.

"Sorry, Charlie," it read. "Charlie Crist will not be Florida's next United States Senator." Not much equivocation there.

Wrote Schale: "Rubio is limiting him to 20% of the Republican vote. If Rubio keeps him at 20% of the GOP vote, Crist needs to get 45% of the Democratic vote in order to win, and according to the latest PPP poll, Crist is only at 38% today with Democrats."

The three-way squeeze, he concluded, was almost insurmountable for me.

It was right around then that the really big conservative dollars started avalanching Marco's way. The Koch brothers gave. Karl Rove's PACs kicked in. So did Dick Armey and his friends at FreedomWorks. These outside givers could spend as much as they wanted. Many of the contributions were difficult to trace. The law prohibited the outside groups from coordinating with any campaigns, but the messages sure did jibe with the ones Marco was delivering. The National Republican Senatorial Committee—ah, my old friends!—contributed $2.5 million, the maximum allowed under federal law, to help elect Marco.

On September 15, he and David Barton—"Glenn Beck's historian and Tea Party favorite," as he was billed—packed 'em in at the

Alaqua Country Club in Longwood. Beck's historian laid out his theory that Thomas Jefferson's "separation of church and state" was intended to be a "one-way wall"—keeping the government out of the church's business but not the other way around.

Wow.

It's hard to quote this drivel with a straight face. But there are a lot of wacky theories in the air.

Marco told the group's overflow crowd at the country club that he was running to defend "American exceptionalism."

"When the story of this election is written, it'll say that it was a year when Americans kind of glimpsed what it would be like to redefine our country and said, 'No thanks,'" he said in an interview from the men's locker room, the only quiet spot in the clubhouse. Inside the Obama administration, he went on, "I think you have people who have dreamed of making America more like Western Europe." The Democratic president, he said, seized on the recession as "a perfect opportunity" to remake America, thereby sparking a response that became the Tea Party movement.

All over America, Tea Party–backed candidates were surprising establishment Republicans. I wasn't the only one the ground was shaking beneath. I was just one of the few who found new ground. On September 15, the same day Marco was standing with Beck's David Barton, political novice Christine O'Donnell, insisting she wasn't a witch, won an upset Republican primary victory over former Delaware governor and congressman Mike Castle for what was once Joe Biden's Senate seat. In New Hampshire, Ovide Lamontagne almost toppled the establishment pick, former attorney general Kelly Ayotte. Two weeks earlier, another Tea Party novice, Joe Miller, upset incumbent Republican senator Lisa Murkowski in the Alaska primary, although she would stage a triumphant write-in return in November. Her initial defeat brought to three the number of sitting senators toppled in primary contests that year, including Democratic senator Arlen Specter of Pennsylvania, who lost after switching parties, and Republican senator Bob Bennett of Utah. With endorsements from the Tea Party Express, the Club for Growth, Samuel "Joe the Plumber" Wurzelbacher, Phyllis Schlafly, and singer Pat Boone, outsider Republican Sharron Angle had won a chance to challenge Senate Majority Leader Harry Reid by easily winning the June 8 Nevada primary against several more moderate candidates.

Something genuine was happening—scary but genuine. Signs were popping up everywhere.

On the third weekend in September, a three-day Values Voters Summit was hosted by the Family Research Council, the conservative Christian lobbying group founded by James Dobson. This was a chance for top social conservatives to remind Republican candidates that low taxes and fiscal austerity weren't the only songs in the conservative hymnal. A keen focus on traditional social issues was important as well. But so much of the Tea Party energy had been devoted to economic concerns, Dobson and his people were concerned that Republican candidates might forget about gays, abortion, prayer in public schools, and other "family" issues.

Marco didn't attend. He probably should have. Michele Bachmann was there, slamming "elitists in Washington" who attended "wine-and-cheese parties."

"I prefer tea parties," she said.

She pronounced herself "giddy" at the prospect of revamping government with GOP electoral wins across the country that fall: "In November, the voter is going to speak again and this time I think they're going to shout."

The three main candidates in Florida's US Senate race met for a debate on October 6. George Stephanopoulos, the *Good Morning America* co-anchor and former Bill Clinton aide, came down to host us. It turned into the liveliest debate of the campaign.

"It's abundantly clear that there's an extreme right faction in the Republican Party," I said. "I'm the only candidate that can both win in November and crash that Tea Party in Washington."

This was the first high-profile televised debate broadcast live with all three of us together. It ran on ABC stations across Florida. As the Independent, I sat between Marco and Kendrick, which gave me a clear eyeshot at both of them. This was a perfect opportunity, I figured, to just be me. It wasn't like I had any party apparatus to please.

"You haven't been drinking the Kool-Aid, my friend. You've been drinking too much tea, and it's just wrong," I told Marco.

The reviews were good. The critics said I seemed loose and, yes, "independent." I couldn't agree more. I even got a tweet from Arnold Schwarzenegger three days after the debate: "I endorse Gov @charliecristfl for Senate. Great leader, works with both parties, and our country needs someone like him in DC right now."

On October 13, Robert F. Kennedy Jr. came down to Deerfield Beach to endorse me. I don't think the environmental lawyer and Democratic senator's son had endorsed too many people who had been elected as Republicans. But he'd come to one of our climate change summits in Miami, and we had really connected there. I think he saw me as an ally on the environment.

"The only person who can win this race and bring common sense to Washington is my friend Charlie Crist," he told the group of about a hundred supporters. Robert always says what he believes, often colorfully. He called Marco a "crackpot," a "radical," and a "sock puppet" who speaks for a "corporate plutocracy threatening to crush our democracy."

So what do you really think, Robert? No reason to hold back!

The Rubio campaign immediately denounced the comments and denounced me. "There's nothing he won't say or do to try to win an election," a Republican spokesman said.

Chapter 20

Talk about a Hail Mary pass! Two weeks before Election Day, during the week of October 18, Bill Clinton tried to convince Kendrick Meek to drop out of the US Senate race.

Twice.

And the former president almost succeeded, though not quite.

I was pulling from Republicans, Democrats, and Independents—people from all groups who were less concerned with labels and more open to moderate, commonsense ideas and policies. The hard political question was: With three candidates in the race, how many votes could I realistically get from each of those three categories? To understand why this was so important, all you had to remember was third-grade math—the lesson on how percentages work. The way I figured it, the hard-core conservative Republicans were all voting for Marco. He was their guy. There was no way Kendrick or I would grab any of that keyed-up Tea Party vote. Between us, Kendrick and I would divide the Democrats and Democratic-leaning Independents. He'd get the party-line Democrats, and I'd get the ones who'd liked what I had done as governor and attorney general. I'd get a big chunk of the Independents, who by definition were not label-focused. But to slightly oversimplify, our side of the electoral pie was being sliced into two pieces. Marco got to keep his piece all to himself. In a three-way race like this one, he had a real advantage.

According to the polls, Kendrick was stuck in third with about 15 percent of the vote. He'd never polled much higher than that. But if he decided to exit the race, wouldn't that throw core Democratic supporters to me? Real Democrats would never vote for an anti-government, Obama-bashing Tea Party darling like Marco. With Kendrick's 15 percent of the vote and my 30 or 35—I'm sure you can do the math better than I can. But the race would be a toss-up again. And with a two-man field, I could turn my full attention to beating Marco.

This was delicate business for all of us, President Clinton especially. It wasn't easy asking a hardworking Democrat and a good guy like Kendrick to leave a race he was running in, especially two weeks before Election Day. Kendrick was a long-standing Clinton ally. He'd supported the former president's wife, Hillary, over Barack Obama for the 2008 Democratic nomination. His mother, former Florida congresswoman Carrie Meek, was a beloved civil rights leader and the first African American to represent Florida in Congress since Reconstruction. It was her seat that Kendrick moved into.

Democrats in Florida and Washington, eager to stop Republicans from grabbing another Senate seat, were focused like a laser on the mathematics of the race. I was intensely interested, of course. Given the realities of the race we were in, consolidating our strengths might be the only hope.

Doug Band, one of the former president's top aides, reached out first to Kendrick, gauging whether he might consider stepping aside.

Only when Kendrick said he would consider it seriously did President Clinton become directly involved. I wasn't directly engaged in the back-and-forth. Some of this I got from the people involved. Some of it I learned from the media, in on- and off-the-record conversations.

Clinton flew down to Florida and campaigned with Kendrick on October 19 and 20. The ex-president spoke bluntly with the Democratic congressman. "There is no way you are going to win this race," he said. But he urged Kendrick to think about the impact leaving could have.

"You can be a hero here," the former president said. "You can stop Rubio from adding another Republican seat in the Senate. You can change this race in one fell swoop."

It sounded like the conversations were taking a while. The president worked on Kendrick one night until after 1 A.M., I was told. Kendrick went back and forth on what to do.

President Clinton never dangled a job in front of Kendrick, who had given up a safe House seat to run for the Senate. He just made the argument that dropping out of this race could advance Kendrick's long-term future.

The president thought he had a deal.

I got the call as I was walking out of a forum at the Poynter Institute in St. Petersburg. "He's dropping out," I was told. "The deal is done." As I was hearing the specific details, I noticed Brendan Farrington standing nearby. Brendan is a talented reporter for the Associated Press who had been covering the Senate race. He'd been asking, "What's up with Meek?" I thought to myself what a great scoop this would be for Brendan. But I didn't dare tell him what I'd just heard on the phone, and I'm glad I didn't. The news might have been true at the moment, but it turned out to be highly premature.

As the week wore on, Kendrick seemed to lose his enthusiasm for what the president had discussed with him. He'd talked it over with his wife, Leslie, an administrative law judge in Washington, he told other supporters. Now he wasn't so sure anymore. Leslie, he said, was convinced he could still win.

The time was ticking quickly. There wasn't much to spare. Election Day was November 2.

Reporters kept picking up little hints. No one had the whole story, but they had some strong whiffs that discussions were going on. The former president shared a few details with CNN's Susan Candiotti on Thursday: "He's trying to decide what to do. I talked to him, and I told him that—we went through everything, we talked about it a couple times. I said, 'In the end, you know you have to do what you think is right.'"

That sounded a lot like a confirmation. But for his part, Kendrick issued a carefully worded denial. "Any rumor or any statement from anyone that says I made a decision to get out of the race is inaccurate at best," he said. There was no deal, he said.

He conceded that Clinton had asked him about reports that he might be thinking of leaving the race. Not urged him to exit, just asked him about the reports. Kendrick said he'd put an end to that talk. "I am looking forward to being the next US senator from Florida," he told the reporters who were camped in front of his campaign headquarters. "President Clinton and I are good friends. He's continuing to be a supporter of this campaign. I count on his support."

But the private conversations continued. Clinton spoke again with Kendrick at the end of the week. By the weekend, the deal seemed back on. Our two campaigns had sketched out a date for the announcement and an outline of what everyone would say.

I was feeling really hopeful. This crazy dream of mine might not be over after all. I'd just have to keep pushing until the end.

On Sunday, October 24, nine days before the election, the Tampa Bay Buccaneers were hosting the St. Louis Rams at Raymond James Stadium in Tampa. There would be a big crowd for the football game, I knew. We were right out front on Dale Mabry Highway with our signs. As game time approached and most of the fans had gone inside, I asked, "Anyone feel like going to the game?" There had to be 65,856 people in there, give or take. Some of them were bound to be registered Florida voters, right? Plus, I figured a couple of hours of NFL football might give us all a break from the race. I bought last-minute tickets at the box office. My two Florida Department of Law Enforcement security agents used their badges to get in.

They weren't great seats, way high up on the west sidelines. During the game, Carole and I, with the officers at their usual discreet distance, headed to the concession area.

We were walking past a beer stand when a middle-aged, heavyset man in a Bucs jersey caught my eye. I smiled, but he didn't smile back.

"Have you lost your mind?" he yelled at me, loud enough to make people turn in a crowded football stadium. "What are you doin'?"

I stopped and looked.

"Why aren't you a Republican anymore? What's wrong with you? You're a freakin' moron."

By that point, he was moving toward me with fury in his eyes. I wasn't close enough to smell his breath, but from his lunging and his slurring, I would guess he'd had a few.

It was one of those moments where I was glad to have two highly trained security agents nearby. Don Schrenker, the larger of the two, stepped calmly between this person and me, urging him firmly to settle down.

He did, though not before a woman who was standing near him—his wife? his girlfriend? I don't know—gave me the most mortified look you could imagine, as if to say, "I'm really sorry. This is so embarrassing."

That's as far as it went, though I'm sure he would have been more than happy to take it out to the parking lot.

It could well have been the beer that was talking. But I suspected his hostile feelings reflected something deeper than that. With all that anger floating just beneath the surface, it didn't take much— two or three beers, maybe—to send it gushing wildly out.

I knew that in the abstract. I'd seen plenty of signs already. But there is something different when the rage is so up close and physical—and directed straight at me.

Thank you, Don.

Clinton had to make a quick trip to Jamaica, where he was speaking in Kingston on "Embracing Our Common Humanity." We picked Tuesday, October 26, as the tentative date for a joint rally in Miami—Kendrick, Clinton, and me—just as soon as the former president got back.

The plan was that Kendrick would explain to his disappointed supporters that their votes could truly save the Senate and stop a highly ambitious Tea Party favorite, a potential national leader, right in his tracks.

As the announcement day approach, there'd been all the maneuvering by intermediaries. But Kendrick and I still hadn't spoken directly. We finally had an opportunity to talk on Monday, October 25. I was eager to share my thoughts one-on-one with Kendrick and to hear his. We were both in Hollywood, Florida, for a meeting of AIPAC, the pro-Israel lobbying group American Israel Public Affairs Committee. He had spoken, and I was about to speak. We were surrounded by local Jewish leaders, but we had a few minutes to talk quietly. I tried to show him the empathy I knew the subject deserved.

"Kendrick," I said, easing into the difficult topic, "I know there have been discussions about leaving the race. I just want you to know that it could produce a very good result from our philosophical perspective. This could be a game-changer."

It wasn't easy finding words for a conversation like that.

"Of course, it would never be forgotten," I said, meaning only that. "It would be such a selfless act. I know Democrats and Independent-minded Floridians would appreciate it immensely. I'll never forget it. Neither will a lot of people who think and feel like you and I do on issues the Senate is certain to face."

Kendrick and I went way back. We had worked on education issues even before he went to Congress. When I was commissioner of education, he was a state senator. He asked me to come down to Miami Northwestern Senior High School in his district. There was some kind of testing issue at the time. I'd always been impressed by Kendrick and considered him a friend. We'd crossed paths at joint-candidates forums since I switched to Independent. With the history we shared, I was happy I was finally addressing this personally with him.

"We've always worked well together," I told him. "Certainly, if you leave the race and I end up being successful, your input on issues would be real important to me. You'd be one of my most important constituents if it works out that way."

Kendrick nodded and said "uh-huh" as I spoke. I could tell he was listening intently. But despite all the plans and discussions and announcement just twenty-four hours away, I could sense he was still struggling. He didn't say more than "uh-huh."

Before we parted, I gave him a small metal cross my sister Margaret had given me. "Just pray on it," I said. "Think about it. Do whatever you think is right."

He was very gracious while he was with me. But he didn't promise anything. The furthest he went was "I'll give it some thought."

I kept hearing the deal seemed on. Then maybe it wasn't. Then maybe it was again. It was quite a roller-coaster for everyone. Lots of people were paying attention from afar. I knew that Senate Democrats were getting minute-by-minute updates. They were itching to gauge who the next senator from Florida might be. I was in Miami with Danny Kanner, our campaign press secretary. We got a call: "Everything is finally worked out. We'll get back to you in an hour."

That hour turned into two and then into three.

As Kendrick's and Clinton's aides tried to button down the final details, Kendrick was backing away again. Finally, according to Clinton aides and other people close to the conversations, Kendrick just said, "Forget about it."

Kendrick didn't want to seem like a quitter.

He didn't want to disappoint his supporters.

His wife still thought he could win.

He went on CNN and specifically denied that any joint rally had been planned. Going even further, his campaign manager, Abe Dyk, vehemently denied the entire sequence of events that Clinton's aides and other Democrats had described.

"Kendrick Meek was not ever dropping out of this race and will not ever drop out of this race," the campaign manager said.

"He's going to stand up for the middle class as opposed to his two lifelong Republican opponents who always stand with the special interests."

That really took the wind out of me. We were so close to salvaging this improbable campaign for the Senate. Right there, I felt it slipping through my grasp. Ultimately, the third-grade math made the race unwinnable for me.

I could also see it from Kendrick's perspective.

He'd worked hard.

If I was so hot about someone dropping out of the race, he might have been thinking, maybe I should drop out instead—and throw my support to him. No way! Kendrick never said that to me, but I can imagine he was thinking it. It's only natural in a situation like that.

I hated what was happening. Things don't always happen the way you expect them to. I'd been around long enough to learn that lesson. It's politics.

We spent the final weekend on a bus trip across Florida. It was Carole and I and Republican State Senator Mike Fasano and our friend Watson Haynes, who is now president of the Urban League in St. Petersburg, and a few others. We had a large sign on the bus that said, "The People's Express." We started the tour very early Friday morning with a pancake breakfast at the Panama City Holiday Inn. I served the pancakes. We made an impromptu stop in Navarre Beach, shaking hands on the beach, slipping into little restaurants and bars. But I skipped my afternoon event in Pensacola to visit two Escambia County sheriff's deputies wounded in a gun battle earlier that day. I was kicking sugar-white sand off my shoes when I got to their bedsides. I was still governor. I couldn't not go there. Mike filled in for me in Pensacola.

The next day was more of the same. We made a stop in Live Oak, up near the Georgia border, where I hit the Dixie Grill, cooked up some mushrooms, and posed for photos with the staff. At a very cool local shop called Good Stuff, I bought a small waterscape painting for fifteen dollars. Carole and I went booth to booth at a yard sale. With two campaign bumper stickers, I taped a Crist poster to the stand of fifteen-year-old Katelynn Gamble and fourteen-year-old Travis Best.

"Way to improvise," Carole said.

"That's it, sweetheart," I agreed. We were definitely improvising.

We stopped into all these little communities and just talked to people. It was politics from a bygone day. Not many events set up. Not a lot of rallying people. Some media in the larger places. It depended on where we were. A couple of reporters rode along on the bus—Aaron Sharockman of the *St. Petersburg Times* and Jane Musgrave from *The Palm Beach Post*. We brought along a large blowup of Tuesday's US Senate ballot. As an Independent candidate, I was listed as an "NPA," no party affiliation. I wanted to make sure people could find me. It wouldn't be the first time Floridians had trouble navigating a ballot. I wasn't eager for a repeat of Bush versus Gore. "I'm number nine in your program," I told people, "but I hope I'm number one in your heart because you're number one in mine. I'm not kidding."

On Saturday, we also hit the Florida-Georgia football game in Jacksonville, campaigning among the high-spirited tailgaters in the parking lot. The Gators always draw pumped-up crowds.

We spent Saturday night in Volusia County at a stock car race in Daytona. Not at the legendary Daytona International Speedway.

This was a gritty old dirt track staffed with the friendliest volunteers you've ever met. I appreciated the symbolism of it. We were a million miles from the Daytona 500, but you know what? It was a real Saturday night.

We stopped by Fort Myers on the way back. My friend Scott Weinstein showed up with his family. We got a special appearance from guitarist Rickey Medlocke of the Southern rock band Lynyrd Skynyrd, which started in Jacksonville. It was special meeting him.

I was feeling okay. We were having fun. We were out there without much encouragement. But we were doing it. I definitely wasn't expecting to win. Our final-lap numbers weren't looking strong at all. Before that weekend, the polling had seemed to be improving a little bit. And I had the tiniest little glimmer of hope. I thought maybe the Independent thing could get us back to where we were in the summer when Marco and I were neck and neck. But then it seemed to all fall apart at the very end.

For six months I'd been campaigning as an Independent. On a personal level, my message did appear to connect. But in the final hours of the campaign, all of a sudden, it seemed very difficult to pull people away from the political parties they'd been comfortable in. Party loyalties aren't shifted overnight. Mine certainly hadn't. In the final analysis, the Republicans, even the moderate ones, mostly voted Republican. The Democrats mostly voted Democratic. That left an Independent like me grabbing for the middle at a huge disadvantage. That's what the polls were showing. As the People's Express rolled toward its final stop, that's how it felt to me.

Before we reached St. Petersburg, we stopped in Bradenton on the other side of the Bob Graham Sunshine Skyway Bridge at a super-friendly little restaurant-bar right on the Manatee River. We shook hands with everyone. I gave a little speech. I kept seeing these little knots of enthusiasm.

A man in the restaurant asked me if I had any regrets about leaving the Republican Party and continuing this race on my own.

"Regrets?" I asked. "You kidding? This is great."

And the funny thing was, that was true.

I wasn't regretting what I had done at all. I was delighted to be an Independent. I really did feel free, even though it certainly didn't seem like we'd be coming in for any soft landings at the end. I couldn't stay in the Republican Party the way it was—and stay true to who I am. I was fully at peace with the decision I had made and had no qualms or remorse or second thoughts—nothing like that. To be honest with myself, I did what I had to do.

Our last stop before we got home was St. Pete Beach at a busy place called the Hurricane in historic Pass-a-Grille. It's a big restaurant with mouthwatering fried-grouper sandwiches.

"Down one road is extremism, Sarah Palin and Marco Rubio," I told a crowd of about a hundred. "And that's not what Florida is all about. I know it in my heart."

We wrapped up there on Sunday night.

I was feeling tired but comfortable, ready to press on.

On Monday, the final day before Election Day, we left from St. Petersburg's tiny Albert Whitted Airport on a one-day fly-around. We didn't have one of those fast leased jets like we'd used on past campaigns. This was a five-seat, two-engine propeller job. Air Charlie had definitely gone downscale. Hoarse from campaigning, I sucked Halls cough drops.

We made several tarmac stops, had a couple of nice rallies, did some local preelection media interviews, and got some splendid views of the Florida landscape. "This race is about mainstream versus extreme," I said several times.

Our last event was back in the airport in St. Petersburg at a restaurant called the Hangar. There was a keyed-up crowd of a couple of hundred people. It was old friends, new supporters, a mix of political and media people—and some who'd gotten inspired by the independent vision I'd expressed in the campaign. I said a lot of thank-yous, and I meant them. Through one of the wildest campaigns in history, these people had all stuck with me. It was a whirlwind final few days, exhausting but also exhilarating. Carole and I went home to our condo for the night.

This was ground-level, nuts-and-bolts politics. The whole thing felt like 1992 all over again, and I was running for the state senate in St. Petersburg again. Only that was a race I had been pretty sure I was going to win.

We woke up on Election Day and did some sign waving with volunteers outside the Tyrone Square Mall. It's a goofy Florida tradition that I know occurs elsewhere—though not with the verve and frequency that it does in Florida. But I like it, and we got a very warm reception, people honking and waving and smiling back.

Our hoped-for victory party was set for that night at the Vinoy Renaissance hotel in St. Petersburg. That's where I'd held my exuberant victory bash four years earlier when I'd won the governor's race and where Carole and I held our wedding reception. We checked in late in the afternoon and tried to get a little rest.

My family was there and a few key supporters from around the state. But mostly it was local people—friends, relatives, campaign volunteers, people I'd known and worked with for years. They didn't care what party I was in or whether I was in any party at all. They believed in what we'd been doing together for decades.

The polls closed at 7. Carole and I had the TV on in the room. They called the race by 7:30.

Marco Rubio, the Republican, 49 percent.

Charlie Crist, the Independent, 30 percent.

Kendrick Meek, the Democrat, 20 percent.

It was another quickie call for me on a US Senate race, almost as fast as my 1998 stomping by Bob Graham. Maybe I'm not supposed to be in the US Senate after all.

It was a very big night for the Tea Party. While Marco was scooting to victory in the three-way Senate race, Rick Scott was winning the governor's race. Rick narrowly defeated Democrat Alex Sink, the state's chief financial officer, 49 percent to 48 percent, a difference of about 61,000 votes. The victory didn't come cheap. When I was elected to the job four years earlier, I'd been the poorest governor in modern Florida history. Rick was definitely the richest. The Election Night commentators all noted he had spent $75 million of his own money on the race.

I still had an election to concede. And Carole really didn't want to go downstairs.

"I can't believe it," she said. "This just doesn't seem right to me."

"Carole," I said, "we gotta kinda suck it up. Put our best face on this thing. It's okay. It's not the end of the world. Nobody died. It's just an election."

She had never been through an election before. This was my third defeat. I knew what losing an election felt like and how to deal with it. But she was hurting.

From the hotel room, I put in a congratulatory call to Marco at the Biltmore in Miami. Out of courtesy, I asked him what time he wanted to give his victory speech. I told him I'd deliver my concession right before that. "You can have the finish," I said.

"Thank you," he said.

It was a short, stiff conversation. We didn't swap any stories or trade any laughs. I just wanted to stay gracious and professional. I think Marco did too.

I talked with Kendrick, as well.

"You ran a great race," I told him. "My best wishes to you."

I didn't say anything about his decision to stay in. I couldn't help but notice that his portion of the pie and mine, added up, together were larger than Marco's. My third-grade math had been proven right. But that was old news already. The votes were counted now.

Around 8:45, Carole and I went downstairs together to face the music. There were many differences between this night and the victory celebration four years earlier, even beyond the election results. This time, the Vinoy's enormous ballroom was cut in half with floor-to-ceiling room dividers. There were fewer lobbyists and elected officials and representatives of special interest groups. Overall, the crowd was smaller. But it was far more diverse. We had Democrats and Republicans and Independents. And they seemed to be getting along. We had people who just wanted a better Florida and didn't identify with any political grouping at all.

I said a few words, thanked everyone, and called it a night.

Chapter 21

I felt disheartened by the defeat, no question about it. To rise from state senator to education commissioner to attorney general to governor, then run into the blades of a political thrasher like that—to go from a 70 percent approval rating to getting just 30 percent of the vote—it wasn't supposed to go like that. The force of this extremism was something to behold. I hadn't really prepared for losing. I didn't have a plan B.

I couldn't help but wonder: How did I let this happen? And what am I supposed to do now?

I'm not normally much of a brooder, but I'd be lying if I said I didn't second-guess myself a little. All kinds of thoughts were bouncing around my head. *I've had a great run, but is it over? Am I politically dead now? What's next for me?*

The two months between Election Day and Inauguration Day were not the easiest time for me. Obviously, I had none of the excitement I'd been feeling exactly four years earlier, staffing up a new administration and canceling that gold-plated inaugural ball. This was more like marking time. I was still the governor of Florida, which is one of the best jobs ever. I was still living in the mansion with Carole. I was going to the big office in the Capitol every day, immersing myself as much as I could in the duties of being governor. But I'd been soundly defeated in the Senate race, and a new guy was preparing to take my old job.

Winners have more friends than losers do. That's true throughout life. But it's especially true in the winner-takes-all world of politics. Some people don't even want to be seen with the guy who's just been defeated at the polls. They don't know what to say. And as a practical matter, there isn't much the loser can do to show his gratitude for past support.

Carole was a terrific strength for me. She made sure I understood that she didn't love me just because I was the governor and she got to be First Lady. I knew that already. Of course, I did. But it was wonderful to see her in action. My parents, my sisters, the rest of the family, and some of my oldest friends—they were all there for me. All of them helped to keep my spirits up. But it was tough some mornings to pick myself up and go to the office and get things ready for the new governor coming in. Temperamentally, Rick Scott and I seemed like very different people. He was a hard-charging businessman. I was the bipartisan coalition builder. He was the government-is-bad Tea Party guy. I'd made much of my career in government, helping people. But he was, in fact, the governor-elect of Florida, and come January 4, he'd be sitting in my old chair. So without a doubt, I would be civil and help him get settled in his new job. It was the right thing to do, and Jeb Bush had done it for me. "He's the man, so treat him well," I remembered Jeb telling the Capitol press corps on my Inauguration Day, before he quietly slipped out of town. That was very classy, I thought. That's how I wanted to be.

Hopefully, we'd have a smooth transition, and Florida wouldn't miss a beat.

Some of my oldest friends made a point of reaching out, Democrats and Republicans. Chris Searcy, a talented South Florida trial lawyer I'd known forever, called just to see how I was. Rodney Barreto, a Republican lobbyist I'd always respected, was very kind. One long-ago day at Pierre's in the Keys, Rodney had told me I should think about running for governor. I knew he'd be with me, coming in and going out. Harry Sargeant, my old Florida State friend now running a worldwide energy and shipping company, called to buck me up. "Don't worry about it," said Harry. "Everything will be fine." You remember calls like those when not too many calls are coming in. It's crickets out there after you lose a race.

Long before I began focusing on my own future, some other people obviously were. The Florida Democratic Party chairman, Rod Smith, came to see me at the mansion. I met with him in the same room where I'd met with Jeb when he was governor. Rod had been around Florida Democratic politics for a long time. He ran in the Democratic primary in 2006. Four years later, he was the party's nominee for lieutenant governor, running with Alex Sink. And now he was state party chairman.

"If you'd been one-on-one with that guy," he said of Rubio, "you would have won that race." I'd already done the math. But it was interesting hearing the Democratic chairman say it to me. Was he hinting at anything?

And then he said it: "I wish you would think about becoming a Democrat."

I got a call from Bob Graham. "I just want you to know," the former governor and US senator said, "you're welcome in my party any time." I wasn't ready to make a jump like that, but it felt great to be asked.

I'm always hopeful about the future, and those calls helped. I wasn't someone who was going to mope for very long. I'm just not wired that way. I am who I am.

I knew I wasn't ready to retire. I was only fifty-four. That's not old, certainly not in Florida. I had to plan something for myself. That's what defeated politicians do. I had to find a job. So along with the daily duties of being governor, I spent some of those sixty-three days trying to figure out what might come next for me. I had some good prospects, several of them, thank God. I got recruited by a large law firm called Blank Rome, which has strong government-affairs and international-law practices. They were very encouraging. The managing partner came to meet me at the mansion to talk about going with them. I got similar overtures from an excellent firm in South Florida, Greenspoon Marder.

The real blessing turned out to be John Morgan. Morgan & Morgan, which John heads, is a large personal-injury law firm whose slogan is "Representing the People, Not the Powerful." The firm has offices across Florida, Georgia, Mississippi, Tennessee, Kentucky, and New York. John, who had a lot of friends and influence inside the Democratic Party, had been a loyal supporter of mine even though I was a Republican. I'd gotten to know him personally, and he stuck with me even as I was on my way out the door. He called me on the phone one day in November and said, "I don't know what you're considering now. But we'd love to have you at the firm. We think you could help us, and I think it would be very good for you—a comfortable situation all around."

I knew a lot of people, he told me. And I had great relationships across Florida and beyond. Despite the crushing defeat, I really stood for something—looking out for people. And that was exactly what the firm stood for.

In those final, lame-duck days as governor, I got a few lingering tasks done. I made an appointment to the Public Service Commission. We struck a long-awaited agreement with the Seminole Tribe to funnel $1.75 million of casino-gambling proceeds to the Florida Council on Compulsive Gambling, nearly doubling that group's funding overnight. And I convinced my fellow members of the Clemency Board to grant a posthumous pardon to rocker Jim Morrison, who was convicted of profanity and indecent exposure after a 1969 Doors concert in Coconut Grove. That may not rank as a major governmental achievement. But it was long overdue. The late singer was a native of Melbourne, Florida. He was a student at Florida State, like I'd been, and a seminal rock-and-roll artist. There was still a lot of confusion over what exactly Morrison did or didn't do onstage that night. He died before his appeal was ever ruled on. And I didn't imagine Rick Scott was much of a Doors fan.

The incoming governor and I didn't have much personal contact, although our staffs worked closely—and amiably—on transition details. He and his wife, Ann, did come by the mansion for the symbolic lighting of the Hanukkah menorah. All the reporters noticed that Rick and I briefly held hands as we danced the hora with several school children.

No, they don't teach that at the Kennedy School of Government.

We stood together for a brief Q&A with reporters, which produced one exchange I thought was funny at the time.

"Are you going to replace everyone in the Crist administration, or will there be some holdovers?" one of the reporters asked Rick.

"He's certainly replacing me," I said, jumping in.

"Well, Governor Crist will be hard to replace," Rick quickly added.

I've always believed that laughter can be the best medicine.

On December 21, eleven days before I was set to go, I sat down with Troy Kinsey, Capitol reporter for Bay News 9, the cable news network for the Tampa Bay area. It was the closest thing I had to an exit interview.

At the Florida Capitol Press Corps Skits every year, Troy was the reporter who had the luck—or was it the burden?—to play me. I have to say, he had my voice and my mannerisms down cold. But what was that ridiculous white wig? Troy was such a talented mimic, I heard that during all the vice presidential talk, the other reporters kept urging him to submit a tape of himself to *Saturday Night Live*—just in case.

But he was all business in our interview. He asked what I was proudest of. I told him that I'd managed to be a genuine populist—"the people's governor"—while still holding the line as a fiscal conservative. "I signed the largest tax cut in the history of the state, reduced government spending more than any governor in the history of Florida, about seven-point-four billion dollars in reductions. I'm very pleased about that. I think it's what the people wanted and needed, particularly in this economy."

Given that, Troy pressed, why such hostility from Republicans?

That was easy. "Because I was kind to President Obama," I answered.

"It was pure and simple," I told Troy. "The hard-right part of the Republican Party really had taken hold. You know, I was anti-tax, pro-life, wanted to do the kinds of things that generally Republicans embraced. But it wasn't pure enough, and I'm not sure what that meant. But it made me uncomfortable. So I became an Independent. It's not about one club or the other."

I'm not sure how Troy got me to unload like that. Maybe his time onstage pretending to be me had taught him to push certain buttons of mine.

Some of the staffers asked if I felt like holding a big good-bye dinner.

"Nah, not really," I said. But we did a few small receptions for staffers, agency heads, and reporters.

We had a lot to be proud of, I thought. In just one term, we lifted Florida's high school graduation rate. We pushed crime down and then down some more. We beat back those runaway property taxes and insurance premiums. I signed a groundbreaking piece of legislation that restored the legal rights of nonviolent felons—including the right to vote—after they'd done their time. We certainly ran a more open and inclusive government than Floridians were used to, welcoming women, minorities, teachers—*even Democrats!*—back to the table in Tallahassee. We got billions of dollars in federal stimulus money from the Obama administration and used them well. We were on the way to winning federal funding for a high-speed rail line from Tampa to Orlando, which would improve transportation, cut pollution, improve our infrastructure, and create twenty to thirty thousand new jobs for Florida.

The list goes on. I think we achieved an awful lot at a very difficult time for the national economy.

And many Floridians seemed to agree. As my term came to an end, my approval ratings were the highest they'd been all year. A Public Policy Polling survey just before Christmas said 50 percent approved of the job I was doing, compared to 39 percent who disapproved. Not so bad for a guy who'd just been clobbered in the voting booth.

I made a point to leave office on an upbeat note. I offered no advice to my successor. Advice from me was the last thing Rick Scott wanted to hear. I had no harsh words for George LeMieux, who I'd appointed to the Senate and who had then supported Marco Rubio, or for Jim Greer, the disgraced Republican Party chairman, or for a handful of others my closest friends were unhappy with.

"I sleep very well at night," I told the reporters on my way out the door. "If you don't follow your heart and your gut instincts, what is it that you're following? I'm very content."

I attended Rick's swearing-in on the steps of the Old Capitol. I sat with his mother, who could not have been nicer to me. I wished the new governor well.

He was gracious to me and thanked me for a smooth transition.

During his address, someone in the crowd yelled at him, very loudly: "You're a crook!" Everyone could hear it, and it seemed to take Rick by surprise. I felt for him. I was barbecued once too.

I didn't hang around Tallahassee for Rick's inaugural ball. No, he didn't cancel his. Right after the swearing-in, I did what Jeb Bush had done on my day. I slipped quietly out of town.

Gina Bovino, who headed my Florida Department of Law Enforcement security detail, drove me to Tallahassee Regional Airport, where a state plane wasn't waiting for me. That part, I didn't care about. The perks were never what drew me to this job. I boarded a US Airways puddle jumper back to Tampa. I drove myself the rest of the way home to St. Petersburg, where Carole was waiting for me. And I got on with the rest of my life.

Chapter 22

Rick Scott didn't only bring a new administration to Tallahassee on January 4, 2011. He also arrived with a wrecking ball. He'd barely unpacked his toothbrush and his custom-made, Florida-seal cowboy boots when he got busy knocking down some of our proudest achievements. Rolling back consumer protections. Reversing the progress on voting rights. Signaling to the oil drillers, utilities, and insurance companies that Florida was open season again. In Tallahassee, the whole tone changed. The bipartisanship that had been such a hallmark of the past four years evaporated with the first morning dew. Democrats were still welcome to their opinions—but no one in power had any interest in listening to them. Teachers, minorities, women's groups, and anyone else suspected of being even faintly Democratic—they were back on the please-don't-bother-us list.

Only I don't believe too many people in the new administration were saying "please."

I didn't have anything personal against the new governor. I barely knew the man. He was born in Illinois, went to college in Missouri, and received a law degree and made his fortune in Texas. From what I'd read and heard from others who knew him, he'd generated quite a lot of controversy on his road to big success. Back in the late-1980s, he'd cofounded a company called Columbia Hospital Corporation, which merged with several other companies including HCA, the Hospital Corporation of America, to become the largest for-profit health-care provider in the world. At one point, Columbia/HCA owned 340 hospitals. Rick made news in 1997 when he was forced to resign as chairman and CEO after the FBI, Internal Revenue Service, and Department of Health and Human Services launched an investigation into allegations of massive Medicare-billing fraud. In settlements signed in 2000 and 2002, the company pleaded guilty to fourteen felonies and paid the government $1.7 billion in fines, which the Justice Department termed the largest fraud settlement in US history. By then, Rick had become a venture capitalist and opened a chain of urgent-care clinics. He moved to Naples, Florida, in 2003, found his way into the national health-care debate, began showing up on the cable-news shows, and entered Florida politics.

You know me. I'm always an optimist. I hoped Rick Scott would do a wonderful job as Florida's new governor. But from the day he took the oath of office on the Old Capitol steps, I have been deeply disappointed in the things he's done to our Florida. There's no other way to say it: He's been a terrible governor, and that's not just because I miss having the job. It's because I care about the people of my state.

There are many, many examples of the new Republican governor stalling, reversing, or sidetracking important progress that we made for Florida during the previous four years. Major things. Petty things. You name it. Taking $1.3 billion from our improving public schools, then grabbing another $300 million from our state universities. Nuking the state's Department of Community Affairs. Packing state regulatory boards with industry softies. Cutting back on early-voting hours—again! Organizing "Governor Rick Scott's Education Accountability Summit" after his third education commissioner resigned, then failing to show up at all at the heavily hyped three-day event. (A few days later, he did find time to attend the Koch Brothers' Americans for Prosperity Tea Party convention.) Announcing he would accept expanded Medicaid funds but then, in the face of a conservative uproar, barely lifting a finger to convince the Republican-controlled legislature to go along, dooming the much-needed benefits. Rick even booted my personal barber off the state Barbers' Board just as he was about to lead the industry's national organization. But there was no single decision any more boneheadedly counterproductive than turning down $2.4 billion in federal money for high-speed rail.

I still find it astounding. For almost three decades, Florida had been discussing high-speed rail. Once I was governor, it took three special sessions of the legislature and some extraordinary work by the state Transportation Department. As my term was ending, everything was all but wrapped in a bow—the politics, the funding, the local approvals, the right-of-ways, literally everything except depositing Washington's check in the bank. Even the Republican House Speaker and the Republican Senate president were on board. People were genuinely excited about what was coming our way: state-of-the-art trains racing along the median strip of Interstate 4 at 170 miles an hour between Tampa, Lakeland, and Orlando, the first major segment of a world-class triangular rail link that could stretch eventually to Miami. Kids in Tampa could go back and forth to Disney on an easy day trip. Orlando tourists could spend a breezy afternoon on a white-sand Gulf of Mexico beach. Development would be spurred along the I-4 corridor, creating more investment and more jobs. And if the modern train service happened to take a few cars off the congested interstate, call that a welcome bonus.

Did I mention the feds were paying for *everything*? Yes, everything.

Private construction firms, thrilled to get the work, had even agreed to eat any unforeseen cost overruns. We'd create 23,000 construction jobs plus another 1,000 permanent positions. One state report concluded that high-speed rail would generate a reliable annual surplus for Florida of $31 million to $45 million within a decade of operation. And we'd leave behind a phenomenal piece of clean-transportation infrastructure for the benefit of generations to come.

How could Rick Scott possibly say no? Actually, it was more like "hell, no!"

On February 16, six weeks after taking office, the new governor announced he was rejecting the entire $2.4 billion.

Every last cent of it.

"This project would be far too costly to taxpayers, and I believe the risk far outweighs the benefits," he said.

What?

It was as if Rick hadn't read anything at all about the project or its funding. As far as I could tell, he just knew the project came from Washington and a Democratic administration—so it had to be bad. That's how blinding this new zeal can be.

I wasn't the only one shocked by his decision. I think most Floridians were. When the formal offer came from US Transportation Secretary Ray LaHood, everyone expected Rick to accept it. He had run for governor on a jobs agenda, after all. Our unemployment rate was up near 11 percent. There are tough decisions that governors have to make. This wasn't one of them. It wasn't like, if Florida didn't take the funding, it would go help pay off the federal debt. That $2.4 billion would just go to a rail project in some other state. Would the new governor really let the money and jobs go to California, where Governor Jerry Brown made clear he'd be more than happy to grab them both? This truly was *our* money. Florida is what's called a "donor state." Our citizens usually send more money to Washington in federal taxes than we get back in federal spending. Finally, we could jump a little ahead of the game.

The newspapers could not believe it. The mayors and county officials from Tampa to Orlando were uniformly aghast. And it wasn't just Democrats. US Congressman John Mica of Winter Park, the Republican chairman of the House Transportation Committee, said the decision "defies logic." Republicans in the Florida Legislature were shaking their heads. Twenty-six state senators, a veto-proof majority and a rare coalition of Republicans and Democrats, signed a letter to LaHood rebuking the new Tea Party governor and asking the US Department of Transportation to send the funds anyway. "Politics should have no place in the future of Florida's transportation," the senators wrote.

"This was going to be a model for the nation," said Republican Senator Paula Dockery of Lakeland, an early Scott supporter who drafted the letter along with fellow Republicans Thad Altman of Viera and David Simmons of Orlando.

Added Simmons, "This is like holding a gun to our heads and telling the federal government: Don't give us this money or we'll blow our brains out."

Two state senators, Republican Altman and Democrat Arthenia Joyner of Tampa, filed a petition in the Florida Supreme Court, trying to compel Rick to accept the funds. They argued that he lacked the legal authority to turn back the funding since it had already been approved by a previous legislature. On March 4, the Florida Supreme Court held that Rick's move did not violate the Florida Constitution.

It might be dumb or irrational or damaging to the Florida economy, the judges seemed to say. But technically speaking, it wasn't unconstitutional.

Rick wasn't entirely alone in his keep-your-money approach to Washington. The Republican hostility to the economic-stimulus plan seemed to have spread a bit. Two other newly elected Republican governors turned down a portion of the Obama administration's national rail system. Governor Scott Walker, who was already dodging recall efforts, rejected a segment in Wisconsin. John Kasich did something similar in Ohio. Like Rick, they also replaced governors who had lobbied hard for the funds. Like Rick, they'd gotten heavy support from Tea Party groups.

Jerry Brown must have had a huge smile on his face when he learned the money really was heading west instead.

Polls aren't everything. Believe me, I've learned that the hard way. But they do deliver a quick snapshot of how people are feeling about their leaders. Right out of the box, the new Florida governor's approval ratings slid into the mid-30s, which is pretty much where they have remained. The Rick years have looked like a consistent case of buyer's remorse.

"My God, is this guy really the governor?" people were asking almost from the start.

He was. And the hits kept coming.

The legislature quickly passed, and the new governor quickly signed, something called the Student Success Act. Nice name, terrible idea. It was really just a retread of the dreadful teacher-tenure bill I'd vetoed the previous year, limiting teachers to one-year contracts and setting up an inflexible student-testing regime. But it pleased the union haters and made Tea Party folks happy.

This wasn't by accident. His very first state budget included a $1.3 billion cut for public schools. It was like he told Florida's teachers and students, "Nice to meet you—here's a devastating budget cut." I understand the need and desire—and the constitutional requirement in Florida—to balance our budget. I balanced four of them. But I'm sorry. I don't believe in doing our balancing on the backs of our teachers and students. Whatever you think about the importance of knowledge and learning, these young people are the economic future of our state. We have to provide them with the tools to succeed in a changing world. We must prepare them for the jobs that are coming next. How else will we ever convince business and industry, "Come on down and let our highly trained workforce help you to grow"?

Cutting $1.3 billion is an enormous assault on education. It's just devastating. That isn't cutting at the margins or trimming bureaucratic fat. With cuts that massive, you're firing teachers and shutting down programs and taking away things that kids really need like phys ed, art and music classes, and in-class teaching assistants. And that's exactly what happened in the first year. And then in year two, adding insult to injury, Rick and the legislature hit Florida's college students with an additional $300 million whack.

But here's what was kind of screwy: In the third year of the new administration, as the question of reelection began to loom, it was like a light went on in the governor's head. It was as if someone woke him up and said: "You know, maybe it actually is important to teach kids about science and math and anthropology. That way, maybe they can realize their dreams of becoming doctors or lawyers or teachers" or whatever they aspire to. So the governor did a fast 180-degree turn and began to restore the cuts that he'd just made. Though not entirely. The reversal wasn't $1.3 billion. It was more like $800 million. But I suspect it'll take a whole lot more than one-time $2,500 bonuses to win the love of Florida's public school teachers. Clearly, the new governor had a highly narrow view of what government can accomplish. As a fiscal conservative, I liked running lean and mean. He just liked running mean.

He ordered welfare recipients to pass drug tests before getting aid for their children. He did away with the entire Department of Community Affairs. That was the state development watchdog, which balanced the legitimate needs of the economy with the legitimate needs of the environment. Both are important, obviously. And the Department of Community Affairs had proven itself over the years with its expertise and sensitivity in balancing all that. Killing the Department of Community Affairs was like killing the federal Environmental Protection Agency. You might get some cheers from industry groups, but the consequences could get ugly over time.

Now, it wasn't just that environmentalists had lost their seat at the table. The table legs were hacked off and tossed into the pulper. The tabletop was also gone.

And there was one other issue that Rick Scott could never seem to get away from: Obamacare, the president's still controversial plan for ending lifetime insurance caps, eliminating preexisting-condition rules, and providing health insurance for tens of millions of Americans who'd been living without coverage.

He hated it, hated it, hated it!

He'd entered politics, after all, as a major funder of anti-Obamacare TV ads.

Before and after becoming governor, he rarely missed an opportunity to claim that the Affordable Care Act would kill jobs, bankrupt America, and—who knows?—maybe even cause halitosis. At his direction, the state was a lead plaintiff in a lawsuit trying to overturn the president's reforms. The suit got all the way to the US Supreme Court. And Rick kept popping up on conservative talk shows, warning that expanding Medicaid, a key Obamacare provision, would put too big a strain on Florida taxpayers. At one point, he asserted that the Medicaid expansion would cost $26 billion over the next decade, although the state's health care agency slashed the estimate to $3 billion after the governor's math was challenged.

With Rick's history, what happened next was a shock at first.

On February 20, two weeks before his first State of the State address, the anti-Obamacare governor told reporters he was now willing to accept a key part of the president's health-care reform plan—the $51 billion Florida stood to receive in expanded Medicaid funds, which would extend health care to an additional 1.1 million of the state's poorest residents. He said he had gained new perspective as his mother was dying the previous year, calling his change of heart a "compassionate, commonsense step forward." He said he couldn't "in good conscience deny the uninsured access to care."

At last.

Florida's always taken Medicaid money. We need it. Medicaid is health care for the poor. It's a compassionate program, one of the most compassionate programs that our country provides to keep needy children and adults well. If you don't get health care, what do you get? You get sick or you die. Under this Medicaid expansion in

Obamacare, Washington would pay 100 percent of the cost for the first three years, 90 percent after that.

Great, right?

Well, not quite. It turned out there's a big difference between a governor telling reporters he supports something—and actually making the effort to get it done. I have no idea what Rick was really thinking, but I know this much. His Tea Party supporters went ballistic at his sudden embrace of "socialized medicine," as some of them called it. They'd helped elect the governor, and they couldn't stand his straying from the anti-government orthodoxy.

"I am flabbergasted," declared Slade O'Brien, Florida director of the conservative group Americans for Prosperity. "This is a guy who said it will never happen on his watch. Well, here it is."

"I'm trying to determine how the Medicaid expansion is going to pay for the surgery to remove the knife planted in my back," Henry Kelley, an important Tea Party leader from Fort Walton Beach, wrote on his blog. "This was his issue, his singular core issue. This is why we rallied around him."

Other Tea Partiers began accusing their good friend of going soft, of flip-flopping, of "throwing up the white flag of surrender," as the governor himself put it in denying he had done any such thing.

The Tea Partiers didn't have to worry. Their tiff with Rick Scott didn't last long. Almost immediately, he seemed to lose interest in any expansion of Medicaid.

In the meantime, the Florida Senate came up with a bill that did what the governor said on TV that he wanted to do. The House did not. Speaker Will Weatherford wouldn't bring the measure up. In Will's defense, he said that Governor Scott never even called asking him to. There was no lobbying, no arm-twisting, no public events, nothing to turn a few lines of warm-sounding rhetoric into legislative action of any sort. It was almost as if the governor sent some deputy press secretary out into the hallway to whisper, "I support it," all the while sitting back in his office and not lifting a finger to actually get it done.

As a result of the governor's inaction, more than a million people in Florida who would have gotten health insurance don't have it now.

In a rare visit to the Florida Senate, where she once served, Florida congresswoman Debbie Wasserman Schultz summed up the situation pretty well.

"While it's very nice that Governor Scott has had a deathbed conversion and decided that he does want to accept the federal funds," she said, "it's time for him to get off the sidelines. Either he is for accepting those funds and is willing to use his clout and his weight and put the full weight of his office behind that position, or he is not."

I have tried. Others have tried. We have urged the governor to call a special session of the legislature and get this done. His aides said that once the legislature's views became known, the governor thought his energies were better spent on issues where agreement could be achieved.

Asked by reporters whether he was forcefully pushing Medicaid expansion, the governor replied: "Both the House and Senate know exactly where I stand."

He went right back to beating the Tea Party drum against Obamacare. "The president's health care law is a disaster," he told WNRP, News Radio 1620 in Pensacola. "It's going to be bad for patients, it's going to be bad for businesses, it's going to be bad for providers. There's nobody that wins in that bill."

Rick Scott was being Rick Scott again.

I wasn't surprised that Rick replaced the vast majority of my appointees. He was the new governor. He had the right to bring in the people he thought would be best. He just seemed to have a funny idea of what was best. For instance, when I was first elected, I appointed Bob Butterworth as secretary of the Department of Children and Families, and he did a heroic job protecting Florida's at-risk children. Rick appointed David Wilkins, an incompetent ideologue who was forced to resign after a barrage of front-page stories about children who died while under the department's care.

And then there was the destructive way he went about the appointment process—I'm sorry, that was just wrong. For instance, Rick didn't only squeeze out Patricia Gleason as director of the Office of Open Government. The new governor's staff "lost" virtually all of the office's documents related to the transition—why some people were hired and others were fired and which special interests were consulted in the process. Suddenly, it was almost impossible for the public or the media to figure out what happened in that crucial period or to hold anyone responsible.

We lost a lot of very good people from jobs large and small—everything from top positions at major agencies to unpaid spots on the tiniest commissions and boards. The new governor and his people took a different approach from the one I learned when I became attorney general and left most of the people in place.

With all the big things to focus on, it's strange—isn't it?—how we sometimes remember the littlest ones, little perhaps to anybody but Carl Troup.

Carl is a wonderful man. He's a barber in St. Petersburg. He's cut my hair since I was in high school. His prices have gone up a little over the years, but his standard men's cut is still ten dollars. He's got a great sense of humor. He's as kind as can be. He seems to know everyone. He even makes me look more or less presentable.

When I became governor, I was surprised how many boards, panels, committees, and commissions the state had. Some of them, I'd never even heard of. Some of them, I'm not sure anybody had, including the people who'd been appointed to serve on them. But I took seriously the job of finding qualified people to sit on all of them. One was the state Barbers' Board.

I asked Carl if he'd like to serve.

"Sure," he said. "It would be an honor."

I put him on the state Barbers' Board, and he got to work. As expected, he did a splendid job.

He attended all the meetings. He worked with other members. He dealt with industry issues. He gained the respect of the staff. He was widely admired as diligent and fair. And soon enough, Carl was elected president of the Florida Barbers' Board.

He did so well, in fact, that he was in line to be president of the National Association of Barber Boards of America, the first time ever for a Floridian. In October 2010, I nominated Carl for a new term on the Florida board. He even had the usual reappointment interview.

Unfortunately for Carl, this was right as the new administration was coming in. Soon after Rick hit Tallahassee, his staff began looking closely at my appointments. After much scouring, I am sure, they found a beloved barber in St. Petersburg who'd cut my hair for more than forty years, and they rescinded his appointment to the Barbers' Board.

I never would have suspected that Rick was so interested in barbering.

But this blew Carl's chance to be president of the national organization since he was no longer a member of the state board. In the scheme of major issues, it might not be the biggest. But it was not something I would soon forget.

Chapter 23

Friends had warned that I might have a tough time adjusting to life as a private citizen. Two years as education commissioner, four as attorney general, another four as governor—it had been a full decade since I hadn't been a full-time state official in Florida.

But I have to say, living on the outside wasn't all that bad. Watching Rick Scott stumble along was still painful for me. Just because I was out of office didn't mean I stopped caring about Florida. But day to day, I was enjoying the rest of my life. Morgan & Morgan turned out to be a great fit for me. I settled in comfortably at the law firm. John and his team practiced law the way I practiced politics. I had been "the people's governor." They were "For the People." That was even their website name. I appeared in TV commercials for the firm—not hard-selling our legal services, just letting people know we were there for them. I never had to serve a single client I felt uncomfortable representing.

The official perks were gone. I didn't get to sleep at the Governor's Mansion anymore. But I still had my rented condo in downtown St.

Petersburg, and it had excellent views. I didn't have Florida Department of Law Enforcement agents providing security and driving me around. But I'd never minded walking or driving myself. So that wasn't any great burden to me.

The state plane, the big office at the Capitol, the attentive staff—all of it was nice when I had it. But that was never the reason I got into politics. And truly, I suffered no culture shock leaving that stuff behind.

I still had my family. I still had my friends. I could spend more hours with them. I still had my boat, *Freedom*. I appreciated my time on the water even more than I had before. And now I had Carole, who I didn't have when I came into office. She made me a far, far happier man.

I knew my public life wasn't over for good. I knew I had time and energy and fresh ideas and a whole lot left to give. I had no idea yet what that might mean, whether I would run for office again or campaign for others or find some other way to serve. But I was sure of this much: I still cared tremendously about my state and about my nation, and I couldn't possibly imagine just sitting quietly and not acting at all.

I kept being impressed by President Obama.

He faced constant distractions. And yet he somehow managed to hold his attention on the things that mattered most—continuing to revive a difficult economy, expanding opportunity for all Americans; continuing to press an international war on terrorism, unwinding our frustrating involvement in Iraq and Afghanistan. Whatever the Republicans threw at him—and something was constantly being thrown—President Obama almost never lost his cool.

Republicans in Congress had taken obstructionism to whole new heights. They turned the most basic functions of government—passing a budget, keeping the bills paid, managing Washington's borrowing authority—into life-or-death partisan slugfests. If the president was for it, they were against it—almost no matter what the issue. With the Republican Party pushed to extremes, that anti-Obama hostility was an unrelenting constant of national politics.

Nothing was easy in this environment. Yet the president navigated as deftly as anyone possibly could have. The personal attacks were never-ending, but the majority of Americans seemed very much to appreciate what he managed to achieve. While Congress's poll numbers sank almost to single digits, the president's remained in the solid 50 percent range—not bad at all in an environment so intensely partisan.

He seemed to get it, and people got him.

On September 8, 2011, Carole and I were at the condo in St. Petersburg. We were sitting on the couch, watching the president on television as he spoke to a joint session of Congress about a new plan to stimulate job growth.

His American Jobs Act called for $447 billion in new and renewed tax cuts and spending. To help those suffering most, he would also extend unemployment benefits rather than let them expire in December, offering states new flexibility in how they encouraged the unemployed to return to work. These moves were necessary, he said, to stop the economy from slipping into a new recession in 2012.

"This isn't political grandstanding," he said, trying to ease the dangerous partisanship that was strangling Washington. "This isn't class warfare. This is simple math."

It was a well-crafted plan and a well-crafted speech. In the spirit of genuine bipartisanship, he made a point of including proposals that had distinct Republican parentage. An infrastructure bank was modeled after a measure proposed by Republican Senator Kay Bailey Hutchison. Using unemployment benefits to retrain the jobless was based on a Georgia program that Republicans had praised. Throughout his speech, the president made great efforts to instill a new sense of urgency in a Congress that had become nearly paralyzed by partisanship. "Some of you have decided that our differences are so great that we can only resolve them at the ballot box," he said to the senators and members of Congress. "The next election is fourteen months away, and the people who sent us here—the people who hired us to work for them—they don't have the luxury of waiting fourteen months."

I jumped off the couch when I heard that.

"*Yes!*" I shouted at the TV like some hyperventilating sports fan. "Exactly right! We don't have fourteen months to wait."

Carole wholeheartedly agreed.

"You're right," my Republican wife said. "This guy gets it."

Later that month, Carole and I were driving to Gainesville for a University of Florida football game. The Gators were hosting the Tennessee Volunteers. We'd been invited by John Morgan and his wife, Ultima.

Somewhere along Interstate 75, she brought up the president's jobs speech and the adamant obstruction of extremist Republicans. "I don't know if I can take it anymore," she said. "This party doesn't represent me anymore. It doesn't represent us. I'm gonna do it. I'm going to become a Democrat."

"Wow, really?" was all I said at first.

Her parents had both been Republicans. She'd grown up on Long Island in a solidly Republican area. I'm sure most of her childhood friends and classmates had been Republicans too. She'd always thought of herself as a Republican. Our backgrounds weren't so different in that way.

But Carole has a way of boiling things right down to their essence. And she is always willing to give a second look. I couldn't deny that what she was saying made a whole lot of sense to me.

Early in August of 2012, my law partner John Morgan received an e-mail from Jim Messina, the president's national campaign manager. John called me immediately. "Hey, I just got something interesting," he said. He read an e-mail to me.

"Not that we are thinking about doing anything like this," the e-mail began, "but if we did think about doing something like this, do you think the governor would be interested in a speaking role at the Democratic Convention in Charlotte next month?"

As John read the e-mail, I was already thinking: *This could be exciting.*

"You think they're serious?" I asked him.

"I don't think it's a random e-mail," he said. "Sounds like they're feeling you out."

A week later, John, Jim, and I got on the phone together.

After a few "Hi, how are yous," John said: "Jim, you want to take it from here?"

Jim explained that the Obama campaign was pulling together a list of speakers for the party's big gathering, which was happening from September fourth through the sixth. "We've been talking about you having a speaking role at the convention," Jim said. "We were wondering if that is something you'd be open to?"

"Of course," I said. "Anything that might be helpful."

I knew the campaign had a large number of slots to fill. The convention ran for three days and nights. I figured they might have me say a few words at some off-hour like 2 P.M. on Tuesday, while the delegates were pinning their badges on and milling in the aisles.

I asked Jim what I should speak about. "Just talk about supporting the president and why he deserves another term. If that's something you feel," he added.

Jim knew I did. "Very strongly," I said.

"We're thinking about Thursday night," Jim added. "The same night as the president, the vice president, and the First Lady."

"The final night?" Wow.

"We'd like to have you, then a military guy, then the vice president, and then the president," Jim said.

A prime-time audience on the final night of a national convention, shortly before the president accepts his party's nomination and delivers the rousing oratory that formally launches the fall campaign? I'd been around politics long enough to know: There isn't a better audience than that.

The convention was inspiring from beginning to end. Despite my Republican history, the Democratic delegates treated me like a long-lost friend. People constantly walked over to shake my hand and thank me for helping the president. From the moment I arrived at the Time Warner Cable Arena in Charlotte, I felt like I belonged with all those high-spirited people in that energized room. They seemed to feel the same about me.

But why was I here?

The president and his people thought that voters might like to hear from an ex-Republican governor who'd had some direct experience with him. In the years since I'd greeted President Obama in Fort Myers, my respect for him had only grown. I'd endorsed John McCain in 2008 and still felt close to John. But I was wholeheartedly supporting the president this time. I very much admired his fresh style of leadership and his natural inclusiveness. And let's be frank, Mitt Romney was no John McCain.

My fish-out-of-water address was received far more warmly than I ever could have imagined. I felt like I was speaking for millions of commonsense Americans who could see beyond partisanship and wanted our leaders to represent all of us.

Carole was there. So were John Morgan and our partner Scott Weinstein. I met tons of new people before and after and ran into many other Democrats I'd known along the way. I received a huge pile of congratulatory notes and calls and e-mails from people back home. I got a few broad grins and shaking heads, as if to say, "Man, I never expected to see *you* here!" For a man who was officially an Independent, this was a party that was really starting to feel like home.

And after leaving North Carolina, I went wherever the campaign wanted me to and did everything I could to help reelect the president. I spent a lot of time in the swing states of Ohio and Florida, two keys to 2012. I was thrilled to be part of the Obama-Biden campaign. And a funny thing about knowing you're on the right track: Even on the toughest days, I was confident of victory.

As the fall campaign hit full swing, more and more attention was focused on Florida. That's what happens when you're America's most populous swing state. It was mathematically possible, most of the analysts agreed, for Mitt Romney to be elected president without taking Florida's twenty-nine electoral votes. Possible, but highly unlikely. The polls were tight, as usual. The campaigns were focused, as usual. Both sides were dumping major resources—staff, volunteers, and advertising dollars—into the state. Romney had to win, and Obama really didn't want to lose. And back in Tallahassee, Governor Scott and those around him were working night and day to make sure a lot of people didn't vote.

They weren't encouraging voting. They weren't making this great constitutional expression easier, more convenient, or less onerous. They were working overtime to put up as many barriers as they could.

This was becoming a maddeningly familiar pattern. A Republican victory in November, party strategists in Tallahassee and Washington seemed to have concluded, was only possible if the overall voter turnout was lowered significantly. So as hard as we'd worked to expand voting in Florida—securing the ballots, broadening the rolls, my executive order before the 2008 election to expand early voting—the new team seemed just as committed to rolling the progress back.

You really had to wonder: After Obama won the state the first time, did someone in the Florida Republican Party say, "We have a problem. We'll lose again in 2012 if we don't keep some of those Democrats away from the polls"?

Rick's campaign slogan had been "Let's get to work." They did—on voter suppression.

They reduced the number of early-voting days from fourteen to eight. They cut the hours back. Despite the pleas of local election officials, they refused to expand the available polling places beyond election offices, libraries, and city halls. They also added a new set of voter-verification rules, an idea that was spreading to Republican states across America. It was like the worst ideas from Florida were suddenly taking hold elsewhere—not the kind of incubator I wanted our state to be. Now, voter IDs were suddenly an issue. Voter signatures had to be matched up precisely. That proved to be a special challenge to seniors. My own mother was having trouble with her handwriting after a mild stroke.

The predictable happened, of course. All those voting cutbacks made it harder for people to vote.

Much harder, in some cases.

Election 2012 was starting to look like a bad combination of the worst from 2000 and 2008, all smushed into one horrible mess.

The early-voting lines were even longer than they'd been four years earlier before I signed my executive order easing them. This time, some people stood in the Florida sun for six, seven, or eight hours just for a chance to vote. Some precincts were all but empty. Others were completely overrun. Again, Floridians were being asked to suffer unreasonable discomforts and indignities just for the chance to vote.

On one level, this was hugely inspiring—that so many people would be willing to suffer in the streets for a chance to exercise one of their most precious constitutional rights. It was also hugely depressing. People in power had decided to make voters suffer on their way to the polls. Make no mistake. None of this happened by accident.

I called on the governor to act. I said he should use his emergency powers like I had. Extend the hours, I said. Open new polling places. Beef up the staffs. It wasn't just me. Many others urged similar measures.

The governor adamantly declined.

By Election Day, Tuesday, November 6, the lines snaked around buildings and circled full blocks. This time in Miami-Dade, a lot of people were still in line at 7 P.M. that many had to wait to vote until well past midnight, after Mitt Romney had already conceded. At

1:52 A.M., when President Obama gave his acceptance speech, people were still voting. I hate to imagine what would have happened if we'd needed a recount. At least we now had optical scanners in all sixty-seven counties where the voters marked their ballots by hand. The touch screens and the butterfly ballots were gone.

It was embarrassing—it really was—to be sitting in a TV studio in Chicago, being interviewed about my home-state election results, in front of a high-definition map of America. The red states and blue states were spread out from coast to coast. And down at the bottom right was one fat finger of yellow—NBC's official color for "we don't know"—Florida.

How could the state have let this happen again?

By late Thursday, two days after the election, Florida still hadn't been called. Governor Scott was getting testy as reporters kept pressing for an explanation. Tony Pipitone, a reporter with WKMG Local 6 in Orlando, asked the governor directly:

"Should you have extended early-voting hours?"

"I'm very confident that the right thing happened," he said. "Four-point-four million people voted"—early or absentee.

When Tony asked again if the hours should have been extended, Rick turned and walked away.

Florida stayed yellow until Saturday, four days after the vote, the last state of the fifty to call the race. With 100 percent of precincts reporting, Secretary of State Ken Detzner finally declared that Barack Obama and Joe Biden had defeated Mitt Romney and Paul Ryan in Florida, 50 percent to 49.1 percent. The difference was about 74,000 votes, far more than the 537 that had officially separated Al Gore and George W. Bush in 2000, really not that close for a modern counting system. And still it took four days. The state's twenty-nine electoral votes were finally awarded to the Democrats. The win meant Obama swept all of the swing states except North Carolina. His Electoral College win was 332 to 206.

By the time Florida was called, I was back home in St. Petersburg. I was on the phone with Tim Nickens, the editor of editorials at the *Tampa Bay Times*, the new name for the *St. Petersburg Times*. My phone started to vibrate and "UNKNOWN" came on the screen. I'd been told to expect an important call.

I asked Tim if I could call him back. I took the unknown call.

"I just wanted to call and say thanks," a familiar voice said. It was Barack Obama. I congratulated him.

"We have to find a way to fix that election system in Florida," the president said.

I told him I couldn't agree more. I promised that if I ever had the chance again, I would.

Once again, the country was looking at Florida and shaking its head.

Rick Scott said he and Ken Detzner would meet to discuss how to improve Florida's election procedures. The secretary of state blamed the problem on the long list of candidates and amendments on the ballot as well as high voter turnout. I hated that he saw high turnout as a problem. To me, it was a sign of democratic health.

A record number of Floridians cared enough to vote—8.4 million, 70 percent of those registered. Of those, 2.1 million voted early, another 2.4 million absentee. Ken Detzner didn't mention how he and Rick Scott had been warned repeatedly.

"We could have done better; we will do better," the secretary of state finally told CNN.

Chapter 24

I t was my old law school friend Mike Hamby who first suggested December of 2012 might be the time for me to finally become a Democrat. Mike had been a Democrat his whole life. He'd watched me inch closer and closer for more than thirty years.

"Aren't you going to the White House for that Christmas reception?" Mike asked me one morning in early December of 2012.

"Yeah," I said. Carole and I had been invited after the election.

"Why don't you become a Democrat there?" Mike suggested.

"At the White House?" I asked.

"What could be more appropriate than that?"

Mike had a point. If I was going to become a Democrat, what better place in the universe to do it than at the White House with a Democratic president, especially a Democratic president I had helped to reelect? I wasn't sure of all the mechanics. I didn't know how the people at the White House would react. But I couldn't see any reason to wait much longer. Given all the things I'd been doing, everyone pretty much considered me a Democrat already.

Duh!

During the 2012 presidential campaign, I thought I was more useful to the president as an Independent. Just about every Democrat in the country was already supporting him, just like the vast majority of Republicans were doing the same for Mitt Romney. That's partisan politics. The real contest in that race, as it so often is, was for Independents in the middle, especially in places like Florida. I understood how unique my position was: an ex-governor of Florida who was neither a Republican nor a Democrat—that had some special value to the Obama campaign, and I'd wanted to share whatever that was worth. I knew how much was at stake.

But now the election was over. The president had won. What was I waiting for? Carole had made the switch fourteen months earlier. She was always a little smarter than I was.

"You really should do this," she'd been telling me. "The Democratic Party is where you belong."

I wasn't a Republican anymore. I'd experienced the three-way squeeze of running for Senate as an Independent. I'd spoken at the Democratic National Convention. I'd campaigned for the president. What exactly was holding me back now?

Carole and I arrived in Washington on Thursday, December 6, a day before the reception. We checked into the Willard hotel. After we got settled, we walked to the White House for a tour.

Our tour was a little different from the tour that most Washington visitors get. A young aide took us into the Situation Room, which I certainly didn't expect. Tucked away in the White House, this high-security communications hub was created by President Kennedy after the Bay of Pigs fiasco, which was caused in part by a lack of real-time information. From the attacks on 9/11 to the killing of Osama bin Laden, some very tense moments have unfolded in there. I don't care who you are—it's hard not to be impressed. We didn't see the president. I'm not sure where he was. Running the country or something, I guess. But we did see senior adviser Valerie Jarrett.

"Hey, how are you?" Valerie asked, greeting Carole and me like old campaign friends.

We had a nice exchange, and then I told her what was on my mind.

"You know," I said, "I was thinking of something I wanted to share with you." Was I stalling? Not really. But I understood, once I blurted out the words, there wouldn't be any turning back.

"What's that?" Valerie asked.

"I think I'm gonna become a Democrat tomorrow," I told her.

"You're always welcome in my party," she said with a big smile. "I think that would be a great thing to do at the Christmas reception."

"I think you're right," I said.

That did it. When Carole and I got back to the hotel, I went to the business center and pulled up the website for the Pinellas County Supervisor of Elections. I printed out the form for switching political parties. I brought it back to the room and showed it to Carole. Then I sat at the desk in the room and filled out most of the form. Name, address, date of birth, and the other blocks. Everything but my signature. I put a check mark in the box next to where it said, "Democrat."

The next night, I folded up the form from the clerk's office. I put it—still unsigned—in the inside jacket pocket of my suit before we left the hotel for the White House.

It was a lovely party. The whole house was dripping in Christmas decorations. Twinkling lights, more trees than I could count—no one could miss what holiday this was. The White House in December is truly the epitome of Christmas in America! We saw lots of people we knew. White House staffers. Folks from the campaign. Other Washington people I'd met over the years. There was a real buzz in the room. The president had just been reelected. A lot of the people at the party had helped. The White House, as it always does, looked gorgeous for the holidays. It was fun, and it just felt special to be there.

Then, around 9 P.M., Carole and I went up to the front part of the White House where the United States Marine Band was playing a mix of holiday and patriotic songs. The president was standing nearby with Michelle.

"You ready?" I whispered to Carole.

She nodded yes. "You bet," she said.

I took the form out of my pocket. Yes, I was definitely ready to do this. I'd thought about it and waited long enough. I was going to sign the form.

But there was one little detail I hadn't thought of.

Precisely where?

I guess the furniture was moved for the party. I didn't see a table where I could bend down and write.

I turned around, and now I was facing the band. The trumpet player—I think it was a trumpet—noticed I had a pen and a piece of paper in my hand and, I'm sure, a slightly quizzical look on my face.

He smiled and waved me over.

He took the sheet music off his music stand. "Here," he said, motioning for me to sign the paper on his music stand.

And that's what I did.

"Charlie Crist."

When I looked up from the music stand, I noticed quite a few people were looking over at me, including the president. The president had a huge smile on his face.

"I just became a Democrat," I called over to him.

I don't believe he was surprised. Valerie must have told him what I was thinking about doing.

He definitely looked happy.

He walked straight to me and gave me a fist bump. I thought that was very cool.

"That's great," he said to me. "I heard you were going to do that."

He certainly deserved a big piece of the credit for my being here.

I don't believe there were any media people at the party—no one that I recognized. But there were people there with iPhones, including the young White House aide who'd given us the tour. He took a picture of Carole and me and said he'd put it on Facebook.

Adam C. Smith, the political editor at the *Tampa Bay Times* and a very well-sourced journalist, called my cell phone. He reached me as Carole and I were leaving the White House and heading to a little celebratory dinner at the Old Ebbitt Grill. I told him what I'd done. Adam's story moved at 10:01 P.M. I thought his lede summed things up pretty well.

"It was just a matter of time," he wrote. "Charlie Crist is becoming a Democrat.

"Crist—Florida's former Republican governor who relished the tough-on-crime nickname 'Chain Gang Charlie' and used to describe himself variously as a 'Ronald Reagan Republican' and a 'Jeb Bush Republican'—on Friday evening signed papers changing his party from independent to Democrat."

He quoted me as saying: "I've had friends for years tell me, 'You know, Charlie, you're a Democrat and you don't know it.'"

I was starting to believe that might be true.

"He has been a strong supporter of higher pay for teachers," Adam wrote. "He works for a leading trial lawyer. He was a leading advocate for civil rights as governor and attorney general. And though he describes himself as 'pro-life,' his voting record in the Legislature was mostly in favor of abortion rights. He has long been more of a populist than a pro-big business Republican."

"What changed is the leadership of the Republican Party," I told Adam. "As I said at the convention, I didn't leave the Republican Party. It left me. Whether the issue was immigration or education or you name it, the environment, I feel at home now."

I sent out my own Twitter announcement from @charliecristfl, staying safely within the 140 characters.

"Proud and honored to join the Democratic Party in the home of President @BarackObama!" I said simply.

I included a link to the photo of Carole and me, which had been taken by the White House aide. You can see me in my best dark-gray suit with a crisp white shirt and a solid, textured blue tie—Democratic blue, blue-state blue. Carole looks sparkling in a sleeveless, holiday-red dress. Both of us have huge smiles on our faces, like we had a giant secret and we couldn't wait to tell everyone. I was holding up a single sheet of paper. The camera on my phone is a little blurry. It's hard to make out every word. But the headline is unmistakable.

"Florida Voter Registration Application," it says.

Chapter 25

How could I stand by quietly as Governor Rick Scott and his band of right-wing extremists kept finding fresh ways to harm the state and the people I loved? As 2013 moved along, that question got louder and louder in my head. It wasn't as if Rick and his cronies were improving with time. If anything, they kept getting worse.

I had long conversations with Carole, my parents, and my sisters. I got a lot of smart counsel from friends I knew I could trust. As well as I could, I tried to gauge the political practicalities of what I was about to do. And on November 4, a breezy Monday morning, I stood in Albert Whitted Park on the St. Petersburg waterfront in front of a couple of hundred relatives, friends, supporters, and a huge throng of media. The rally was organized by my good friend Michelle Todd, who has been with me on much of the journey these past few years. This was the day I announced I was running for governor of Florida in 2014—as a proud member of the Democratic Party.

"My friends," I said, "I don't have to tell you that what we have here in Florida today isn't working. Tallahassee is out of control.

Governing for the people has been replaced with cronyism and government on the fringes. The voice of the people has been silenced by the financial bullies and the special interests. Other than a few legislators, you the people have no advocate."

I spoke very simply and very directly. I spoke the only way I knew how to—from my heart. "You deserve a governor who wakes up every day thinking about you," I said, "who you can trust to govern honestly and in our collective best interests, who will make this economy more fair for hardworking taxpayers and who will move Florida forward, not by giving every break to big business but by leading on the things that matter to you. Good schools. Affordable health care. Respect for our environment. Dignity for our seniors. That's who I am. That's what I believe in, and that's what I'll do if you help me become your next governor."

It felt wonderful saying those words, like a load had just been lifted, like the path in front of me had just turned bright.

I knew this wasn't going to be easy. I knew that in the annals of American politics, hardly anyone has ever been able to achieve a party switch like this. I knew I'd be attacked viciously by an opponent with a nearly limitless bankroll for trashing me. Rick Scott had already vowed to spend $100 million. I had no doubt he would. I knew I would need tremendous support from my fellow Floridians.

I also knew I had no other choice. Quiet wasn't an option anymore.

I'd already decided we'd keep the same campaign slogan we had used eight years earlier. "The People's Governor." I saw no reason to change that. And the core values of my candidacy would be the same they'd always been: honesty, common sense, bipartisanship, never forgetting that the people are the boss. That's the kind of Republican I was. It's the kind of Democrat I am.

"When the people give you the honor of being their governor," I said in my announcement, "you aren't the governor of any one party. You are the governor of all Floridians. No matter what they say, it is not a sin to reach across the aisle. It is your obligation to work together."

What a change that would be for Florida! But it was hardly any change for me at all. I've just found a better place to be me. That's all.

I am convinced of it: The Democratic Party is the right home for me. The causes I have fought for, the values I hold dear, the issues I care most deeply about—they aren't welcome in today's tormented Republican Party.

I've always stood up for the things that I believe in—for freedom, for fairness, for opportunity. But now I notice that the people standing near me aren't rolling their eyes and shaking their heads when I speak out for what I know is right. They're not mumbling, "Really? Do you have to?" My fellow Democrats are encouraging me. They're saying, "Go for it, Charlie!"

And I will.

I love my new allies, from the president on down. It's a far more open environment than I had lived in before. We don't always have to march in lockstep. We can even disagree. The tent really is a large one here. Democrats, even those in politics, tend to be positive people and speak their minds. They are not inclined to display phony anger just to rile up the troops. Going forward, I am certain I won't agree with every Democratic policy on every imaginable issue. I'm still a fiscal conservative. I'm not a tax-and-spend liberal with other people's money. I'm still a Second Amendment guy with common-sense limits like background checks for gun buyers.

Florida still runs through my veins. But I know that if my positions feel right to me and the people I serve, we can expect a respectful hearing inside the party and a reasonable debate. In good faith, we can always trade ideas and compare different strategies. Together, we will achieve great things. I am sure of it.

I am hugely upbeat about the future. I am grateful for the new opportunities I have to serve. I used to think I could do that and still be a loyal Republican. I discovered that was no longer true. The forces of intolerance and extremism, fueled by the passion of the Tea Party and funded by a tiny knot of super-rich guys, had taken too strong a grip on the party I'd grown up in. They didn't seem to care about the people. They'd shut down the government on a whim. The candidates they were fielding were total goofballs. Did they really believe the crazy stuff they were spouting? Their ideas were so loud and out there, some of these characters sounded like they'd just climbed out of clown cars. The issues they promoted played to the worst of our nature, not the best. There was no room left in their once-proud party for moderation and common sense. I am a Democrat because I believe in democratic values and I have seen what's become of the Republicans. I cannot be a part of that and stay true to myself.

Some things haven't changed at all.

I am not motivated by money. I never have been. I don't need glory or acclaim. They're fun, but they're not why I'm here. However much the ground has shifted in the past couple of years, I know who I am and I am still me. I love my friends and my family. I care about our nation and our state. I treasure the wonderful people I have been privileged to serve. The real thrill for me, as it's always been, is confronting large challenges on behalf of decent people and making the world better for us all.

Really, it's not a bad way to spend a life.

I don't need to renounce all things Republican. As far as I'm concerned, great ideas can come from anywhere. I believe in civility even toward people who disagree with me—especially toward them. Great leaders bring people together, helping everyone find a contributing role. And no, I won't be changing the name of my boat. I don't believe Republicans should own the Freedom franchise. But if I ever get another boat, I just might call it *Justice* or *Fairness* or *Equal Opportunity*. The world can always use a little more of those.

No political party is perfect. I don't expect the Democrats to be. I will never lose my independent spirit. I have a brain and a heart, and I plan on using both of them. I'll keep speaking the truths that I believe in. I won't sign away my values and judgment just because there's a "D" beside my name, any more than I did when there was an "R." No one should. We can confront the issues one by one. We certainly have enough of them.

As a start, we simply must achieve real immigration reform. We have waited long enough. Eleven or twelve million men, women, and children have been waiting far too long. The vast majority of today's immigrants are the very same kind of people who built America— hardworking, decent, patriotic, eager to provide for their families and build new lives. As Marco Rubio found when he tried to promote immigration reform inside the Republican Party—and then pulled abruptly back—bitter partisanship has stalled our progress. I refuse to believe that we cannot find a process to welcome these immigrants fully into the land of the free, the home of the brave.

All Americans deserve decent health care. That's a principle we must fully meet. No child should ever be denied a trip to the doctor.

No adult should ever be thrown into bankruptcy because of a hospital stay. President Obama's health care reform is an important step down that road of decency, bringing health insurance to 30 million uninsured Americans, ending cruel limitations like preexisting conditions and lifetime caps. We must not rest until all Americans have high-quality health care. We are too decent a people—we are too affluent a nation—to look into the eyes of the sick and the suffering and heartlessly shrug: "Too bad."

The middle class is the foundation of our society, and it is terribly squeezed right now. Stagnant incomes, shaky jobs, unaffordable prices, too much debt—the people in the middle and those working hard to get there desperately need some relief. At the same time corporate America is reaping huge profits. A very few people are enriching themselves enormously. We have always been a nation that rewards hard work and enterprise. I believe in that. But we have to strike a better balance between the strivers and the already-haves. We shouldn't dim the hopes of the vast majority of Americans. They must see the path of opportunity open to them. They must know that they too can succeed.

We must always ensure that consumers are treated fairly. Free enterprise helped to build America. But government is the balance that makes our system work. There are big corporations that will take advantage of people. They just can't help themselves. Unless they are kept in check by fair and reasonable rules and regulations, the powerless will inevitably be taken advantage of. Insurance rate payers, phone-company customers, mortgagees—they all need and deserve protection. They are depending on us.

Our hearts and minds and laws must remain open to people who live a variety of lifestyles. What business is it of anyone's who someone else loves or chooses to marry? I've been heartened by how quickly Americans have accepted gay marriage. Ten years ago, the idea seemed politically unthinkable. Now, it's hard to remember what all the fuss was about. There's a basic question of justice here. Gay men and women have the right to be accepted fully and to honor those they love. Who are we to judge them? Especially, who is government to judge them?

We must fight vigorously and everywhere to preserve and expand the right to vote. It's inexcusable how today's Republicans have been scheming to undermine such a hard-earned right. It's an affront to anyone who believes in fundamental fairness. It's an insult to the Constitution of the United States. Having failed to persuade voters with Republican arguments, party operatives are pursuing a cynical suppression strategy instead. Limiting early voting. Restricting mail-in ballots. Carelessly purging the rolls. Demanding precise signature matches. Insisting on state-issued identification cards. Doing everything they can think of to keep minorities, college students, and others away from the polls. It's happening in many states where Republicans have power, including my beloved Florida. We should be helping people to vote in America, not daring them to try.

In today's complex world, education is more important than it's ever been. It's what will help us to thrive and compete in the global economy for decades to come. It's the gateway to the future, even more than it was in my grandfather's day with his third-grade education and his seven children completing college. Excellent schools will never be cheap. First-class universities and technical colleges won't be either. But aren't our children worth investing in? If they're not, who is? We need to recommit ourselves immediately to the priority of education. It's what makes the future bright.

It's time for genuinely fresh thinking on crime and drugs. There are some people who need to be locked away in prison. Society must be protected from their violence and abuse. But our prisons today are packed with nonviolent drug offenders and others who don't need to be there nearly so long. It's expensive. It's counterproductive. It's rarely rehabilitating. It wrecks families and lives. Forty years into the war on drugs, we have learned what works, what doesn't, and why. We must pull our justice system into the modern age.

Government must always keep its distance from the personal decisions that individuals and families make. On birth control. On abortion. On medical treatment at the very end of life. People have very strong feelings about issues as personal as these, as they should. These beliefs are informed by religion, family, upbringing, and the cultures we live in. As I like to say, "Change hearts, not laws." Issues like these are the very last place government should be stomping around.

Infrastructure is the easiest thing to skimp on. The bridge that isn't repaired, the transit line that isn't built, the training and upkeep that get deferred again—no one notices at first. But real leaders take the long view. Failing to invest in infrastructure is almost always foolhardy. Real people will suffer from the school that isn't built, the sewer that isn't laid, the growth that we aren't prepared for. We are Americans. We build things, big things. Justifiably, we are proud that we always have. And all that building has created—will create— many new jobs.

The environment is incredibly important, the opportunity for our children and grandchildren to see God's beauty as we have been blessed ourselves. We must be good stewards for this earth of ours, and we must be guided by facts. We can't renounce science. We can't twist logic. We must constantly learn from experience and results. We need energy to run our modern economy. But thankfully, we can now find that energy in clean ways. From the sun. From the wind. From the tides of the ocean and the heat of the earth. From places we haven't even imagined. Other parts of the world are ahead of us, but America is awakening—just in time to save our planet and pass it on.

Finally, we have to return civility to government and our public lives. The partisanship that has taken over political debate must be drained of its poisonous rancor. We must achieve together. It's one of the things I am proudest of: changing the tone in Tallahassee. Republicans and Democrats working together. Bringing in people and groups from all perspectives and from all across the state. The achievements that we had all flowed from that. And everyone felt invested. We must reach out to others. We must sit at the table with them. We must remember that almost nothing can be accomplished alone.

I face the future with appreciation, optimism, and energy. Appreciation for the chances to serve that I've been given. Optimism about the future we have in front of us. Energy to get up every morning and ask, "How can I make things better today?"

With my new allies, I am off on another great journey. I hope you will join us. Together, I know, we can achieve amazing things.

A 150-YEAR PUBLISHING TRADITION

In 1864, E. P. Dutton & Co. bought the famous Old Corner Bookstore and its publishing division from Ticknor and Fields and began their storied publishing career. Mr. Edward Payson Dutton and his partner, Mr. Lemuel Ide, had started the company in Boston, Massachusetts, as a bookseller in 1852. Dutton expanded to New York City, and in 1869 opened both a bookstore and publishing house at 713 Broadway. In 2014, Dutton celebrates 150 years of publishing excellence. We have redesigned our longtime logotype to reflect the simple design of those earliest published books. For more information on the history of Dutton and its books and authors, please visit www.penguin.com/dutton.